THE ACADEMIC GATEWAY

THE ACADEMIC GATEWAY: Understanding the Journey to Tenure

EDITED BY

Timothy M. Sibbald
Victoria Handford

University of Ottawa Press
2017

uOttawa

The University of Ottawa Press gratefully acknowledges the support extended to its publishing list by Canadian Heritage through the Canada Book Fund, by the Canada Council for the Arts, by the Federation for the Humanities and Social Sciences through the Awards to Scholarly Publications Program, and by the University of Ottawa.

Copy editing: Michael Waldin
Proofreading: Robbie McCaw
Typesetting: Counterpunch Inc.
Cover design: Éditscript enr.
Cover image: Dr. Victoria Handford

Library and Archives Canada Cataloguing in Publication

The academic gateway : understanding the journey to tenure / edited by Timothy M. Sibbald, Victoria Handford.

Includes bibliographical references and index.
Issued in print and electronic formats.
ISBN 978-0-7766-2437-2 (softcover).--ISBN 978-0-7766-2438-9 (PDF).--
ISBN 978-0-7766-2439-6 (EPUB).--ISBN 978-0-7766-2440-2 (Kindle)

1. College teachers--Tenure--Canada--Case studies.
I. Sibbald, Timothy M., 1966-, editor II. Handford, Victoria, editor

LB2335.7.A33 2017   378.1'2140971   C2017-902114-1
                                          C2017-902115-X

@ University of Ottawa Press, 2017

Canada

About the Cover Photo

The cover photo carries symbolic meanings, both aesthetic and geographical, about tenure-track experiences.

The photo was taken over Kluane National Park and Reserve in southwestern Yukon. It is part of the largest international protected wilderness area in the world and it contains the world's largest non-polar ice field. The region is a UNESCO World Heritage site. The glacier seen in the picture is a frozen river, well over a mile deep, and thousands of years old. In spite of this, it is in a constant state of change, something not immediately apparent to those unfamiliar with glaciers.

The isolation, ruggedness, and the expertise needed to master this domain are all part of the metaphor for academia. Like the frozen river, academia is founded on knowledge and thinking that extends back for millennia, yet the processes of thinking and the knowledge base itself are in a constant state of change. Mount Logan, Canada's highest peak, is just beyond the view in the cover photo. The stature academics strive for in their tenure-track navigates paths like the glacier, all in search of that peak—tenure, promotion, and academic opportunity. The uncertainty that tenure-track faculty feel about what they are trying to achieve is familiar, but unique to each individual path.

Photo Credit: Dr. Victoria Handford

Table of Contents

Acknowledgements ix
Introduction... xi

Section I

Editors' Preface—Late Tenure-Track 13
1   On the Tenure-Track: Navigating Research, Teaching, and Service Responsibilities in a U15 Institution
Frank Deer... 17
2   Meet Jill—She Fell Down the Hill but Came Back up Again: Struggling with Mental Illness While on the Path to Tenure
Joan M. Chambers 29
3   Re-Locating: Moving Between the Field and the University
Lee Anne Block 41
4   Belonging Differently: Immigration, Identity, and Tenure-Track
Cecile Badenhorst 51
5   The Three-Headed Monster
Greg Rickwood... 63

Section II

Editors' Preface—Tenure-Track Collaboration 75
6   Women Reflect on Becoming an Academic: Challenges and Supports
Memorial's Education Writing Group 79
7   I Think You Are Ambivalent: The Realities of Indigenous Scholarship in Mainstream Universities
Onowa McIvor, María del Carmen Rodríguez de France, and Trish Rosborough 93
8   A Dynamic Duet: Fluid Mentorship and Holistic Co-Teaching
Manu Sharma and Cam Cobb... 111

Section III

Editors' Preface—Mid-Tenure-Track 129
9   Practitioner to Academic: A Composition of Transitions
Timothy M. Sibbald 133
10   Surviving and Thriving in the First Years of Tenure-Track: A Journey Through France, Spain, and Québec
Margarida Romero 145
11   For Academy's Sake: A Former Practitioner's Search for Scholarly Relevance
Lloyd Kornelsen... 159
12   Transitioning to the Academic Tenure-Track at Mid-Career: Exploring Adaptive and Maladaptive Responses to Challenges and Adversity
Peter Milley 179

Section IV

Editors' Preface—Early Tenure-Track 199
13   From There to Here
Victoria (Tory) Handford... 203
14   The "Ten-Year Road" to Tenure: A Personal Narrative of the Beginning Phases of the Journey
Greg Ogilvie 217
15   Professor, Student, Mother: Can You Have It All?
Kathy Snow 233
16   Just Today and Just Tomorrow: Building Capacity on the Tenure-Track in New Brunswick
Lyle Hamm 249

Conclusion—Tenure-Track Advice 265
Contributors 273
Index 281

Acknowledgements

Like many authors in this collection, the editors have prior experience in the field of education. Perhaps unusually, they also have significant experience writing reports. However, while such experiences can aid the process of proposing, editing, and seeing a book through to completion, they do not necessarily open the doors within academic publishing. For that reason, we would like to acknowledge the University of Ottawa Press for taking on two relatively unknown tenure-track editors for this volume. Their support and thoughtful advice provided professional guidance that was well suited to our stage of editorial growth.

Additionally, we would like to acknowledge the financial support we have received for the production of this book. Specifically, we wish to express appreciation for funding from the Faculty of Education and Social Work at Thompson Rivers University, the Seymour Schulich Benefaction, and the Schulich School of Education at Nipissing University. The timely support facilitated moving this book to in-press status, and was significant to the editors and all the tenure-track authors who contributed.

Introduction

Joining academia in a tenure-track role affects all aspects of one's life. It is not clear, in advance, how it will develop for an individual, and information about the experience is scarce. Within the academy there are many different departments and areas of expertise where one can hold a tenure-track role. That diversity confounds the study of individual experiences. However, the process has characteristics that are shared by many who begin the journey. By narrowing the field to Education faculties, we have sampled people who typically have a background in teaching and service, most of which is well matched to the university environment. For many, only the research component is truly new, notwithstanding differences arising from engaging adult learners and changes in the way service is provided. In a sense, this is a best-case scenario, as it should have the least amount of role change. As we will see, this does not mean it is without challenges! This book will be informative for many because the experiences described are relevant beyond Education faculties.

The context for this book is the lived experiences of people pursuing tenured positions in Canadian faculties of Education. This context was selected because it provides common values and beliefs and a national understanding of the role of higher education. There are differences in the tenure process from one institution to the next, but in all cases, the chapters have been written before the authors knew what the outcome of the tenure process would be. In this respect, the authors share a degree of uncertainty about their future and are writing about a process in which they are immersed.

As a process, progress towards a tenure decision should highlight increased clarity about the role. There are choices and interpretations along the way, but in general, it is believed that a person who has worked three years in a tenure-track role will be more informed than a person who has worked one year. This supposition led to the organization of sections and chapters within those sections, according to the duration that each individual has spent in academia. The writers in Section I have been in the tenure-track the longest. This section includes contributions from late tenure-track collaborators, as their collective effort may mitigate the fewer individual years in the tenure-track. The authors appearing in Section III and IV are in the middle and early stages of the tenure-track. The book can be read in whatever order the reader finds interesting, but we hypothesize that the given order will benefit understanding the progression of the journey, a sort of view of the process that begins with the end in mind. If the supposition that duration affects clarity about the role is accurate, then, as one progresses through the volume's sections, the level of uncertainty about the transition should generally increase as the amount of experience in the tenure-track decreases. However, as no writer of a chapter had tenure at the time of writing, the uncertainty is omnipresent.

The 16 contributed chapters in this book were written by academics in eight different provinces spanning from the University of Victoria on the Pacific Coast to Memorial University on the Atlantic. The individual chapter authors are balanced in terms of gender. The collaborative authorships have more women than men, reflecting the responses received from the call for chapters, rather than action by the editors. Prior career experience was varied and considered as a possible means to organize the book; however, there was too much variation among the "first careers" for this to be used for this purpose.

It is notable that a few of the larger, more prominent universities in Canada are missing from this book. We posit two explanations for this. First is the question of whether entry-level tenure-track positions are to be found in these locations. Tenure-track faculty may move from smaller institutions into more prominent institutions, thereby reducing the number of tenure-track faculty initially entering higher education at prominent institutions. A second explanation was brought to light by a proposal from a tenure-track faculty member at a well-known

Canadian university. Having written a proposal, the writer sought advice from a colleague and, as a result, changed the proposal. The advice received caused concern about potential negative repercussions within the faculty for voicing the individual's experiences. The modified proposal was written from a stance of advising how to be successful at achieving tenure. While it was well intentioned, the proposal was not accepted because it did not speak about personal experience.

A challenge that a book about tenure-track faces is clarifying details of the context of the tenure-track. Consider that the use of lecturing has been around for millennia, yet it has changed because of projection equipment and multimedia options. Since the same modernization may be true of tenure-track, we sought a systematic approach to looking at university roles. Statistics regarding full-time education faculty members were collected from the annual almanacs of the Canadian Association of University Teachers (CAUT, www.caut.ca/resources/almanac). The statistics are only to 2010/2011 because that is all that is available. The number of education faculty, by year, is provided in table 1, according to role.

Table 1. Full-Time Education Faculty in Canada

Number in Role					
	Full Professor	Associate Professor	Assistant Professor	Lecturer	Total for Year
2010/2011	582	804	537	189	2,112
2008/2009	774	1,032	807	240	2,853
2007/2008	762	1,002	813	234	2,811
2006/2007	768	978	780	225	2,751
2005/2006	777	984	753	204	2,718
2004/2005	663	858	717	186	2,424
2003/2004	681	852	636	210	2,379
2001/2002	725	861	610	186	2,382
2000/2001	709	848	553	153	2,263

The table shows the overall number of faculty members generally increased through the years, but there was a drastic decrease between 2008/2009 and 2010/2011. The decrease occurred at all levels, which suggests tenure may not mark the level of stability that is commonly associated with it. All levels of professorship show similar patterns, suggesting that all universities had similar experiences with respect to hiring, tenure, or promotion in the last decade. However, comparing the 2010/2011 values to the corresponding 2000/2001 values shows that all categories have declined, except that of lecturers. This suggests a disproportionate increase in the number of lecturer positions, which are positions entailing teaching, service, and additional programmatic roles or other leadership, but requiring no research. When the values are expressed as a percentage of the 2000/2001 values, full professors are decreased 18%, associate professors decreased 5%, assistant professors decreased 3%, but lecturers increased by 24%. This suggests that the level of support available to tenure-track individuals from their tenured peers, particularly for research, may have been diminished in recent years. We leave it to the reader to consider this as they read through the book. Though it is beyond the scope of this book, we wonder if the balance of priority between teaching and research may be changing in a fundamental way. The reader will find the chapters of this book useful for thinking about this question, but will find this book has too narrow a focus to determine if we are in the midst of a change in university priorities writ large.

An additional diminishing of tenure may arise through a reduction in full-time roles. To explore this possibility, CAUT statistics were gathered for the number of people completing an undergraduate degree in education. The counts are shown in table 2.

Table 2. Graduates in Education by Year

Year	Graduates in Education	Students per Full-Time Faculty
2012	21,792	
2011	22,080	10.5
2010	22,053	
2008	19,875	7.1
2007	19,512	7.1
2006	19,056	7.0
2005	18,219	7.5
2004	18,480	7.8
2002	18,181	
2001	16,797	7.4
2000	20,779	
1998	19,374	

The number of graduates has generally increased through the years. In many cases the ratio of full-time faculty members per graduate is between 7 and 8. However, a significant increase in the number is evident in the 10.5 value. Unfortunately, statistics are not available after 2011, and confirming a trend was not feasible. However, since collective agreements do not allow drastic changes in the student-to-professor ratios, it is likely this actually reflects an increase in the number of part-time sessional instructors in education. This would point to additional instructors with no research mandate. It also suggests a diminishing of the number of role models for tenure-track professors. If, alternatively, the ratio of graduates to full-time professors really does mean that class sizes have gone up, then professors will have increased work associated with teaching, which poses an additional challenge in balancing their research, service, and teaching proportions.

The CAUT statistics also provide details regarding gender in different roles. For simplicity, only the percentage of females is provided in table 3. This shows, remarkably, that in education, the number of females has been steadily increasing in every type of faculty role. It is notable that gender equality has been achieved for full professorships. However, at all other levels the gender inequity in faculties of education favors females.

Table 3. Percentage of Female Faculty Members

By Year	Full	Associate	Assistant	Lecturer/Other
2010/2011	49.5	57.5	61.5	69.8
2008/2009	43.0	52.6	57.2	57.5
2007/2008	39.8	53.3	57.2	56.4
2006/2007	38.3	53.1	57.7	56.0
2005/2006	35.9	52.1	43.0	58.8
2004/2005	35.3	52.1	57.3	58.1
2003/2004	33.3	49.9	56.4	57.1
2001/2002	29.9	48.1	55.4	54.8
2000/2001	29.5	47.1	54.6	57.5

The overall portrait derived from the few statistics provided in this introduction show that changes have been taking place in academia. The number of people being hired as lecturers has been increasing disproportionately, which implies increased hiring in non-research roles. The proportion of females shows that gender equity has been achieved for full professors, but also implies that equitable promotion of individuals through the ranks will lead to a female majority at all ranks.

The editors had to negotiate changes that are occurring with the tripartite definition of a professorship. While this is historically recognized as research, service, and teaching, issues with this definition exist (Watermeyer, 2015), with the focus being predominantly between research and public engagement. In the context of teaching, the latter speaks to professional leadership and community engagement. Our emphasis was on the traditional definition because it was the overwhelming majority among the responses to the call for chapters. We did receive a proposal from an assistant professor in a Canadian university that did not fit the traditional definition—they had a leadership component rather than research. This suggests readers may want to consider how tenure should be defined rather than simply accepting it as having a static, unchanging definition.

The changing circumstance of tenure led to concerns about the suitability of different methodologies that might be applied to interpret the chapters in this book. If tenure is dynamically changing, then how could we develop a norm for comparisons of different individual experiences? There are uncertainties around the level of tenured peer support for new faculty members, which potentially vary from one university to another. For this reason, we did not attempt a detailed analysis of tenure itself, nor did we examine structural aspects of the academy itself. Instead, we consider each tenure-track author in this book to be a lens on a lived experience within a changing organizational environment.

We, the editors, wrestled with issues of whether imposing a need for each chapter to have an explicit methodological framework might obscure details of the development of the natural use of such frameworks as one progresses through the tenure-track years. At the same time, the use of auto-ethnographic or autobiographical frameworks (Ellis, Adams, & Bochner, 2011) could explicitly provide a framework for chapter development. We ultimately decided not to impose a need for a framework, in order to facilitate the authentic emergence of this aspect of systematizing. We do feel that the result is "encouraging change through 'evocative stories'" (Sharp, Riera, & Jones, 2012, p. 326), and, in that respect, the book does achieve a goal of auto-ethnography. It is also addressing a gap noted by Ponjuan, Conley, and Trower (2011) that ". . . the current literature provides little insight on how pre-tenure faculty members in different career time points experience their work life" (p. 321).

A further complication was the need to respect that all of the authors are in a period of growth. The editors provided extensive feedback regarding chapters. However, in writing the section introductions we were concerned that analysis could be viewed as critical or evaluative of individuals. Doubtlessly, part of becoming an academic entails learning from some misguided thinking, but we felt it would be disrespectful as editors to challenge authors' thinking in the section introductions. The reader is advised of the need to consider the possibility that any chapter may reflect a growth in understanding that remains under development.

Numerous social and psychological issues are found in this book, most stemming from the double-edged sword of having a large degree of autonomy to carve out one's academic expertise, while finding this an isolating and lonely experience. This may be exacerbated by, to use Maslow's hierarchy of needs, having been self-actualized individuals in their prior roles and, upon moving to a university, finding themselves addressing issues as fundamental as safety in a new place, financial changes, and health needs. In the new institutional setting, there is a desire for a sense of belonging that was lost with the move from a prior role.

The need for belonging also extends to family members, including spouses and children. They are also exposed to changes of environment or, at the very least, changes that result from the family member's career change. Hours of work are no longer the same, and work-home balance is affected by the pursuit of tenure and flexibility within the academic's work schedule.

All these challenges, and many more, are found in the chapters in this book. However, while these factors must be known to graduate-school professors, there is little mention of communication about them from authors when they reflect on the preparation they received for the current role. Graduate supervisors play a role as many authors launch their tenure-track careers. However, the authors focus on the work element and the role of the supervisor in launching the new career. They do not extend their commentary to the supervisor offering advice about the larger issues of personal change of circumstance.

The editorial process of the book had some challenges. With respect to early tenure-track authors, there was a need to provide revisions that would improve clarity, while balancing that against too much editorial polishing. Group authorship had issues of just how many authors would be included in the list, and the difficulty of coordinating multiple authors in the writing process resulted in some delays in this group. Some mid- and late tenure-track individuals were anxious for the book to be published, in order for their chapter to support their application for tenure. In addition, the two editors also contributed chapters (originally written as part of the book proposal submitted to the publisher), and a conscious effort was made not to revise those chapters after receipt of any other chapters. Where minor revisions were needed, the other editor provided oversight to make sure that the meaning had not been changed. Despite the various struggles pulling this together, the volume provides significant insight into the tenure-track years and the experiences of working to earn tenure.

There are four brief prefaces that introduce the late, collaboration, mid-, and early tenure-track experiences. It is in these prefaces that individual chapter authors will be introduced. The prefaces were written by the editors based on the themes that emerged from the chapters in the respective sections. We hypothesized that duration in the tenure-track would be a significant organizing consideration and used a systematic approach to confirm that there was nothing better available. The systematic approach considered the collection of chapters and compared the chapters with each other. Our dialogue served to refine the themes to the extent needed to introduce the chapters. Readers should be careful to appreciate that the editors have not passed through all the stages that these sections represent. In this respect, we have done our best, but the reader should exercise his or her own critical appraisal.

We would be remiss if we neglected to point out a couple of potential shortcomings of the organization of this volume. It is possible that the duration of experience in a university attunes one to the norms of that institution. In this respect it may be that, rather than being more informed, experience simply gives a better understanding of how far one can push the limits. That is, a possible shortcoming of the organization may be that an alternative explanation for the progression in the level of clarity from early to late tenure-track could be at work; future research may reveal an unknown explanatory factor or mechanism. A second challenge is that prior experience may trump experience in a university, which defies an assumption that all persons in transition are equal. Is a person with a newly earned doctorate that was founded on a minimum of teaching experience to be considered equivalent to a second person who was a principal and who had considerable teaching experience prior to moving to academia? Informal expectations may simply reflect the level of competency each individual brings to their role.

References

Ellis, C., Adams, T. E., & Bochner, A. P. (2011). Autoethnography: An overview. *Forum: Qualitative Social Research, 12*(1), Art. 10.

Ponjuan, L., Conley, V. M., & Trower, C. (2011). Career stage differences in pre-tenure track faculty perceptions of professional and personal relationships with colleagues. *The Journal of Higher Education, 82*(3), 319–346.

Sharp, M. D., Riera, J. L., & Jones, S. R. (2012). Telling our stories: Using autoethnography to construct identities at the intersections. *Journal of Student Affairs Research and Practice, 49*(3), 315–332.

Watermeyer, R. (2015). Lost in the 'third space': the impact of public engagement in higher education on academic identity, research practice and career progression. *European Journal of Higher Education, 5*(3), 331–347. doi: 10.1080/21568235.2015.1044546.

SECTION I

EDITORS' PREFACE

Late Tenure-Track

The late tenure-track authors have two-and-a-half to five years of experience in academia. They have developed the role, and become more focused. The process of changing institutional settings is no longer emphasized because it is part of the story; it is integrated into a longer journey if it is mentioned at all. In this respect, the authors in this section highlight a variety of paths toward tenure, and their writing emphasizes a particular aspect of the journey. It is, to draw an analogy, as if one gets to peer through a series of microscopes that are properly focused. These multiple, clear views facilitate thinking about not only each view, but also the larger picture.

There is clarity of purpose in the writing, and the task has a structure that facilitates the clarity. These chapters have strong alignment between framework and message. The additional experience of the late tenure-track writers has facilitated improvements in their ability to convey their thinking. A small, but possibly telling, detail we noticed was that these authors conformed to style standards (for this book, APA formatting) on first submission. For example, having volume numbers italicized or a space between initials in author names in citations (e.g., Smith, A. B.) was consistently performed on the first draft. While a seemingly minor point, the editors wondered if the mastery of APA provided the opportunity for the authors to focus more on the delivery of the text itself. Suffice to say, we did very little style-guide editing in this section of the book.

The difference extends beyond style issues and the clarity of the writing, to extending and articulating the episodic focus as an integrated message. There may be better comprehension of the goal they are aiming to achieve, which contributes to increased confidence (Coke, Benson, & Hayes, 2015). Immersion in the academic environment has resulted in a perspective that clarifies the types of goals academics can realistically and meaningfully attain. Initial growth and casting about has given way to intentionality as efforts gain focus through experience. The experience includes teaching and student feedback, writing, peer review of writing, multiple rounds of editing, and an understanding of the contributions of the academy beyond the university gates. The authors reflect this grounding.

Their chapters are detailed stories that point to some of the challenges of the academic environment. More than once the editors found themselves engaged in conversation that was not about the message, but about the larger implications the messages convey.

Frank Deer is the author here who is furthest along the tenure-track. Deer addresses his journey using the research, teaching, and service demands to articulate his experience in each of these domains. His most recent experience as acting Associate Dean of Undergraduate exposes an experience some have during the tenure journey—the institutional rush to move pre-tenured faculty into significant leadership roles, making the journey itself much more complex.

Joan Chambers writes about her struggles with mental health as she progressed on her journey. She highlights resilience in the face of unanticipated challenges, which the tenure process was not designed to accommodate. Chambers has found collegial and institutional support, patience, and caring, which have been critical to her transition.

Lee Anne Block identifies issues of agency and the validity of the success or failure paradigm. She writes a careful analysis of how this dualistic view, so deeply imbedded in the tenure process and in the lives of those in the tenure process, models outdated and inappropriate reasoning for teacher candidates, as well as for others we are hoping to help on their academic journey.

Cecile Badenhorst shares her story of immigrating to Canada from South Africa. She speaks of cultural differences that include English-language usage. Her arrival revealed challenges of having her background understood and fully appreciated. While her experience in South Africa was significant, it was not necessarily perfect preparation for a Canadian university.

Greg Rickwood is our final, and least experienced, late tenure-track author. He identifies the importance mentors have played in his "long walk down a short road" to tenure. As with the other late-tenure authors, Greg has divided his chapter into clearly delineated sections. He addresses his perspectives about successfully lopping the heads off the "three-headed" hydra that tenure can seem to be.

Reference

Coke, P. K., Benson, S., & Hayes, M. (2015). Making meaning of experience: Navigating the transformation from graduate student to tenure-track professor. *Journal of Transformative Education, 13*(2), 110–126.

CHAPTER 1

On the Tenure-Track: Navigating Research, Teaching, and Service Responsibilities in a U15 Institution

Frank Deer
Faculty of Education, University of Manitoba

Introduction: Entering the Academy

In July of 2009, I accepted a tenure-track position as assistant professor in the University of Manitoba's Faculty of Education. This position, in the Department of Curriculum, Teaching and Learning, was intended to develop the faculty's capacity in the area of Indigenous education. Having completed a PhD at the University of Saskatchewan, where I studied citizenship education as it was manifest in Manitoba's then-new social-studies curriculum, I felt I was prepared to serve the emergent area of Indigenous perspectives in curriculum and learning. I remained in my tenure-track position for just over five years and filed for tenure and promotion in June. In that time, I've acquired rich experiences as a scholar—experiences that are associated with the three principal areas of concern for faculty members: teaching, research, and service.

In the area of teaching, I have had the opportunity to engage in course development, specifically in the relatively new area of Indigenous curriculum and learning. With a focus on language and literacy (in English- and non–English-language contexts) across the curriculum, I've been afforded the chance to create opportunities for students in initial teacher education to interface with Indigenous perspectives. In a provincial jurisdiction where imperatives associated with Indigenous perspectives have become more espoused by legislators and school administrators, this is an exciting time to be involved. I've also had the opportunity to teach in graduate and post-baccalaureate classes while supervising MEd and PhD level students. The organizational structures at my university, as well as within the provincial ministry, have supported my work greatly. The institutional and collegial realities have empowered me.

In the area of research, I've benefited from a relatively rich, supportive, and diverse group of colleagues, some internal to the university, others external and in the professional field, and still others in the communities in which I work. As Indigenous education research is still a developing area that has become respected, there are many opportunities to engage with novel, unique areas of research that can inform policy, pedagogy, and curriculum in positive ways. As a recipient of a research grant from the Social Sciences and Humanities Research Council of Canada (SSHRC), I am now studying the community capacity to re-establish and maintain Indigenous languages in Canada. My journey toward establishing my program of research as a tenure-track assistant professor is a departure from my experiences as a doctoral student, in so far as the standards for rigor of research and the primacy assigned to partnerships have become more significant. Although my graduate-student experiences offered valuable lessons in grant acquisition and effective research, it is in my current role with the support of my colleagues and partners where I've experienced the most scholarly growth.

In the area of service, I've been afforded the opportunity to work in campus-based and off-campus environments in literacy activities, games for underprivileged youth, board membership in public organizations, lectures to secondary-school students, professional development work, and other activities that support the field of education.

In spite of these activities that may represent the diligent and faithful execution of the duties of a tenure-track assistant professor, there are questions I continue to ask myself: Have I done enough? Are the journals in which I am published of appropriate standards? Are my teacher evaluations sufficiently favorable? Will my research be viewed as sufficiently acceptable? Who will be the members of my tenure and promotion committee and will they see things as I do? I hope the following will communicate the vagaries of tenure criteria, the lack of firm guidelines, and pressures to perform in the first years of a professor's career.

Navigating Research

Research, which is described more broadly at my university as "research, scholarly work and other creative activities" (University of Manitoba, 2010, Article 19.A.2.4.1.6), may be seen by many of my colleagues as the reason they wished to become a professor. Indigenous research as a field of study that is significant and worthy of consideration for social and scientific betterment is a relatively new sentiment (Wilson, 2008). Some may suggest that the progress, quality, and foundational values of recent and contemporary research in the field of Indigenous education has its political/legislative roots in the final report and recommendations of the Royal Commission on Aboriginal Peoples (RCAP; Indian and Northern Affairs Canada, 1996). There may be some justification for such suggestions—although federal officials responded to some of the recommendations of the report (Niezen, 2013), many initiatives on the part of provincial education authorities as well as that of universities cite RCAP as a principal point-of-inquiry (Castellano, Davis, & Lahache, 2000). The effects that RCAP and other socio-political developments in the last three decades have had on my area of scholarship, Indigenous education, have been significant. The interest in Indigenous issues has been reflected in new areas of scholarly exploration funded by the SSHRC as well as within the U15 group (www.u15.ca) of Canadian research-intensive universities. This interest appears to be driven by the desire to better understand the Canadian Indigenous experience (Kanu, 2011). My research interests have corresponded with these developments; it is possible that the progress I've experienced in my research (e.g., grant acquisition, partnership development) has been facilitated by the increased interest in Indigenous issues across Canada and abroad.

Like many tenure-track professors, the research activities with which I was engaged in my doctoral studies extended into the initial stages of my tenure-track professorship. Facilitated, in part, by the fact that only eight months separated the completion of my doctoral studies and the commencement of my role as a tenure-track assistant professor, I believed that I bore a sort of scholarly agency; I had something unique to say about my research, and I had scholarly forums in which to say it. The topic of my doctoral dissertation yielded some discussion at conferences and a small number of publications in the 12 months following my graduation (accounting for the first portions of my professorship). The legacy of my doctoral work was a belief in myself as a researcher and the potential that what I research and disseminate can have a desired effect upon the field of Indigenous education.

During my tenure-track period, I've received a number of small and internal research grants as well as a few travel grants to support the dissemination of my research. These grants supported the development of a program of research that explored the use of Indigenous perspectives in teacher education, the development of culturally relevant secondary-school learning to support the post-secondary aspirations of Indigenous students, and Indigenous curriculum studies. There were a number of crucial lessons I learned with these initial studies, of which two merit elaboration here. First, prior to my role as a tenure-track assistant professor, I had only one significant interaction with the process of research ethics boards—that being associated with my doctoral work. In that instance, the acquisition of clearance to proceed with my research was not very rigorous compared to the amount of work necessary to do so now. There appears to be one important reason for this: the *Tri-Council Policy Statement: Ethical Conduct for Research Involving Humans*, the governing document for ethics in research in my area of scholarship (Government of Canada, 2010), was renewed, and new requirements and issues emerged, placing an increased burden upon the researcher. Much of what became required by research ethics boards of universities, in order to conduct research, is included in the requirement of completing an online tutorial for which one receives a certificate. Developments such as this were part of a greater sensitivity towards ethics in university research in recent years (Bogdan & Biklen, 2007). The development of research ethics applications during my tenure-track period allowed me the opportunity to refine my own sensitivity toward human ethics as well as temper my work with the expectations of ethics boards.

In addition to ethics, the importance of funding acquisition has also been a lesson of sorts in my journey as a tenure-track assistant professor. As a new member of the professoriate in my faculty in 2009, I was provided a small amount of money via a research start-up fund. Although this resource funded some of the work I did in the initial stages of my time in my faculty, there was pressure to seek out and acquire funds from elsewhere, in order to continue with my program of research. Internal grants of a few thousand dollars each and a few travel grants facilitated my progress. However, internal funds for research were granted with the tacitly understood notion that external funding, particularly tri-council funding, would be pursued. Tri-council funding is seen as important for a variety of reasons—supplementary institutional funding (from the SSHRC, the Natural Sciences and Engineering Research Council, and the Canadian Institutes of Health Research), partnership opportunities, and prestige (among others). The portion of the tri-council from which I would solicit funds, the SSHRC, is one in which the application and review processes are rigorous. It took some time before I was comfortable with and attuned to the application process as a principal investigator. In addition, I was fortunate that my faculty is home to a Research Grants Facilitator, who is responsible for assisting in grant writing and other research-related activities.

What has been important for my development is that these experiences led to the successful acquisition of research funding from the SSHRC. My current area of research that is funded by this SSHRC grant, Indigenous language education, has the potential to bring the same personal and scholarly rewards that I described earlier in regard to my doctoral work. My experiences as a tenure-track assistant professor, which have included committee work, tenure workshops, and professional dialogues, have revealed an important truth regarding research: grant acquisition is essential for conducting even modestly sized studies. Also, the sort of external grant sources one pursues to support research may have important affects upon how one is judged in the acquisition of tenure and promotion.

Navigating Teaching

When I began in my role as a tenure-track assistant professor, I saw the three principal areas of responsibility that were described to me at the outset—research, teaching, and service—to be three relatively equal areas of responsibility in terms of importance as well as demands upon my time. Faculty administrators have informed me that the tenure and promotion process will look upon these three areas in this way. However, it is clear that the discharge of my duties in the area of teaching is administered with departmental oversight in a manner that does not occur in the other two areas. Otherwise stated, my research and service activities take place at (principally) my initiative, with very little administrative oversight. With regard to teaching, I am assigned teaching duties from my department head at a rate commensurate with the credit hours for which I am responsible each year. Perhaps understandably, teaching is the portion of the three areas of responsibility that is most regularly scrutinized by administrators outside of the tenure and promotion process. There is a clientele, in the form of students, to whom we provide courses, supervisory support, and, in many cases, requisite practical experiences. The accountability associated with the provision of these services requires careful administrative planning, diligent and faithful management, and quality control in the form of instructor evaluations. In my experience, when the duties of professors are discussed by administrators, outside of tenure, promotion, and annual progress reports, it is teaching that is of principal concern. There are times in my experience when I see myself, principally, as an instructor—so great is the overt pressure to perform in this area.

The courses I have been assigned have been those that cover content that aligns with my scholarly interests. Every undergraduate, post-baccalaureate, and graduate-level course that I've been assigned for the first time has required development on my part. Recent developments in my area of scholarship have led to a need for such new courses. As mentioned previously, the release of the report of the Royal Commission on Aboriginal Peoples (Indian and Northern Affairs Canada, 1996) informed developments in provincially controlled sectors such as health and education (Dickason & Newbigging, 2010), and many changes in the area of Indigenous education occurred in Manitoba. In regard to primary and secondary education, teacher resources and grade-specific curricula were developed. Cross-grade and cross-discipline resources that utilized an integrative framework were introduced, and the discipline of Native Studies (Manitoba Education, 2011) became an accepted teachable subject (i.e., it became possible for teacher candidates to major or minor in Native Studies in a teacher-education program). In a relatively short period of time, provincial authorities (amongst others) had begun responding to a new socio-political development—that the Canadian Indigenous experience merits exploration in primary and secondary schools and is relevant to all future teachers. The implication for faculties/colleges of education was the need to respond with appropriate programming that reflects the emergent area of Indigenous education. In 2006, education authorities in the Manitoba government created the mandate that all students graduating from an initial teacher-education program would complete three credit hours of course work in the area of Indigenous studies. My faculty has created numerous courses that may be used for this purpose and, at the time of writing, about 80% of my teaching has been in courses that fulfill this requirement.

Teaching in a relatively new area of scholarship that is required by the government for all students of initial teacher-education programs—an area of study that has the potential to cover content that may be seen as politically and racially charged—can be a challenge. Through discussion within the relatively small community of instructors in Canada that teach such courses, I've found that some have had positive experiences while others have experienced resistance. It has become clear that there is an important dimension in the teaching of Indigenous education—the sometimes relentless reference to history and Indigenous historical narrative. It seems that the balance between discourses in history that explore colonial and post-colonial experiences and the need for practical knowledge that will be applied in classrooms is important. I would characterize my position on this as being responsive to the need for discussion, resources, and exploration of best practices in the areas of Indigenous curriculum and pedagogy. The task that I feel I must set for myself in the tenure and promotion process is to make this position clear to my committee, and to demonstrate how this position, and the way in which it informs my teaching, is responsive to the field of primary and secondary education.

Navigating Service

The service component of my responsibilities is perhaps the most undefined of my three principal areas of work. Service, which is defined at my institution as "those internal and external activities which arise from the research and teaching functions of the University" (University of Manitoba, 2010, Article 19.A.2.4.3), can be understood as a responsibility that exists in order to ensure that professors serve as public intellectuals whose raison d'être is the acquisition and dissemination of knowledge. Activities such as campus governance, committee work, consultation on academic matters with students, and support of external community activities that are commensurate with one's area of work may fulfill the service component. The description of service in my university's collective agreement is rather open in so far as it allows for many different sorts of activities that may be undertaken on the judgment and initiative of the professor.

One of the perennial concerns regarding service is how a professor, especially those who are tenure-track, may act appropriately in order for service to be favorably assessed during the tenure and/or promotion process. There is an aspect of service in my particular experience that is not as prevalent for most tenure-track assistant professors. Currently, my university is aggressively negotiating how it will respond to the discourses and imperatives associated with the Canadian Indigenous experience. As an Indigenous faculty member who works in the area of Indigenous education, I have received many invitations to participate in activities internal and external to the university from Indigenous people and organizations as well as from the field. Many feel that it is important to have an Indigenous voice in administrative activities, consultations, and internal/community events; I've had more opportunities to participate in such activities than I can perhaps manage. Although service activities may be available in virtually all disciplines, there are fewer Indigenous faculty like myself to fill these roles. I have had to make judgments regarding where I will commit myself based on, amongst other criteria, where my efforts will have most benefit for the field of primary and secondary education.

Much of my recent activity in the area of service may be characterized as attempts to affect the scholarly dimensions of Indigenous education in Canada—activities that have afforded me the opportunity to meet and collaborate with faculty from across Canada and abroad. In 2012, I was elected to serve as the first vice-president of the Canadian Association for the Study of Indigenous Education (CASIE). A constituent association of the Canadian Society for the Study of Education, CASIE was established in 2008 and provides forums for scholarly presentations and discussion in the field of Indigenous education. Now serving as president of CASIE, I am responsible for conference planning, management of the CASIE executive, publication opportunities, and other activities. The required travel, teleconferences, and other tasks make this portion of my service perhaps the most onerous—but possibly the most rewarding.

The forums in which I work through CASIE reflect a truth about service as it is manifest in my professional identity: I often feel as though I have the most impact upon the field of primary and secondary education through my service activities. Perhaps this feeling is informed by the opportunity to interface with teachers and other stakeholders who voluntarily attend, listen, or otherwise consume my ideas, thoughts, and insights. In taking advantage of frequent speaking opportunities, writing of op-ed news pieces, and discussions I've initiated in a podcast I host with a colleague at another university (Podbean.com, n.d.), I've received appreciative and critical responses to my work and views that are not always forthcoming in respect to the two other sets of activities. I am of the opinion that the tenure and promotion process will entail articulating service as the principal means of disseminating my work in a way that promotes my field as well as the work of my university.

Conclusion

The culmination of my tenure-track activities will be my attempt to acquire tenure and promotion in September. This involves the declaration of my intent to move forward with the process, striking of the requisite committee, developing a package of materials that will serve as evidence of my activities during my tenure-track period, and the final tenure and promotion hearing that resembles (I'm told) a dissertation defense. Along the way there will be a variety of formal and informal meetings to discuss the process and my application. It has been stated that the three areas discussed above—research, teaching, service—will be the principal foci of my eventual tenure and promotion committee.

In my situation, there is another significant aspect of my time as a tenure-track assistant professor that may or may not positively affect my efforts to acquire tenure and promotion. In December of 2013, I was asked by my Dean to serve as acting Associate Dean Undergraduate in our faculty for the first six months of 2014. In this role, I was, in part, responsible for administrative, staffing, and disciplinary issues associated with the Bachelor of Education program. This meant that I chaired numerous committees, received and frequently adjudicated disciplinary issues, and managed the areas of admissions, student services, school experiences, and student awards. As a member of the Dean's administrative team, I also had opportunity to confer with others in administrative roles (e.g., department heads and directors) in order to ensure the effective management of the faculty.

Following the completion of this term as acting Associate Dean, I was appointed to the role of Director of Indigenous Initiatives—a new and ongoing role intended to support the improvement of Indigenous research, teaching, and service in the faculty, as well as academic achievement for Indigenous students. Both of these positions are administrative in nature—the consequence being that I have had less time to devote to teaching and research. From my perspective, the acquisition of administrative duties as a tenure-track assistant professor does not appear to be a common experience at a U15 Canadian university because the administrative duties associated with such positions reduce productivity in relation to the tenure application. This was a possibility that I considered prior to accepting these appointments.

I currently believe there is a fundamental, new quality to my field that may not be as significant in other disciplines. This governs the professional choices I have made and appears to govern the administrative choices of others who have influence or authority over my activities (e.g., my current Dean, who has made possible for me many opportunities for professional growth). That new quality may be best understood by considering university responses to the growing desire/need for Indigenous content, Indigenous perspectives, and the affecting of culture and climate in our institutions. Because the provision of Indigenous content, perspectives, and relevant institutional changes are relatively new initiatives, many existing institutional structures may not be readily responsive to this new imperative. In recent years, universities across Canada have ventured to improve their programs and campuses in a manner that is responsive to the Canadian Indigenous experience. In a sense, my current professional context is the result of my university's efforts to improve itself in this way. Faculties such as mine require staff, instructors, and professors who will inform the undertaking of appropriate institutional improvements. I'm currently involved in the creation of new programs that are essential to the emerging field of Indigenous education. The institutional, academic, and social-justice importance for such programs is what I hope to communicate to the tenure and promotion committee in order to justify my professional choices during my tenure-track experience.

I've dedicated some space in this chapter toward articulating my perspectives on the vagaries of what I experienced on the journey toward acquiring tenure and promotion at a Canadian university. In those experiences, two things have been made clear to me about the process that I have undertaken: first, that the tenure and promotion process has the potential to be very appreciative and comfortable. Second, the realization of an appreciative tenure and promotion process depends upon the quality of work that I present and how I articulate that work in the context of research, teaching, and service. I can appreciate that the needs of the university, in part codified in my original letter of offer for my tenure-track professorship, are closely associated with my productivity in these three areas. However, essential to any professor's scholarly identity is the consideration of research, teaching, and service with the use of a discipline-based framework that will allow one's self to participate effectively in the acquisition and dissemination of knowledge for the betterment of all people.

My entry into my chosen career path was borne out of a desire to bring my perceived aptitudes and skills to bear in such ways as to affect the quality of human knowledge and discourse for the better. I think this is true of many professors: we want to make a difference. As a coherent whole, the initial stages of my career may be understood through my activities over the tenure-track period, but it is my hope that it is also understood as being the scholarly trajectory I've chosen in an effort to discover knowledge and moral truth, and to help others to do likewise.

References

Bogdan, R. C., & Biklen, S. K. (2007). *Qualitative research for education: An introduction to theories and methods* (5th ed.). Boston, MA: Pearson Education.

Castellano, M. B., Davis, L., & Lahache, L. (2000). *Aboriginal education: Fulfilling the promise.* Vancouver, BC: University of British Columbia Press.

Dickason, O. P., & Newbigging, W. (2010). *A concise history of Canada's First Nations* (2nd ed.). Don Mills, ON: Oxford University Press.

Government of Canada. (2010). *Tri-council policy statement: Ethical conduct for research involving humans.* Retrieved from http://www.pre.ethics.gc.ca/pdf/eng/tcps2/TCPS_2_FINAL_Web.pdf.

Indian and Northern Affairs Canada. (1996). *Report of the royal commission on Aboriginal peoples.* Ottawa, ON: Author.

Kanu, Y. (2011). *Integrating Aboriginal perspectives into the school curriculum: Purposes, possibilities, and challenges.* Toronto, ON: University of Toronto Press.

Manitoba Education. (2011). *Grade 12 current topics in First Nations, Metis, and Inuit studies: A foundation for implementation.* Retrieved from http://www.edu.gov.mb.ca/k12/abedu/foundation_gr12/full_doc.pdf.

Niezen, R. (2013). *Truth and indignation: Canada's Truth and Reconciliation Commission on Indian Residential Schools.* Toronto, ON: University of Toronto Press.

Podbean.com. (n.d.). *The Frank and Kevin Show: In Colour.* http://frankandkevin.podbean.com

University of Manitoba. (2010). *University of Manitoba—University of Manitoba Faculty Association 2010–2013 collective agreement.* Retrieved from http://umfa.ca/pdf/collective_agreement/20102013/1013_collective_agreement.pdf.

Wilson, S. (2008). *Research is ceremony: Indigenous research methods.* Halifax, NS: Fernwood.

CHAPTER 2

Meet Jill—She Fell Down the Hill but Came Back up Again: Struggling With Mental Illness While on the Path to Tenure

Joan M. Chambers
Faculty of Education, Lakehead University

Jack and Jill went up the hill
To fetch a pail of water.
Jack fell down and broke his crown,
While Jill came tumbling after.
~ Traditional 18th-century English nursery rhyme

This is my story of becoming an academic. My story is not unlike the story of *Jack and Jill*, minus the Jack. I'm Jill. I fell down a hill, but I came back up again. It is not an easy story for me to tell because it reveals the truth of me for all to see: the vulnerable me. Though my story reflects who I am, my personal experiences, and my journey—that does not mean snippets of my story might not be reflective of your own. Reading my story just might resonate with you, the academic-to-be or current tenure-track assistant professor, and help you realize that we are not alone on this arduous journey to tenure—there are commonalities and shared experiences. Depending on your place within your own journey, perhaps my story may ease your journey, feel familiar, or at least remind you that we are all human, complete with human frailties and vulnerabilities. It may (or may not) validate your own story, thoughts, and feelings. You are not on your own, even within the siloed halls of academia.

The Academic Journey Begins

My journey through undergraduate to graduate school and finally on to academia and the tenure-track has taken me along a path that often curved where I thought it ran straight, or forced me to climb hills steeper than I imagined. My journey has been adventurous, shifting, bewildering, and challenging in unexpected ways. Though I graduated in 1985 with my Bachelor of Education, I did not teach in a formal school setting. Instead, I chose the path of motherhood, caring for my children at home for a number of years. I began graduate studies at the University of Alberta in 2000 in the Master of Education program, specializing in Instructional Technology. I graduated in 2002 and ventured out into the workforce but left a toehold in the world of academia through my continued work as a research assistant. Following a year of part-time work (teaching part time and supply teaching in the K-12 school system, as well as continuing as a research assistant), I entered the doctoral program at the University of Alberta in 2003 in Elementary Education, focusing on science and environmental education, graduating with a PhD in June 2007. My graduate studies did not end there, however; I began postdoctoral studies in September 2007 with the university's Department of Secondary Education and a focus on climate-change education. Though my postdoctoral research was not complete, I began my current position as a tenure-track assistant professor in January 2009 at Lakehead University, a northern Ontario university located in the city of Thunder Bay.

How I Arrived at Graduate School

I suppose my story, thus told, appears fairly uncomplicated, but that was not my experience of events as they transpired. I had been a stay-at-home mom from the time of graduation with my Bachelor of Education degree in 1985 (eight-months pregnant while writing finals) until I found myself a single mother of three and began looking, unsuccessfully, for work as a classroom teacher in 1997. Obtaining a teaching position following a twelve-year career hiatus to raise my children was not as straightforward as I had (naïvely) hoped. I upgraded, taking three fourth-year university courses in reading and reading diagnostics, but to no avail.

It was at this time that I decided a complete career change was in order—I trained as a computer network specialist and acquired a position at a local school board as a network technician. I repaired computers, updated servers and computer labs, and helped support personnel, teachers, and staff with their technical needs. The two most frequent calls for help? "I can't print!" and "I forgot my password!"

Not enamored with my job as a network technician, combined with daily exposure to schools, classrooms, and children, resulted in feeling compelled to upgrade once again. I wanted that elusive teaching career. I entered into a Master of Education in Instructional Technology program within the Department of Educational Psychology at the University of Alberta. My hope was that a Master's degree would help me to gain employment as a classroom teacher. Finally my plan worked; the local public-school board hired me as both a supply teacher and as a part-time computer teacher for Grades 7, 8, and 9. I was also working as a research assistant at the university at the time, and was thoroughly enjoying the research work.

My work as a research assistant concerned the integration of climate-change education within the enacted elementary-science curriculum. My future PhD supervisor was my research supervisor; she and my Master's supervisor were the ones who pushed me to complete a doctorate. And so, I began my journey through doctoral studies in an area of study completely different from my Master's work. I switched to the Elementary Education Department at the University of Alberta and began my studies in elementary science and environmental education. This was clearly a good choice, as I had the good fortune to receive a doctoral grant through the Social Sciences and Humanities Research Council of Canada (SSHRC).

My four years as a doctoral student were followed immediately by postdoctoral studies (also SSHRC funded) in the Department of Secondary Education at the University of Alberta. It was during my time as a postdoctoral fellow that I began applying for tenure-track positions at various universities in Canada and in the United States. After four interviews and two offers of employment, I chose the university I am currently with, ultimately ending up as a tenure-track assistant professor.

Beginning on the Path to Tenure

I thought I was well prepared to enter the world of academia. After all, I had received two SSHRC research grants and several awards; had publications (six peer-reviewed papers, three conference proceedings, and one book chapter); had travelled with my supervisor to present at international conferences; taught undergraduate and graduate courses; and had served as president of a graduate students' association, on a postdoctoral fellows association, and on faculty council in the University of Alberta's Department of Secondary Education while a postdoctoral fellow. I knew about scholarship and research, teaching, and service before I even began searching for a position at a university—my supervisor was absolutely amazing and had prepared me well, or so I thought. However, it was as a beginning tenure-track assistant professor that I learned how being a top-notch student much of my life did little to prepare me for the realities of my new life as an academic at a university in an unfamiliar city and province.

Though I eagerly headed east to begin a new stage in my life, I was not prepared for the demands of a nearly full teaching load, service duties, writing, and beginning new research projects, essentially all on my own. I was also not prepared for the challenges of moving away from Alberta, leaving my family and home to begin life anew at 50 years old. My children did not fly the coop; I did, with no concept of "empty nest syndrome" (Harkness, 2008). In the field of education, especially for women, academic careers tend to begin later in life, though the demands for tenure "make few concessions for late entry" (Acker, 1997, p. 72). I struggled both professionally and personally in a world that does little to accommodate for either area of challenge.

I frequently stumbled along the way, felt alone and abandoned, and was, for the most part, left on my own to figure things out as I went along. A caveat, however: I recognize that it may come across as though I landed in an uncaring or uninvolved faculty, which is far from the truth. I am surrounded by very caring and understanding colleagues (faculty, administration, and staff), but as an introvert and a newbie, it took time to discover how to reach out for support and just how fortunate I really am in my place of work.

On my first day as an assistant professor, in January 2009, I found myself wandering the education building, trying to find someone who might give me a key to an office I assumed I had; a computer and email address would also have been helpful, especially considering I was to teach my first class that very afternoon. I soon discovered that a January start date is less than ideal as it leaves little to no time for preparation by both the faculty and the beginning professor. Somehow, miraculously, I made it through that first teaching term, I thought, unscathed. Little did I know that was the beginning of my personal and consequent professional unravelling.

The Intertwining of Personal and Professional Challenges

Because we (perhaps I, but I suspect not) cannot easily separate who we are from what we do, especially in the world of academia, I have chosen to explore both personal and professional contexts dialogically, as they are interwoven with my progress through the tenure process.

Throughout graduate school, I was driven onward by my personal need to succeed; I was also drawn towards the notion of new experiences and a chance to begin life anew. However, I, like many other graduate students, experienced feelings of being an impostor, defined by Clance (1985) as, "individuals [who] experience intense feelings that their achievements are undeserved and worry that they are likely to be exposed as a fraud" (cited in Sakulku & Alexander, 2011, p. 75). These feelings of being an impostor did not diminish once I was hired as a tenure-track assistant professor; rather they intensified.

In my new surroundings—living alone for the first time in 29 years, feeling lost and lonely, and having left family and friends behind—I began to seriously doubt my ability to cope. The responsibility I felt and the demands of my work were more than I had anticipated. At 50 years of age, I felt a decrease in both physical energy and mental stamina compared to my younger self, and in comparison with my younger colleagues. Though tenure was a far-off goal, I felt the pressure of achieving tenure almost immediately. After all, I was 50! What would my options be in six years' time if I were not successful in achieving tenure? So I worked as hard as I could, but it just did not seem quite good enough; I felt unable to keep up with the demands placed on beginning faculty on the road to tenure—a road with a long history, which, in my opinion, needs some "road work" to upgrade it to a travelable condition.

The beginning roots of what we now refer to as tenure are old, commencing in the 12th century as a way to protect academic freedom (Cameron & College, 2010). Though it has undergone significant revision over time, the contemporary tenure process in Canada and the United States more or less follows and is essentially unchanged since "the 1940 Statement of Principles on Academic Freedom and Tenure …, published by the American Association of University Professors (AAUP)" (Cameron & College, 2010, p. 1). Tenure was traditionally designed for white males who were at the beginning of their long and illustrious careers as academics. Quinn, Edwards Lange, and Riskin (2004) state, "the tenure-track is modeled on a traditional career trajectory that either had a full-time caregiver in the home or had no family obligations" (p. 1). As such, the tenure process was not designed with women (or men) in mind who wanted to balance family life with career (Trower, 2006). Nor was the tenure process designed for delayed entry into the world of academia, such as those in education, who typically have teaching careers prior to entry into graduate school, or for women, like me, who had delayed their entry while raising their family. Life experience, of which I have plenty, is unrecognized in the tenure process. Furthermore, "this outdated model has been shown to jeopardize the attainment of tenure for the growing ranks of women and men faculty who are caregivers" (Quinn, Edwards Lange, & Riskin, 2004, p. 1), including those often termed the "sandwich generation" (Canadian Press, 2014)—those people (primarily women) caring for and/or supporting children while also caring for and/or supporting aging parents. I'm a sandwich.

September 2009—a new academic year, new courses to teach, the daylong seminar for new hires (not offered in January due to the size of the university), and the official start of my tenure clock. Tick, tick, tick … Unfortunately, it wasn't until the new fall term began that I realized I was suffering from mental illness. Having no access to a family doctor, a concern for anyone moving to a new city in Canada given the current pressures on the health-care system (Muzyka, Hodgson, & Prada, 2012), I went to the hospital emergency department to seek help. "Depression," the emergency-room (ER) doctor said, and he sent me on my way with a prescription for Prozac and the address of the city's only walk-in clinic that will see patients who do not have a family doctor.

I do not want to construct a notion of cause and effect—that the pressure of work and the tenure process led to my depression. The causes of depression are complex (Mood Disorders of Canada, 2013), involving environment, biology, past and present experiences and our interpretations of those experiences, and so forth. The stressors I was facing at work did not cause my depression but formed part of the environmental factors leading to the emergence of the illness. I do not want to get into all the gory details of my struggles with mental illness; I could not possibly begin to describe what it is like as eloquently and powerfully as Barbara Jago (2002) does in her auto-ethnography *Chronicling an academic depression*—an amazing read. Suffice it to say that it took me two years to find a family doctor, several medication changes, and more than two years, along with a few trips to the ER, to find a psychiatrist. My saving graces were, and still are, my amazing therapist (confidentially recommended to me by a colleague), a close friend I found (or who found me) within the faculty, a supportive and caring psychiatrist, my family, and as my illness became manifest in later years, my Dean (I kept my condition hidden from him at first), neighbours, and colleagues.

Armed as pitifully as I was in the 2009/2010 academic year, with my pills and my determination to succeed, I plowed on, teaching courses as fervently as I could and providing service to the faculty, the university, and my professional community. Scholarship and research? That fell by the wayside as I had my hands and head full with all I could manage. I also did my utmost to keep my struggles with mental illness a secret, known only to a very select few—a secret that is possible to keep hidden within academia where you are not visibly "on the job" daily. I was afraid of the stigma associated with mental illness and the possible repercussions on renewal and tenure; I felt incredibly vulnerable and disempowered. Surprisingly, perhaps shockingly, however, I received a nomination for a Contribution to Teaching Award that academic year, but since I was considered to be in my first year of teaching at the university, was ironically ineligible for the award.

My progress in my second academic year (2010/2011) was much the same as the first, though I did manage to publish a book chapter. Fortunately, a graduate student from a spring course I taught asked me to collaborate with her in order to obtain research funding from the Teacher Learning and Leadership Program (TLLP)—a teacher-initiated, government-funded action research initiative sponsored by the Ontario Ministry of Education. She was a vice-principal at a local school and hoped to initiate a project in her school, integrating environmental education with literacy. Since my doctoral research was conceptually framed by the notion of environment as text (Chambers, 2007), we based our proposal on the theory behind my doctoral work and were successful in receiving funding. I finally had some research set in motion.

The spring and summer of 2011 were spent preparing for the TLLP project, driving to Alberta for a visit with family, and planning for fall teaching, all the while feeling stressed about maintaining the pace and feeling so very alone upon my return to Ontario. The halls in the education building seemed eerily empty through the summer period. However, establishing the research protocol, obtaining ethics approval though the Research Ethics Board (REB), providing the teachers involved in the study with professional development, acquiring additional research funding through the Faculty of Education, hiring a research assistant, and obtaining consent from parents and children was completed by mid-fall 2011, allowing us to proceed with the study. Everything seemed to be going well—the research, my teaching, and my service, all seemingly balanced with my personal life as a mom and daughter. Though Jill's pail was full, perhaps overly full, she thought she was managing, when it suddenly tipped, spilling its contents. The slope became horribly slippery ... Jill fell tumbling down the hill. I suffered a serious mental-health crisis, landing me in hospital for three weeks in October/November, the middle of the fall teaching term. The secret was out. The faculty scrambled to cover my classes, my co-researcher and research assistant carried on with the research project, and my family and friends ensured my home and dogs were well taken care of. It was at this time that I took a six-and-a-half-month leave of absence in order to literally claw my way back up the hill towards mental health. Cognitively, I was forever changed. The hope, and belief, that I could succeed as an academic vanished, whisked away by the shifting winds of depression. I came precipitously close to resigning and moving back home with my tail tucked between my legs. I didn't though. I'm not entirely sure why, but I worked damn hard, harder than I ever have in my life, in order to regain that life and return to the university and my position as a tenure-track assistant professor. All was not sunshine and daisies though.

Despite the intensive therapy I had undergone, my psychiatrist and therapist were very concerned about my return to work after only a six-month recovery period. They were taken aback by human resources' insistence that I return to work full time; they presumably thought I was able to take on the full duties and responsibilities of an academic. Unfortunately, there is no contingency within academia, at least not at my university, for a graduated return to work for faculty. No accommodation, such as temporary reduction in workload to allow for reintegration and building of resiliency, for mental illness was allowed. I was counseled by my health team to consider delaying my return to work for a full year, but I was far too concerned about renewal and tenure, so I started back May 2012.

I returned to my office, feeling anxious and afraid. My illness was no longer a secret—how would my colleagues treat me? How would they react to the invisible and visible scars of my illness? What would my Dean say to me? I remember those early days, hurrying from my office to the washroom and back again, hoping against hope that I would pass unnoticed and unseen. But my fears were not grounded in reality. My colleagues genuinely welcomed me back, expressing their care and concern. And my Dean offered me his full support; he wanted to see me succeed. Arrangements were made, and I met with him monthly for close to a year to discuss my progress towards tenure, strategically planning how I could best meet the academic requirements.

The next year and a half was not easy. It took every ounce of strength I could muster to walk into class to teach that first day in fall 2012. I visibly shook with anxiety, hoping my students wouldn't notice. But I now had the support and help of my colleagues and my Dean, and there was no way I was going to let them down. So I taught my full-course load as best I could. I served on faculty and university committees, reviewed papers and conference proposals, examined theses, and saw my first thesis student to completion. I managed to analyze the data collected from the TLLP research, which had carried on in my absence, and with my co-researcher, presented our research at two high-level academic conferences: the American Education Research Association (AERA), and the National Association of Research in Science Teaching (NARST). Together, we authored and published two peer-reviewed academic papers. I was back on the road to tenure.

Jill, my other self, was not gone during this time; she appeared over and over again—recovering from major depression does not have a straightforward trajectory—but I never fell quite so far down the hill as I had that October, and each time I climbed back up the hill, I knew I was no longer climbing on my own.

Conclusion

The tenure process is challenging for any beginning academic. It has to be one of the longest probationary periods in the world of work. With it comes enormous pressure and a heavy workload because it continues to be modeled after an outdated old-boys system. No matter the faculty, the demands of the tenure process do not easily allow for a balance of life and work, and the exigencies continue to disadvantage women, especially those in the sandwich generation. Within faculties of education, where late entry is not uncommon, inadequate consideration is accorded beginning academics at a different stage in their lives, nor is recognition of life/work (i.e., teaching) experience made note of on the tenure balance sheet. The clock starts ticking anew once employment at the university has begun. Finally my struggle with mental illness could very well have ended my career before it had begun, but I am very fortunate to be in a faculty where the people see me as more than my illness and have unquestionably supported me on my journey to achieving tenure.

Jill is with me still, perhaps always will be, but I now acknowledge her presence and continue to work towards maintaining mental health and well-being. In order to do so, I know I must take the necessary steps to create balance in my life, whatever that may mean in terms of tenure. At my age and stage of life, I feel I really have no other choice. Besides, being a professor in education is a part of who I am; it's what I want to do.

References

Acker, S. (1997). Becoming a teacher educator: Voices of women academics in Canadian faculties of education. *Teaching and Teacher Education, 13* (1), 65–74.

Cameron, M., & College, D. (2010). Faculty Tenure in Academe: The Evolution, Benefits and Implications of an Important Tradition. *Journal of Student Affairs at New York University 5*, 1–9. Retrieved from http://steinhardt.nyu.edu/scmsAdmin/media/users/lh62/CameronJoSA_.pdf.

Canadian Press. (2014). *'Sandwich Generation' squeezed by caring for parents and kids: BMO,* August 12, 2014. Retrieved from http://www.cbc.ca/news/business/sandwich-generation-squeezed-by-caring-for-parents-and-kids-bmo-1.2734126.

Chambers, J. M. (2007). "Ecological literacy materials for use in elementary schools: A critical analysis" (unpublished doctoral dissertation). University of Alberta, Edmonton, AB.

Clance, P. R. (1985). *The impostor phenomenon: Overcoming the fear that haunts your success.* Georgia: Peachtree Publishers.

Harkness, S. (2008). Empty nest syndrome. In S. Loue & M. Sajatovic (Eds.) *Encyclopedia of aging and public health* (pp. 318–319). New York, NY: Springer. doi: 10.1007/978-0-387-33754-8_156.

Jago, B. (2002). Chronicling an academic depression. *Journal of Contemporary Ethnography, 31* (6), 729-757. doi: 10.1177/089124102237823.

Mood Disorders of Canada. (2013). *What is depression?* Retrieved from http://www.mooddisorderscanada.ca/documents/Publications/DepressEng-Master_v18_Nov_2013.pdf.

Muzyka, D., Hodgson, G., & Prada, G. (2012). *The inconvenient truths about Canadian health care* (CASCH Research and Report). Retrieved from The Conference Board of Canada website: http://www.conferenceboard.ca/cashc/research/2012/inconvenient_truths.aspx

Quinn, K., Edwards Lange, S., & Riskin, E. A. (2004). *Part-time tenure-track policies: Assessing utilization.* Paper presented at the WEPAN 2004 Conference June 6–9, 2004, Albuquerque, New Mexico. Retrieved from https://journals.psu.edu/wepan/article/viewFile/58344/58032

Sakulku, J., & Alexander, J. (2011). The impostor phenomenon. *International Journal of Behavioral Science, 6* (1), 75–97. Retrieved from https://www.tci-thaijo.org/index.php/IJBS/article/view/521/pdf

Trower, C. (2006). "Gen X meets theory X: What new scholars want," *Journal of Collective Bargaining in the Academy*: Vol. 0, Article 11. Retrieved from http://thekeep.eiu.edu/jcba/vol0/iss1/11

CHAPTER 3

Re-Locating: Moving Between the Field and the University

Lee Anne Block
Faculty of Education, University of Winnipeg

I completed my dissertation, *Locating social justice issues in middle years classrooms: Not all pumpkins are orange* (Block, 2006), and received my PhD in December 2006. I was 54 years old and had taught in the public-school system for 20 years. In 2010, I was appointed to a tenure-track position at the University of Winnipeg's Faculty of Education. Prior to that, I had worked with two other education faculties in term positions. As a tenure-track professor, I believed I had achieved my objective of becoming a teacher of teachers in a university setting. Now all I had to worry about was tenure, which seemed so far away. I joked that if I didn't achieve tenure, I could retire content at having taught for five years.

My tenure package is due in seven months. My fifth grandchild is due in seven days. Although they bring wonder and wisdom, grandchildren are not part of one's curriculum vitae. However, 20 years of teaching schoolchildren and adult learners, facilitating professional development, and working with teachers' organizations *are* experiences that directly impact my production of knowledge as a professor of education. How can those experiences be integrated in a tenure package whose requirements "fit all sizes"?

My academic career has not been a direct trajectory; rather it has evolved through personal and professional commitments. Those commitments can be framed as teaching, service, and research, although in practice those categories are not always separate. The literature

(Caruth & Caruth, 2013; Trower & Chait, 2002) and my colleagues emphasize that for tenure and promotion purposes, the balance of teaching, service, and research is skewed in favor of research. This orientation goes against the grain of my personal and professional identity. Reshaping my teaching identity from teacher to professor has been interesting and validating. Subsuming that teaching identity to my role as researcher is complex.

This chapter will discuss the value of praxis for an education faculty, and the tensions inherent in moving between the field and the university. It will also explore the difficulties of shifting identity in the transition from established professional to tenure-track professor. How does one position oneself, and how is one positioned?

The transition from teaching public school to the university was deliberate. My route into the teaching profession was less than direct. Becoming a public-school teacher was a socio-economic decision as much, or more so, as it was a calling. As a divorced mother of two, I was fortunate that, after jumping through many administrative hoops, I was accepted into an after-degree program in education. This acceptance meant that I had the option of giving up part-time private teaching of drama, part-time theatre work, and part-time waitressing. The hoops that were necessary to jump through centered on my unteachable philosophy degree, which meant I had to take five additional courses in teachable subjects. Having met the requirements, I was equally fortunate to find a teaching job right after graduation. I could support my family, do meaningful work, and recover the respectability I felt I had lost.

In the early years of teaching in the public schools, my teaching identity was linked to my previous work with disadvantaged and/or creative young people. I wanted to be nurturing, thought-provoking, and inspiring, and sometimes I was. Much of the time, I was exhausted. I rejected being an authority figure at the same time as I resented not being given respect by my students. I critiqued my pedagogy and was not a team player. Over time, I became less dogmatic, more flexible, and perhaps more socialized into the profession. A new middle-years school with an innovative and deliberate approach to teaching and learning in grades 6 to 8 was opened, and I asked for a transfer. In this new building, the classrooms were grouped in pods and had big windows. The experience of being isolated behind the door of my individual classroom was diffused both structurally and emotionally. The context of the new school addressed my need to question pedagogical habits and to reform curriculum, instruction, and assessment. It was affirming to be in a setting where teachers worked collaboratively to construct practice. The collective energy of working in theatre that I had enjoyed was partially replicated in the dynamics of this school.

Although I was in a better teaching situation, I was still conflicted about whether I wanted to teach grade 8 forever, or return to theatre or work with adults. After ten years of teaching in Winnipeg, Manitoba, I took a leave of absence from the school division and completed a Master of Arts in Curriculum, Teaching, and Learning at the Ontario Institute for Studies in Education, University of Toronto (OISE/UT). Graduate school was transformative, and a substantial change from teaching thirteen-year-olds, as was a part-time position teaching pedagogy to college instructors. It became clear to me that teacher education was the direction I wanted to pursue, a conviction which was reinforced by a year-long term position teaching methods courses in the Faculty of Education at Brandon University. I spent that year on a treadmill of preparing, teaching, and grading five new courses as I tried to convince myself that I was fit for university teaching. In the end, I did convince myself, and decided I needed a PhD to qualify.

I applied to doctoral programs at OISE/UT and the University of North Dakota (UND) and was accepted with a teaching assistantship to both. The criterion for where to study was not based on which academic position was best; rather the decision, like many others, was made in relation to my family situation. At North Dakota, I could commute home every weekend, as I had from Brandon. Toronto was much farther away. I spent three years in graduate school at the University of North Dakota, crossing the border and commuting 220 kilometers twice weekly and teaching courses every term. The program was oriented to practicing professors in adjacent colleges. It was at UND that I began to identify as a researcher, and specifically as a school-based researcher. However, my program and teaching load, in addition to the commute, left little time for research beyond the parameters of my dissertation.

Teaching my first university courses at UND was very intense, as Brandon University had been. The courses were assigned to me and yet I wanted to make them mine. I spent many hours prepping, creating materials, grading, and reflecting, while also working on my own graduate studies. Teaching was always a priority during my doctoral program. I was in the program because I wanted to teach and my studies were financially supported because I could teach. The time spent in K-8 classrooms was the source for instructing teacher candidates in the first to third year as I theorized and narrated my practice. Teaching was experienced both as an act of service and as an act of self-preservation. I knew that my record as a teaching professor would be of substantial influence in gaining a position at UND's College of Education (where I was actually hired for a one-year term position) and at any other education faculty. The faculty at UND supported my scholarship but they needed my teaching—at least that was my perception. Perhaps it continues to be my perception that teaching is the priority in my academic life. Sometimes I believe I will get tenure just because I am a good teacher.

At the University of Winnipeg I teach undergraduate courses in Social Studies methods, Foundations of Teaching and Learning, Social Justice, and a post-baccalaureate course in Cultural Sustainability. Building awareness of context, what I have termed "the interactive curriculum," is foundational to my work with teacher candidates. This concept requires the teacher candidate to consider the inter-relationships of content, students, and the teacher(s) themselves as part of the curriculum. The interactions, structured and unstructured, of these three components construct curriculum. These interactions also create a milieu, the human and physical environment or location within which teaching and learning takes place. In turn, that milieu is embedded in cultural and socio-political institutions, power structures, and discourses. Thus, discussion of my teaching will necessarily include the teacher candidates I work with. The majority of teacher candidates in Manitoba faculties of education are of the dominant culture (Manitoba Education, Citizenship, & Youth, 2006). Their varied personal experiences are rooted in a shared dominant perspective (Tupper, 2011). In many schools in Manitoba, however, the majority of students are *not* of the dominant culture. To meet the needs of all students, teacher candidates need to learn how we name and engage with difference in educational locations.

I am a good teacher partly because I teach against the grain of dominant culture (Simon, 1992). I am an effective education professor because I identify my values, question myself, and critique my practice. I am not (too) afraid to raise uncomfortable issues (Block, 2013; Boler & Zembylas, 2003) and to ask students to question their assumptions. I am also effective because I was a public-school teacher for 20 years and that experience informs my teaching at the university. Student evaluations of my courses regularly include comments that students appreciate stories of my experience, and that those school experiences "legitimize" my role. The stories situate me in "the real world" of the school. Much as I welcome this validation of my teaching experience, I object to the school/practicum being identified as the real world to the exclusion of the work being done in the university. I take up students' use of the phrase "real world" and propose that our class and the university are just different real places. I want us to honor the time we share through our course and within that course make deliberate connections to the practicum, to the field.

In general, teacher candidates understandably value their practicum more than their coursework. In the practicum they experience agency, they are doers; they are givers, not receivers, of knowledge. No matter how I structure my courses for agentic action, I cannot compete with the practicum, with the authority students' experience being a teacher. The gap between theory and practice is not bridgeable for most of the students in the program. Ironically, when I introduce "praxis," it often remains a concept, not an experience. Teacher candidates will verify a connection between some assignments and their practicum. Certain course readings will also provoke that connection. Teaching praxis requires performing praxis. My capacity to demonstrate praxis derives from my ability to move between the field and the university.

The Faculty of Education is an academic context where the dualism of practice/theory is experienced directly within the program because the practicum is intrinsic to the program. Teacher candidates' opposition of practicum and coursework, a dualism which designates one aspect as less real than the other, is replicated by tenure and promotion committees' valuing of research over teaching (Ragoonaden, 2015). This dualism reinforces the theory/practice divide.

I believe that in education faculties, teaching and research should inform each other. In my own practice, research emerges from the problems that I encounter in relation to teacher education and to social justice and sustainability issues. Much of my research takes place in school and community settings. This research is embedded in a theoretical framework and an educational philosophy that has evolved over time through practice and study. That practice includes my teaching in the real world of the Manitoba public-school system.

My field experience, teaching public school, is very real to me; but it is no more and no less real than the years in the academy. If I had been a biologist working in the field in the Amazon basin, that field experience would be valued when I was hired to be a professor of biology. Similarly, for an education professor, the time spent teaching in the public school should be valued beyond a half step on the pay scale.

My research focus is also affected by my age and life stage. It was strange to be positioned as a novice professor at the same time as being positioned as a mature educator in late middle age. I had unreservedly elected to make a career change and to develop my abilities for the university context. However, my previous work context is not unrelated to those abilities. It seems pedagogically unsound that a faculty of education should have the same criterion for research from a 58-year-old beginning professor as it does from a 28-year-old beginning professor. Nor should the criterion for teaching be the same for the two. The two professors have different skill sets.

The term "skill set" implies measurable qualities of performance. Clearly, not all of a professor's performance is measurable, such as a professor's ability to focus colleagues' discussion of complex academic issues or a professor's concern for students' intellectual, emotional, and/or spiritual growth (Meng, 2009). These abilities are talents, not skills. One could suggest that in addition to considering that the two professors at different life stages have different skill sets, they should also be considered as offering different talents (Richardson, 2015). An inclusive faculty of education would value the talents of both.

"Talent" is not a popular term within the discourse of neo-liberalism, which is a driving force in contemporary higher education (Broom, 2015; Giroux, 2004; Meng, 2009). Neo-liberalism is an economic theory, which has become an ideology that includes both an overt and a hidden agenda. In higher education, neo-liberalism is manifest in the commodification of knowledge and in the emphasis on accountability, standards, outcomes, and skill sets, all of which must be measurable. The tenure/promotion process requires that we be measured by our peers. In addition, we measure ourselves against these standards, which we have internalized. Foucault's (1988) term for this internalized regulation is "self-surveillance." Boal (1996) refers to the process as "cops in the head" and develops popular theatre techniques to reveal the internalized regulation. Self-policing has valid social functions, but it also preserves dominant values, values that need to be inspected and modified or rejected.

Some part of me believes I will get tenure only if I have followed the rules for getting tenure and have self-policed, despite the rules being somewhat unclear to me and despite my questioning of the system that constructed them. Mason, Casey and Betts (2010) delineate the tension between constructing one's identity as a professor and meeting tenure expectations. Perhaps my need to critique dominant values is offset by the need for respectability.

Boal's popular theatre is educational theatre, theatre for social change. Educating for change has been the focus of my teaching. I imagined that working at the university would be a vehicle for social change. I find working with teacher candidates a form of activism. The experiences generated through my courses may provoke changed understandings of equity and of interlocking oppressions and relative privilege in my students. These understandings may alter how the teacher candidates position themselves as teachers. A critique of neo-liberal approaches to education can aid in rejecting the commodification of knowledge and can question monolithic value systems. The affirmation that knowledge is partial and emergent, that it is embodied, meaning that minds and bodies interact to know (Davis, Sumara, & Luce-Kapler, 2008) and that it is embedded in socio-environmental contexts (Robbins & Aydede, 2009) creates a framework which authorizes teacher candidates both to teach within the context they are located and to question that context. That is, they learn to understand teaching and learning as related to context, and they learn to deconstruct the culture of the social and institutional contexts they work within.

Success in school settings often involves succeeding in relation to others, competing and winning against others in the spelling bee, the math competition, the science fair. Teacher candidates bring these experiences from their schooling to their studies in education (Britzman, 1999). Most teacher candidates have experienced moderate to full success in the school system, an experience that impelled their choice to become teachers. Unpacking the concepts of at risk and success, which are embedded in our program and in educational discourse, is another strategy for questioning dominant assumptions.

My pedagogy attempts to interrupt the dualism of success and failure through alternative discourse and approaches. An incident from the foundations course I taught illustrates how such an interruption can evolve: It is the end of term and groups within a cohort of after-degree teacher candidates are presenting the school-based projects they had organized and facilitated at their practicum schools. The grass-roots projects were intended to address an educational need at the school and also to offer teacher candidates a context to collaborate with each other and the school community. Agentic experience for teacher candidates was another objective of the assignment. The presentations are intended as a celebration of their efforts. PowerPoints of kindergarten to Grade 6 students and their families engaged in yoga, crafts, and other activities are the backdrop to the presentations. Most groups present with a sense of accomplishment; they also reference difficult experiences. One group's presentation focused only on their difficulties because they had not accomplished much. They described the process of developing their club and then asked the rest of the cohort for ideas to improve the project for next term, as they had had minimal attendance. The teacher candidates in this group could admit the limitations of their agency and their discomfort, within the support of the cohort. The pedagogy that shaped the cohort was focused on collaboration, competences, and agency, and on possibilities for transformation. In that context a lack of competence is not experienced as failure but as something more to learn.

Schoolchildren, as well as teacher candidates, want to be competent, to experience themselves as agents of learning. I expect teacher candidates to learn to build relationships with students that foster competence, confidence, and collaborative learning. I want them to work with individuals and to build communities. I wish that their experiences in schools will give them time to collaborate meaningfully with other teachers.

This research into the discourse of success resonates with my approach to tenure. If I get tenure, I succeed within an academic system I chose to compete within. If I do not get tenure, it is because I failed to meet the expectations of that system. And where is my agency in the tenure process? In these five years, I have been an agent of my own learning in research, have struggled to maintain authentic teaching and learning, and have participated in the communities I found within the university and the field. I have also remained engaged with family and friends who are the fabric of my life and who supported my academic career. If I ask my students to reject the limitations in the discourse of success and failure, can I reject it for myself?

References

Block, L. A. (2013). Locating difference in teacher education. *In Education, 19*(2), 57–71.

Block, L. A. (2006). "Locating social justice issues in middle years classrooms: Not all pumpkins are orange" (unpublished doctoral dissertation). University of North Dakota, Grand Forks, ND.

Boal, A. (1996). *The rainbow of desire: The Boal method of theatre and therapy* (A. Jackson, Trans.). New York, NY: Routledge.

Boler, M., & Zembylas, M. (2003). Discomforting truths: The emotional terrain of understanding difference. In P. P. Trifonas (Ed.), *Pedagogies of difference: Rethinking education for social change* (pp.110–136). New York, NY: RoutledgeFalmer.

Britzman, D. (1999). *Practice makes practice: A practical study of learning to teach.* Albany, NY: State University of New York Press.

Broom, C. (2015). Ideology, performativity and the university. In K. Ragoonaden (Ed.) *Contested sites in education: The quest for the public intellectual, identity and service* (pp. 32–48). New York: Peter Lang.

Caruth, G. D., & Caruth, D. L. (2013). The octopus, the squid and the tortoise. *Policy Futures in Education, 11*(5), 490–496.

Davis, B., Sumara, D., & Luce-Kapler, R. (2008). *Engaging minds: Teaching in complex times* (2nd ed.). New York, NY: Routledge.

Foucault, M. (1988). *Madness and civilization: A history of insanity in the age of reason* (R. Howard, Trans.). New York, NY: Vintage.

Giroux, H. A. (2004). Public pedagogy and the politics of neo-liberalism: Making the political more pedagogical. *Policy Futures in Education, 2*(3–4), 494–503.

Manitoba Education, & Citizenship and Youth. (2006). *Belonging, learning, growing: Kindergarten to grade 12 action plan for ethnocultural equity.* Retrieved from http://www.edu.gov.mb.ca/k12/docs/reports/equity/belonging_learning_growing.

Mason, R. T., Casey, C., & Betts, P. (2010). Toward tenure: Developing a relational view. *The Journal of Educational Thought, 44,* 85–98.

Meng, J. C. S. (2009). Saving the teacher's soul: Exorcising the terrors of performativity. *London Review of Education, 7*(2), 159–167.

Ragoonaden, K. (2015). Setting the path towards emancipatory practices. In K. Ragoonaden (Ed.) *Contested sites in education: The quest for the public intellectual, identity and service* (pp. 9–20). New York, NY: Peter Lang.

Richardson, P. (2015). Dwelling artfully in the academy: Walking on precarious ground. In K. Ragoonaden (Ed.) *Contested sites in education: The quest for the public intellectual, identity and service* (pp. 21–31). New York, NY: Peter Lang.

Robbins, P., & Aydede, M. (2009). A short primer on situated cognition. In P. Robbins & M. Aydede (Eds.) *The Cambridge handbook of situated cognition* (pp. 3–10). Cambridge, U.K.: Cambridge University Press.

Simon, R. I. (1992). *Teaching against the grain: Texts for a pedagogy of possibility.* Boston, MA: Bergin & Garvey.

Trower, C. A., & Chait, R. P. (2002). Forum: Faculty diversity why women and minorities are underrepresented in the professoriate, and fresh ideas to induce needed reform. *Harvard Magazine, 104*(4), 33–37.

Tupper, J. (2011). Disrupting ignorance and settler identities: The challenges of preparing beginning teachers for treaty education. *In Education,17*(3), 38–55. Retrieved from http://ineducation.ca/ineducation/article/view/71/415

CHAPTER 4

Belonging Differently: Immigration, Identity, and Tenure-Track

Cecile Badenhorst
Faculty of Education, Memorial University

Introduction

In 2011, I accepted a tenure-track position in the Faculty of Education at a university in an Atlantic province in Canada. This was not my first academic appointment. I had worked previously in South Africa at one of the country's most prestigious universities. The narrative that follows is an account of my experience as an immigrant or international scholar. This is not an easy narrative to write because my experiences of feeling "othered"—feeling different and not belonging—were often the result of subtle and complex interactions. Additionally, I work with wonderful colleagues who have gone out of their way to make me feel welcome and at home. My story is about how my reality of being an immigrant, with all its accompanying feelings of loss, insecurity, and uncertainty, intersected with implicit processes of being othered. The consequence of these overlapping processes was that I tried to reduce the difference by fitting in and being the same as everyone else. Despite the strong imperative to conform, the sense of loss and alienation persisted until I realized that *difference* is essential, for my identity as a research scholar and as a teacher. I drew on key sources to help me negotiate my way back to a comfortable place of difference—where I could be both different and belong. My story speaks to the experience of many other international faculty and indeed professionals who immigrate to a more developed country.

I am South African by birth and of Indian Ocean island heritage. My mother came from the Seychelles islands and my father was a generation away from his Mauritian roots. I lived in South Africa for most of my life. I did, however, spend six years as a graduate student completing a Master degree and PhD at Canadian universities. After finishing my doctoral program, in 1992, I moved back to South Africa where I managed an adult basic education non-governmental organization in the rural areas in the arid and poverty-stricken northwest parts of the country. As the country shifted from apartheid into democracy, I moved into the field of adult education more broadly, and this eventually led me to an academic position at one of the largest and well-respected universities in South Africa, the University of the Witwatersrand, colloquially known as Wits. The school I joined was then called the Graduate School in Public and Development Management. It was a new school that had been established in 1994, before the country's first democratic elections. The purpose of the school was to provide education for those in the new public sector, many of whom were returning exiles. In a context where education, under the apartheid government, was racially divided and poorly resourced, the majority of the population had received inadequate schooling. Structural and legislated inequalities meant that many learners had few choices or opportunities to cross the threshold into universities, let alone graduate schools. The school offered graduate degrees in public management and a range of post-graduate certificate programs aimed at building skills and capacities in a number of government sectors, such as health care, agriculture, civil service, national defense and others. While the goal of the school was educational redress, there was also a political agenda. "Public Administration," the civil-service discipline under apartheid, had been discredited for its decontextualized and neutral characteristics since it had administered the apartheid state unquestioningly. Public management was a paradigm shift intended to meet the needs of social development in a new democracy led by one of the most progressive constitutions in the world. I was hired in this position because of my practical experience on the ground in adult education. My role was not to teach content but to work with these mature students and academic staff across the sub-disciplines of the school on academic and research literacies using my knowledge base in adult education. Although students were managing the coursework relatively successfully, the thesis component of the Master's degree proved to be a major stumbling block for many. My job was to teach students research genres and academic literacies such as writing, reading, writing proposals, literature reviews, and dissertations, as well as developing academic-staff capacity as thesis supervisors. By the time I left, 10 years later, I was managing the school's large doctoral program, which contained between 20 and 30 active students annually. This position involved working closely with students and supervisors on writing proposals, writing their final dissertations, and teaching courses on research methodology. In addition, I was delivering workshops to faculties across the university for both faculty and graduate students on research writing, writing for publication, and developing supervisor capacity. I had also written two books on research writing.

Moving to Memorial

The decision to move to Canada was the result of a number of complex intersecting pushes and pulls. My husband was offered a position at Memorial University, in Newfoundland, and while I did not have employment initially, I had a contract to write a third book. After I completed the book, I applied for short-term contract position as grants facilitator in the Faculty of Education at Memorial. My job there was to help faculty write SSHRC and other grant proposals. While I was doing this work, a faculty position in adult education was advertised. It was this position that I competed for and was subsequently offered.

I tell this backstory to indicate that I was not a novice or junior, definitely not young, and quite confident when I joined the faculty. I had ten years' experience of teaching in a university, conducting research, and participating in institutional politics. I had completed two graduate degrees at Canadian universities, and I felt I knew the environment, at least on some level. I thought my transition into Canadian academic life would be relatively easy and familiar. However, as I started my new job I realized that there were many unwritten rules in a system that seemed more hierarchical and structured than I had experienced before. Although I had a clear idea of my research agenda, the pressure to produce research was coupled with the ever-present anxiety to compete for grant funding.

Teaching, an area I had always felt comfortable with, ended up being even more stressful than research as I had to find my way around a new learning management system and online classrooms. Service was an unknown to me and defined in a more structured way than I had experienced before. I was never sure what counted as service since my research, teaching, and community work overlapped extensively.

Yet, these challenges are similar to those experienced by most new faculty (Lawrence, Celis, & Ott, 2014; Tierney & Bensimon, 1996). The tenure years are a process of socialization, where one tries to get accepted into the organization and prove one's worth. However, as many international scholars will know, tenure-track is notoriously hard for those who are different and considered outside the norm, even if they are experienced academics in other contexts. Minority scholars, academics of colour, and women fall into this category (Boyd, Cintrón, & Alexander-Snow, 2010; Calderon 2014; Henry, 2012; Tierney & Bensimon, 1996; Trower, 2009; Varpalotai, 2010; Young & Wright, 2001) as do international scholars (Munene, 2014). As I muddled my way through the first years of promotions and tenure, tensions continued to surface, and I locate these as the experiences of immigrant or international new faculty. Alongside the new discourses, different procedures, and, sometimes, unfamiliar language was the constant insecurity and second guessing so as not to upset anyone unknowingly.

Leaving History Behind

How does one become othered? I found myself reading on this subject, and I even introduced it into the advanced qualitative research course for doctoral students that I taught, believing that they could relate to this concept. One article, *Writing against Othering* (Krumer-Nevo & Sidi, 2012), resonated with me profoundly. Although it is written in the context of researchers writing about their participants, I found myself drawing parallels with my own experiences. There's a paradox with otherness because it contains the restraints of stereotypes, but also the exoticness of being unique; essentially, a person gets caught in a "network of interpretations and representations" not of her or his own making (p. 299). The representations are a potential source of dominance as the person is unable to maneuver out of preconceptions of stereotypes, uniqueness, exoticness, and difference. The effect of othering is exclusion, where one lives and works together with people but feels a sense of not belonging (Krumer-Nevo & Sidi, 2012).

I experienced what I imagine otherness to be. In my imagination, otherness involves feeling different, a vague awareness of inferiority without understanding why, and of never really fitting in. Unlike fellow Africans, my fair skin allowed me to blend in visually as long as I was silent. Even though I am English speaking, I stuck out when I opened my mouth because of my accent, because I used the wrong words, and because I was initially so lacking in local knowledge and know-how. There were times when the exoticness of living in South Africa, the Mandela iconology, and the proximity to wildlife and warm weather shaped my otherness. At other times, it was general stereotypical perceptions of Africa as dark, technologically backward (and therefore intellectually backward), disease-ridden, and hungry that served to represent me in ways that I could not control. Out on the street, I did not mind these perceptions and could shrug them off easily. In the academy, however, I found myself startled when these perceptions affected how academics around a committee table perceived my (lack of) abilities. My early contributions to discussions sometimes resulted in a pause in conversation, but many times were just ignored. This happened in other cross-faculty meetings as well. I raise this to highlight how perplexed I felt. I felt the *same* yet I was seen as *different*. Whereas, in meetings at the University of the Witwatersrand, my opinions would be sought after as critically reasoned, possibly insightful contributions, now my opinion was overlooked and ignored because they were simply opinions—and from a new, junior faculty member.

After some reflection, I realized what was missing. I had lost my history. My opinions were just opinions because no one knew the experiences they were based on. The person I had been, with various elements of expertise, had disappeared in the crossing of continents and oceans. Prefacing my contribution to a meeting by saying "In my experience ..." did nothing but irritate my colleagues. Expertise is dependent on reputation, and reputation on long experience. I realized that for many academics I came in contact with on a daily basis, I only existed from the moment I arrived at this university. That's why I was new and junior. Whatever had happened in South Africa in my work did not seem to count for much. My published work was similarly to do with Africa and therefore apparently not relevant. My history had effectively melted away. I only existed in the present. This was a revelation to me.

The Immigrant Experience

Understanding one's own experience is also a paradox—can we ever really understand ourselves? Can we escape the processes of self-disciplining to fit the norms of discourses as Foucault describes (1977)? What does it take to see through the hegemonic trends? Self-reflection often becomes a means of self-service lacking the discursive *nous* to challenge deep taken-for-granted normalized "truths" (see Nishimura, 2010). Becoming an immigrant began a process that challenged my unacknowledged assumptions about immigrants, immigration, and being South African. In South Africa, I didn't see myself as African, or as an immigrant, although my family had only recently planted roots in the country. Living in a place like South Africa, with its racially divisive politics, it is difficult not to be aware of oneself as a classed, ethnic, or gendered being, and the privilege that occurs when these align with economic and political power. It is abundantly clear that gender, race, and class do matter. But even within this knowledge, there is a normalization, a natural order of living with diversity, as one goes about one's life in a neo-liberal globalized world, where time is money and there isn't enough time to think deeply.

Becoming an immigrant disrupted that for me. It decentered my confident, privileged world and replaced it with vulnerability, insecurity, and an overwhelming consciousness of being different, where difference was not something positive. There were few overt incidents but more a collection of ongoing small occurrences, which left me wondering: Did that happen because I'm different? Did they assume I wouldn't understand that because I'm from away? I must be imagining this. Any bits of cohesive stable identity I had brought with me—academic and personal—shattered in the onslaught of a desperate need to belong and not to be different. Conforming and fitting in became important. I almost did not notice how much I was disciplining myself to fit in, to be normal, and to be just like the others. The promotions and tenure process itself is a significant force of disciplinary power. In addition, the overwhelming silence on gender, race, and ethnic issues more broadly within academia encouraged and rewarded assimilation (see Chan, 2010).

However, as Dressman (1998) argues, our consciousness includes a range of liminal states where sometimes, just within range of comprehension, we access the thoughts that we shove away while living up to the consensually *normal* behavior. The self comes apart and then reassembles. It was through this liminal state, this borderland of shifting between trying to fit in and sitting on the outside, that I began to find my way.

Writing to Resist Othering

Krumer-Nevo and Sidi (2012) suggest *three modes of writing* that have the potential to resist othering in the context of conducting and writing research. The three modes are: 1) writing *narrative*, which allows the participant to tell her story and to be the protagonist in foregrounding events and experiences and to retrieve her subjectivity; 2) *dialogue*, which involves including multiple voices in the writing and multivocal perspectives; and 3) *reflexivity*, where the researcher writes in his or her own subjectivity. This provocative eye directs the gaze inward "towards one's self, one's history and position, and as an articulation of one's analytically situated self" (p. 306). Usually this involves "a cognitive process that focuses on one's own thoughts, memories, or sometimes, emotions" (p. 306). While these authors write about these concepts in the context of a researcher writing about research participants, I applied all three to my own life.

I learned to provide a strong *narrative* with my promotions and tenure file to contextualize and personalize my work. For each of the three areas—research, teaching, and service—I told a story of how my *now* work related to my *then* work. When I mentioned being published in a South African journal, I was sure to include lineage, pedigree, and ranking. Rather than letting my CV stand as it was presented, I told the story of the significance of some of the entries in relation to what I was now currently doing and what intellectual traditions these were drawing on. I pointed out the continuities of my research and how they depended on previous knowledge.

As one of eight non-tenured faculty, I found when *talking* to others that I was not alone in my sense of otherness. We all felt alienated to some extent, but for very different reasons. For example, some colleagues had been teachers in the K-12 school system and, by moving into a university position mid-career, were experiencing similar processes of disaffection. Many also felt the loss of their previous expertise and history. By openly talking about these micro exclusions, we began to realize that while exclusion is individually felt, it is also institutionally enacted. In other words, while we individually felt at fault for not fitting in, we collectively began to realize that we could not all be the problem. We formed a writing group to help us negotiate the borders between our past lives and our new lives and the thresholds we needed to bridge. By joining together and sharing our knowledge, we found collegiality, companionship, but, most importantly, a safe borderland where we could mesh who we were with who we are becoming. It was in these spaces of dialogue that I first began to feel a sense of belonging.

I also started to be *reflexive* on my own interactions with people and the ways in which I inadvertently othered others from my positions of privilege. I incorporated this new insight into my online courses, where I knew many learners felt alienated by technology and ageism. I also joined committees, like the LGBTQ and diversity committees, where I could not only learn about the subtleties and the complexities of othering but also possibly find further solutions for my own problems. I began to focus more on gender, diversity, and international students in my own research work, and to work with international students more consistently and more reflexively than before.

Re-Writing History

Ultimately, I realized I had to recover my history. I discussed this in the writing group, and other members of the group showed an interest in writing their own stories. We initiated a project called *On Becoming a Researcher*. We sent out a call for narratives to the whole faculty to be published in an in-house journal (http://www.mun.ca/educ/faculty/mwatch/fall12.html). We invited all contributors to tell their history as researchers. We received 20 papers in total, and the special issue of the journal generated interest and further dialog in the faculty. I wrote a narrative about my history as a researcher to humanize my story and to reposition myself. Ostensibly I wrote it for the members of faculty who saw me as African and as a way to disrupt the stereotypes, but essentially I wrote it for myself. I wrote it to reclaim and recover a history I felt I had lost. I wanted to reflect on who I was before and how that linked to who I am now. What I did before had direct bearing on what I do now, but the now me has altered as well. The context has changed, my thinking always evolves, yet epistemologically I maintain strong roots. The process was reaffirming for me. Writing the narrative allowed me to situate myself with agency and reposition myself in relation to the representations of others. It focused my thoughts about my identity as an immigrant and helped me to reaffirm the value of my previous experiences, memories, and emotions, and then to re-experience and decontextualize them as valuable in this new context. In a small way, I was able to recognize what Mudimbe (1988) argued when he wrote "history is both a discourse of knowledge and a discourse of power" (p. 188). Since othering is often the "attribution of inferiority to difference" (Krumer-Nevo & Sidi, 2012, p. 307), through the narrative I wanted to change that and attribute *creativity* to difference; perhaps also *possibility* and *opportunity*.

Concluding Thoughts

Research in the US shows that international faculty experience, alongside the regular stresses of being tenure-track, additional stresses such as "dealing with immigration rules and regulations; different cultural values; discrimination; difficulty in socialization and interaction with colleagues, administrators, and students; and the challenge of determining both implicit and explicit academic expectations" cause isolation (Kim, et al. 2012, p.36). These faculty members often feel isolated because they are expected to seamlessly fit in without any orientation to the prevailing culture (Munene, 2014).

My story, although an individual one, feeds into the stories of many others who can identify with these experiences. Otherness is created by other criteria as well. For example, being a young academic can sometimes be as lonely as someone who is culturally different (Boyd, Cintrón, & Alexander-Snow, 2010). When practitioners become university faculty they also experience similar processes of exclusion (Saito, 2013). Universities by design and economic circumstances send their doctoral students further and further afield to find jobs. Education faculties recruit from the K-12 system. In an increasingly globalized world, international scholars are common. Gender diversity, ethnic multiplicity, and minority cultures exist. Difference is the order of the day. Yet the push towards acculturation is strong, particularly in institutions with less experience of internationalization, and the consequence is that individual identity is homogenized

(Tierney & Bensimon, 1996). The denial of difference means that we, faculty, do not appreciate the diversity that exists, and we implicitly we teach our students not to. As Tierney & Bensimon (1996) argue: "we must work toward the creation of a community that does not demand the suppression of one's identity in order to become socialized into abstract norms. We support the development of organization in which interrelatedness and concern for others is central. A community of difference implies that the community is de-normed" (p. 16). Creating a comfortable space for difference—acknowledging different voices—allows for more opportunities to work productively together (Monk-Turner & Fogerty, 2010) and to be teachers in a multi-cultural world. However, it requires a commitment to, and an investment in, difference, and there are many models of mentoring and collegiality in the research literature to turn to (see Thomas & Goswami, 2013; Wasburn, 2007). It also requires an institution that rewards change and faculty that are willing to risk censure, at least in the beginning. The ultimate goal is worth it though—an organizational culture that is stronger and richer because of the diversity and mix of its community.

Acknowledgements

Thanks to Gabrielle Young and Sharon Penney for their "old" wisdom and deep support when reading through an earlier version of this paper.

References

Boyd, T., Cintrón, R., & Alexander-Snow, M. (2010). The experience of being a junior minority female faculty member. *Forum on Public Policy Online*, 2. Retrieved from http://forumonpublicpolicy.com/spring2010.vol2010/womencareers2010.html

Calderon, D. X. V. (2014). "The socialization of international women faculty" (unpublished doctoral dissertation). University of Maine, Orono, MA.

Chan, A. S. (2010). Women at the boundaries. *Forum on Public Policy Online*, 2. Retrieved from http://forumonpublicpolicy.com/spring2010.vol2010/womencareers2010.html

Dressman, M. (1998). Confessions of a methods fetishist or the cultural politics of reflective non-engagement. In R. Chávez & J. O'Donnell (Eds.). *Speaking the unpleasant: The politics of (non)engagement in multicultural education terrain* (pp. 108–126). Albany, N.Y.: State University of New York Press.

Foucault, M. (1977). *Discipline and punish: The birth of the prison*. New York, NY: Vintage.

Henry, F. (2012). Indigenous faculty at Canadian universities: Their stories. *Canadian Ethnic Studies/Études ethniques au Canada, 44*(2), 101–132.

Kim, D., Twombly, S., & Wold-Wendel, L. (2012). International faculty in American universities: Experiences of academic life, productivity and career mobility. *New Directions for Institutional Research, 155,* 27–46.

Krumer-Nevo, M., & Sidi, M. (2012). Writing against othering. *Qualitative Inquiry, 18*(4), 299–309.

Lawrence, J. H., Celis, S., & Ott, M. (2014). Is the tenure process fair? What faculty think. *The Journal of Higher Education, 85*(2), 155–188.

Monk-Turner, E., & Fogerty, R. (2010). Chilly environments, stratification, and productivity differences. *American Sociology, 41*(3), 3–18.

Mudimbe, V. Y. (1988). *The invention of Africa: Gnosis, philosophy and the order of knowledge*. Bloomington, IN: Indiana University Press.

Munene, I. (2014). Outsiders within: Isolation of international faculty in an American university. *Research in Post-Compulsory Education, 19*(4), 450–467.

Nishimura, A. (2010). Negotiating the line between masculine and feminine rhetoric within the academy. *Forum on Public Policy Online, 5*. Retrieved from http://forumonpublicpolicy.com/vol2010no5/womencareers2010.html

Saito, E. (2013). When a practitioner becomes a university faculty member: A review of the literature on challenges faced by novice ex-practitioner teacher educators. *International Journal for Academic Development, 18*(2), 190–200.

Thomas, J., & Goswami, J. S. (2013). An investment in new tenure-track faculty: A two-year development program. *Journal of Faculty Development, 27*(1), 50–55.

Tierney, W. G., & Bensimon, E. M. (1996) *Promotion and tenure: Community and socialization in academe*. Albany, NY: State University of New York Press.

Trower, C. (2009). Towards a greater understanding of the tenure track for minorities. *Change, 41*(5), 38–45.

Varpalotai, A. (2010). The status of women at Canadian universities and the role of Faculty Unions. *Forum on Public Policy Online, 2*. Retrieved from http://forumonpublicpolicy.com/spring2010.vol2010/womencareers2010.html

Wasburn, M. H. (2007). Mentoring women faculty: An instrumental case of strategic collaboration. *Mentoring & Tutoring, 15*(1), 57–72.

Young, D. S., & Wright, E. M. (2001). Mothers making tenure. *Journal of Social Work Education, 37*(3), 555–56

CHAPTER 5

The Three-Headed Monster

Greg Rickwood
Schulich School of Education, Nipissing University

Introduction

Stepping away from a secure, secondary teaching career into the unknown world of tenure-track refuted my better judgment. However, after 14 years as a secondary-school teacher and administrator, I believed that post-secondary education was where I needed to be, and it was where I could make the biggest difference for Ontario's next generation of students and teachers. I knew that working within a faculty of education would offer multiple opportunities to teach hundreds of teachers who, in turn, would teach thousands of students. Moreover, having access to funds that would help me answer some of my long-standing questions around physical education, and teaching students who were as passionate as I was about this subject area sparked my curiosity. These perks were what I needed as a mid-career teacher who had already explored the many facets of the secondary-school system in Ontario.

As a father of two young children, learning that my salary would drop $20,000, a tenure-track position, on paper, was a step backwards. In addition to the financial sacrifices of pursuing my dream career, the emotional price continues to be steep. I live five hours from my family home for several weeks at a time because my wife and daughters want to remain in close proximity to our family members and friends. My daughters are young, and expecting my wife to operate as a single parent brings personal feelings of guilt and neglect. As well, my daughters are involved in several extra-curricular activities, forcing us to seek out daily assistance from family members to fill in the gaps. Are these fair requests to ask of the people closest to me? Are the short-term financial and familial pains going to be worth the long-term gains?

Reflecting back on day one of the job, I distinctly recall sitting at my desk at 42 years of age having gained a tenure-track position at a reputable university. As I looked around my basement office out into a secluded courtyard, the question came to mind: "Were the personal and family sacrifices worth it?" I am now completing my third year of tenure-track and can, with vigor, respond, "Yes."

Teaching

I sought a tenure-track role because I wanted to teach students with a purpose—students who made the conscious choice to enter the Bachelor of Physical Education program, and who understood the challenges and commitment associated with their decision. Students like me, I guess, because I chose the same path as they did. I could relate to their experiences, and we (teacher/student) could create collaborative learning activities that advanced our growth in the subject area. This proverbial picture was painted when I was a Master's student and taught courses within the university's kinesiology program. As a mature graduate student who had never formally taught a class, developing course expectations, pedagogical strategies, and student evaluations for courses with no formalized curriculum was outside my comfort zone. However, I learned to appreciate this academic freedom and harboured memories of positive student relationships that would fuel my pursuit of a PhD many years later.

During the winter term of my first year in tenure-track, I was asked to teach a required physical-education course to fourth year, Bachelor of Physical Education students. I felt confident about delivering the content, and combined with my teaching background, I was ready to teach senior-year students about exercise prescription and assessment. As I would have in any other new course, I reached out to my colleagues who had taught the course before and constructed what I thought was a calculated and intriguing course syllabus. From their feedback, I learned it was a course that no other faculty member wanted to teach because of the less-than-favorable student responses to the material, and the time associated with meeting course expectations. Being the new guy in the department, it appeared that it was my turn to take one for the team. To test their interpretation, I surveyed the class on day one of the course, asking how many students had plans of venturing into physiotherapy, massage therapy, personal fitness training, or athletic therapy—natural extensions of this course. Of the 95 students, only three raised their hands. The other 92 students had already applied to a Bachelor of Education program and bluntly stated, "We are only here because we need this credit to graduate." Having taught secondary students for many years in required courses, I knew what was ahead and reality soon set in. Teaching the weekly, two-hour lecture became a burden as students voluntarily left and entered the class, or sent last minute e-mails stating their friends would give them the lecture notes. This was not what I had envisioned—a laissez-faire student group who just wanted the credit. I tried various motivational strategies to engage the students, but it simply felt like I was back teaching Grade 9 health and physical education.

As part of the learning curve, I found the demands of post-secondary students to be much greater relative to my secondary teaching experience. Students expected a ten-minute response time to their e-mail requests, instructor-modified percentages attached to each course component that complemented the areas in which they were more successful, and a reduction in labs/assignments to accommodate their busy personal lives. I discovered quickly that it was not the course I wanted or needed to deliver, but a course that students could fit, without duress, into their daily timetable. Comments like, "The test was unfair," "There are too many quizzes," "We do not have enough time to finish our labs," were consistent "shout outs" in the classes. Did I have to listen to and accommodate their wishes? The short answer is yes. Knowing that these students were evaluating my performance and course structure, I had to marry the integrity of the course curriculum with student requests (demands).

Unlike my secondary-school teaching experience, these students formally evaluated the course and my delivery of it. Initially I thought, "Why do undergraduate students, in a non-elective course, without any teaching and/or course development background have the ability to influence my career?" At the time, I grumbled to my wife explaining, "To me, it is like a Grade 9 student evaluating a fourth-year, undergraduate thesis paper—there is no way they can fairly assess the final product—they do not have the skills or experience to do so." Looking back on the course evaluations, several students were absent on course-evaluation day, leaving me to wonder if their feedback would have altered my evaluation average. Essentially, my focus became less about student learning and more about student approval. This was contrary to my core teaching and personal values, but I recognized that positive student evaluations would influence my track to tenure. In my opinion, there is value to student feedback—it guides the evolution of education relative to the dynamic nature of student needs and interests. On the other hand, if the feedback is directly associated with an instructor's future in education, it encourages that person to teach for approval.

Service

As a secondary teacher, service to my school was a cultural expectation. Coaching school sport teams, supervising school events, and connecting community-based resources to school operations were what I believed to be professional practice. Although highly valued for promotion in the secondary system, service is perceived as less important for gaining tenure and/or enhancing one's profile within the university. Recently, a tenured colleague and prior tenure-and-promotion member reaffirmed my perception by stating, "I have never known someone not to gain tenure due to lack of service." With this in mind, I serve the university when the opportunity arises, but its priority is a distant third.

During the first years of tenure-track, I was struggling to invest in service, not knowing the time commitment or if my contributions would be valued. Therefore, I reached out to my director, and collaboratively we established a productive service plan that aided my understanding of university operations. I was appreciative of the director's guidance because he knew what I could handle along with my teaching and research responsibilities. My first months of university service included membership on various internal committees, which, in turn, introduced me to new faculty members and new research opportunities. Also, being mentioned in faculty council meetings as someone who helped further a cause that benefitted the collective, generated feelings of inclusivity and acceptance among my colleagues—it gave me a perceived position within the institution.

Prior to service work, I failed to understand where I fit within the fabric of the university. I was vacating my office each day feeling emotionally isolated and insignificant beyond my students.

Early in my second year, I welcomed the opportunity to serve as a faculty facilitator on a three-week international teaching practicum in Kenya with concurrent education students. The position required me to work with another faculty member in selecting, preparing, and mentoring 25 teacher candidates on this excursion. What I enjoyed about this eight-month commitment was the mentorship provided by my faculty partner. Rather than fumbling through practicum expectations, I was able to watch and learn how the program unfolded with an experienced colleague. Until this juncture in my tenure-track experience, I received very little mentorship and learned the ropes through trial and error. Overall, I cherished the international service experience and agreed to lead the following year's group; I had found my service niche. Working with education students in the field and forming relationships with international colleagues was gratifying both personally and academically.

Research

The significance of research became apparent when the Dean of Education met with me before my first day on the job, to reinforce the importance of applying for an internal research grant and establishing a research program. She highlighted how few publications I had, and for tenure, I needed to enhance this part of my portfolio. The Dean made no reference to achieving positive course evaluations or sustained service to the university—the conversation was publish or perish. This feedback caught me somewhat by surprise. I always heard how important publications and funding were to attaining tenure, but this conversation solidified the rumors.

As a newbie in the Physical and Health Education Department, I was hoping to piggyback on some of my colleagues' research and funding for the first year to learn more about the process. The university provided an internal research grant, but I needed to know how the research cycle worked. Unfortunately, there was only one other faculty member in the department who mirrored my research agenda, and she transferred into administration the month I arrived. Outside of this individual, my potential mentors were exercise physiologists, sport psychologists, and community-health planners. Thus,

I needed to diversify my research agenda to profit from collaborative research projects with my departmental colleagues.

My saving grace was an individual in the university's research department who took the time to explain the university's ethics application process. She provided me with an overview of the external granting agencies that might invest in my research. She reviewed previously successful grant applications with me and even proofread my applications prior to formalized submission. She also offered motivation and sound advice throughout the application process. I did not obtain a nationally funded grant in my first year of tenure-track, but did receive an internal research grant that helped jumpstart my research program. To further the cause, the Dean of Education made several calls to her contacts in the local school boards to inform them that I would be seeking their approval for future research.

What surprised me the most about external funding applications was the onerous nature of producing the final draft. Being my first time through the process, I recall thinking that securing funding could be a full-time position in itself. After committing at least 60 hours to the preparation and refinement of my grant proposals, not being successful was discouraging—it made me ponder my decision to enter academia. I had never dedicated so much time and brainpower to a project within the education field and not been rewarded in some way. I learned of my fate through a generic letter from the granting agencies that stated my project was not prioritized for funding and, in turn, failed to meet the minimum standards for consideration. Instead of dwelling on the negative, I focused on the positive feedback and understood that denial was going to be a part of the growth process in gaining funds. In my second year of tenure-track, I applied for smaller grants and recruited colleagues to join me in these projects. This team approach helped me obtain external funding to initiate projects that were of great interest to me, and gave me the confidence to push forward on future funding opportunities.

Now in my third year of tenure-track, I believe I have established myself in the department as a valued research partner. Many of my departmental colleagues are now reaching out to inquire if I would like to be a co-investigator on some of their projects. Two of my colleagues have willingly partnered with me on a few of my more recent studies. Generally, I sensed that I needed to prove my worth—defend my research in nationally recognized conferences, and produce peer-reviewed publications. My colleagues needed to hear about me from their academic contacts before I was accepted as one of them. I understand the rite of passage and the notion that because "we" had to go through it, I had to as well. In talking individually with my colleagues over the past three years, they stressed the desire to know how my research agenda complemented theirs before collaboration could be mutually beneficial. With many of my colleagues being in their first years of academia (three to five years), they were concerned with sustaining their own research programs, not with helping me start mine.

Research Realities

Being able to develop research questions and protocols that would help me answer some of my long-standing questions in physical education was, in my estimation, a perk of tenure-track. Funding was the first hurdle, but I quickly learned that is was not the only barrier in the way of accomplishing my research agenda. After submitting my ethically approved study to the local school board and finding out a month later that they were not accepting any more research projects for that academic year was devastating. The rejection of my study meant that I had to wait until the start of the following school year, an eight-month lag, to resubmit my proposal. I presented my study again in the new year to the school board, and this time they accepted. However, shortly after I was approved to start working with teachers, administrators, parents, and students in the board, the teachers went on strike and my study was put on hold. When the strike ended, my ability to recruit participants for an extracurricular project diminished exponentially. Instead of reaching my goal of 20 participants, I received consent from four teachers who were willing to fulfill participation expectations. I also learned from speaking with the participants that the schools in the board had been inundated with requests for research, and many schools were declining involvement. This finding was contrary to the information I received during my interview for the tenure-track position. The search committee told me that the local school boards had been untapped in terms of research opportunities. Looking back, the individuals on my search committee did not conduct research in local schools and, therefore, could not have known about the surplus of research demands imposed on the local school boards.

Another reality associated with research in physical education is the limited value that some school leaders (i.e., administrators) associate with the importance of daily physical activity and regular physical-education classes. With the ongoing drive to improve student scores on standardized tests, and to expand curriculum expectations in the academic subject areas, the thirst to enhance the daily physical activity levels of students across the school day is minimal. Therefore, recruiting diversified school members (i.e., non-physical-education teachers, parents, students) to engage in research regarding school-based physical activity is challenging, and has slowed the evolution of my research productivity.

Conclusion

The tenure trilogy that is teaching, service, and research embraces a long-standing philosophical approach to promotion within academia that forces tenure-track employees to choose failure in one evaluative component. Given the time frame to achieve tenure (four to five years), the energy associated with developing and delivering new courses, and the urgency of acquiring funding and collaborative partnerships for valued research, it can be a long walk down a short road. If shortcuts are not taken early, the road ends and the efforts made to get to that point in the process are forgotten.

The shortcuts, based on my experience, are the mentors who have guided my professional growth. These individuals were not appointed to me but are people that I have sought out and continue to rely upon for direction. I fondly recall one colleague who took three hours out of her afternoon to teach me how to geocache and incorporate this activity into my Teaching and Learning in Physical Education course. Geocaching is an outdoor treasure hunt using global-positioning handheld devices. The majority of students have not engaged in this type of activity during their educational journeys, so it can be an enriching pedagogical tool. I also remember another colleague who led me on a tour of the university's athletic complex explaining how to use the facility to my advantage for teaching and research. Additionally, engaging in daily conversations with tenured faculty to learn how they cope with the internal and external pressures of academia has been instrumental in helping me find my way. In general, mentorship is available in the post-secondary system for those who are willing to ask.

The path to tenure is murky and unique to the individual. There are many days where I feel as if I am floundering to the tenure goal line. With feedback drawn mainly from undergraduate students, journal editors, and a one-page review of my annual progress report, the track to tenure lacks tangible boundaries. What I can control are my actions leading up to the tenure application; observing and learning from tenured colleagues and applying this knowledge to my personal experience could be the equation for success.

SECTION II

EDITORS' PREFACE

Tenure-Track Collaboration

The collaboration section highlights colleagues who have chosen to write a chapter together because they have some sort of cooperative relationship with each other. In terms of the organization of the sections of this book, the chapters in the collaborative section represent a mixture of more and less experienced voices. We determined that the best placement was after the late tenure-track section and before the mid-tenure-track section, having considered rationales for various locations. The section is somewhat disruptive to the flow of individually written chapters, but adds an important dimension, in that authors frequently do not research or write alone.

Each team here is unique in terms of the origin of the writing group: The first existed before all of the current members joined; the second arose from shared interests that aligned with an organizational structure within a faculty; and the third arose from sharing around teaching. There is little doubt that collaboration has benefits both in terms of each chapter and in ways that extend to other tasks and goals (Coke, Benson, & Hayes, 2015).

These authors have a wide range of years of experience in academia. Each group contains late tenure-track members who likely provided a degree of mentorship to earlier tenure-track faculty participating in the writing process, hence many comments for the previous section apply equally well to this section. There was evidence, in communications with the editors, of scheduling and negotiations between members within the groups.

Memorial's Education Writing Group is unique in this book. It is a group of 14 authors! Some have migrated to other universities as their careers have developed, but it was during their time at Memorial University that they were engaged directly with the group. While two authors have taken the lead on the chapter, the other authors contributed through group participation. The group extends beyond the 14 authors and engages some tenured faculty. This does not diminish the challenge the group faces; it should be considered in positive terms, offering a way that universities, or their faculty, might contribute mentorship on the tenure-track journey.

Indigenous scholarship is well represented by three strong voices situated on the Coast and Straits Salish territory at the University of Victoria. It is interesting that their distinct geographical roots come together in a unified voice where a tradition of respect challenges conformity to non-Indigenous styles found in many academic journals. They face unique challenges because of attention that is being focused on Indigenous scholars, while they are making their way on the tenure-track.

The dynamic duet of Manu Sharma and Cam Cobb began as two independent responses to the call for chapters. The editors realized the two were respectively writing about shared experiences and suggested they unite and co-author a single chapter. This effort is consistent with their message. The initial collaboration was co-teaching and expanded to include shared research.

Each group of collaborators has a focal message that conceptually goes beyond individual stories by bringing together a variety of perspectives. During the editing process, we drew attention to some critical alternative interpretations that may have been considered but not expressed because of shared understandings that developed within the context of the collaboration. Alternatively, they may reflect a process where compromise is made. The latter can arise for many reasons; it could reflect available time or a dynamic of respect. In terms of respect, mentees may avoid voicing or supporting protracted dissent that is contrary to the mentor when they know there is an external editorial process that the writing has to pass through.

In terms of the book, the editors had not anticipated having collaboratively written chapters and were delighted to see them. They point to a shared approach that can address common feelings of isolation or uncertainty within the tenure-track. In many ways, these chapters are a call to action to address a multitude of issues that are apparent within the single-author chapters of this book. We think these chapters are an interesting and illuminating component of the book—and we hope you will find many moments that cause considered thought.

Memorial's Education Writing Group (authors' names are given at the end of the chapter) is a large group that meets regularly to assist each other with scholarly writing. The chapter is a qualitative examination of the needs of tenure-track faculty members. In the same way that the writing group itself was a constructive approach to addressing needs of new faculty members, the chapter highlights constructive ideas for improving the experience.

Onowa McIvor, María del Carmen Rodríguez de France, and Trish Rosborough address the challenges of representing Indigenous education. They speak of struggling to find balance between a politically motivated drive for the academy to have thorough Indigenous representation and their personal needs to develop their own research programs. The distinction between service and research within Indigenous settings is a further difficulty they share.

Sharma and Cobb speak passionately about collaboration within the academy. They articulate the benefits of co-teaching and give details that highlight experiences that arose from their collaboration. The move beyond co-teaching to conducting research and publishing together has further benefited their relationship. They highlight the benefits of multiple perspectives throughout their chapter.

Reference

Coke, P. K., Benson, S., & Hayes, M. (2015). Making meaning of experience: Navigating the transformation from graduate student to tenure-track professor. *Journal of Transformative Education, 13*(2), 110–126.

CHAPTER 6

Women Reflect on Becoming an Academic: Challenges and Supports

Memorial's Education Writing Group
Memorial University of Newfoundland
(The authors from the writing group are listed at the end of the chapter.)

Little research has been conducted regarding faculty members who have had a previous professional career. Some researchers have addressed moving from practitioner to academic careers (see Crane, O'Hern, & Lawler, 2009; Fogg, 2002; LaRocco & Bruns, 2006), reporting that individuals who have been in practice may be at a disadvantage compared to those who took a more direct pathway to academia and may experience challenges surrounding understanding the structures of the university, adopting the language and culture of academia, meeting research expectations, establishing a work-life balance, and defining roles and responsibilities. In addition, moving from an education practitioner career, where there is daily interaction with students and colleagues, to an academic environment can result in a sense of loneliness and isolation (Crane et al., 2009).

Method

Participants
In this collaborative self-study project, personal narratives were used to understand the perceptions and experiences of 14 women (aged 32–56) who pursued careers in academia. The participants, who are the authors of this study, are part of a writing group located within the Faculty of Education at Memorial University of Newfoundland. Members of this group agreed to participate in this study and opted

to employ writing as a lens of inquiry (Richardson & St. Pierre, 2008). These individuals came from qualitative and quantitative research backgrounds and various fields of education including Aboriginal education, adult education, art education, counseling psychology, math education, music education, science education, second-language education, social studies, and special education. All but one of the writing group members had previous careers, having invested from two to twenty years as teachers (in varying disciplines), guidance counselors, school psychologists, and clinical psychologists prior to transitioning into academia. At the time the narratives were written, four women were on contract and the remaining women were in their first, second, fourth, fifth, and sixth years of their tenure-track positions.

Data collection and analysis procedures
The first two authors asked participants in this study to write personal narratives surrounding their career paths prior to entering into academia and their initial perceptions of becoming an academic. Participants were also asked to reflect on factors that helped to make them feel at ease in their new role as an academic. In order to shed light on the emerging themes, members of the writing group were asked to share their narratives with others and to write down pertinent phrases that came to mind as the narratives were read aloud. Utilizing a modified concept mapping approach (Kane & Trochim, 2007), the first two authors independently sorted the key phrases that arose from the narratives into separate thematic groups. The first two authors re-read each narrative in order to select segments of text that were instrumental in highlighting participants' experiences surrounding their transition into academia. The selected excerpts were coded using the themes that were identified from the keywords when the narratives were read aloud, and a few segments of these excerpts are presented below.

Results

Varying pathways and driving forces into academia
With the exception of one individual, participants could be described as second-career academics, a term used by Barrett and Brown (2014) to describe individuals who have moved from a career in K-12 education to a tenure-track faculty position in a post-secondary

environment. Participants' transitions into academia could be described as non-linear: "My career path prior to entering academia was quite varied," "somewhat accidental," and "My path to becoming an academic has been a bit like a journey through a labyrinth." Participants felt "finding myself in a tenure-track position is one of surprise—definitely unexpected."

Passion for their subject area fueled participants' ventures into academia. One individual noted, "I had no intention of becoming an academic, but I loved Geography Honors ... I don't remember making a conscious decision to do a PhD. It was more a case of things unfolding and I went with the flow." Others described their passion which drove their career, with one individual saying, "Three months ago I became an academic; a reluctant academic I might add. This was not a goal of mine. I am here because of my passion for Aboriginal education."

Some participants pursued a PhD to seek answers to their questions: "learning and curiosity has always lain beneath the surface, scratching away at who I am so that I get nudged into certain directions." Individuals also pursued graduate studies to challenge themselves and further develop their skill set; however, experiences within graduate studies paved the path towards a career in academia and participants described how encounters with people, educational theories, and research methods transformed their academic journeys. One participant attributed her desire to pursue a career in academia to her supervisor, saying, "I had the support of a great supervisor .... She was a great mentor, and with her as a model, I knew it was possible to simultaneously perform the role of a parent and academic."

Encouragement from other faculty drove a participant to pursue a PhD and a career in academia: "His encouragement for me to publish my Master's final paper in a journal gave me the piece of my career that was lacking when I applied for my PhD." Another participant said,

> In my Master's, my instructors encouraged me to realize that I had more capacity than I gave myself credit for .... As my Master's came to a close, my supervisor encouraged me to apply for a PhD.... Again I was encouraged to think about academia by my supervisors and advisors.

Encouragement provided the needed confidence to pursue further graduate education and a career in academia: "with the encouragement of professors I continued on with my graduate work ... knowing that professors I respected felt I was ready for the program gave me a huge boost in confidence."

Difficulties encountered as a new academic
Participants noted that the journey towards becoming an academic was not an easy one. Various participants discussed their experience with the imposter syndrome: "wondering whether or not this average student did not somehow get into this role that she did not deserve is a constant question that I face." Another individual said, "struggles with self-doubt, anxiety, imposter syndrome and depression all plagued the thesis-writing process ... while I suppose now I have a career in academia, without a tenure-track appointment, I struggle to feel like an actual academic."

Others questioned their rationale for pursing academia and their ability to perform as an academic: "While the idea of helping to train future counsellors was exciting, it was also daunting! I worried whether I would be able to do the work; whether I would be successful." Another participant said, "I continue to feel like I am grappling around instead of settling down into this new career. I have a lot of uncertainty about how to do research ... ."

Individuals described their transition into academia saying, "My initial perceptions of becoming an academic were that it was both exciting and overwhelming. I could see so many opportunities, but it all seemed complex. I felt somewhat lonely." Participants commonly referred to academia as a lonely place:

> In my first couple of months as a new hire I was lonely... While some of the faculty attempted to support my transition, there was no formal system of support or mentorship. I can honestly say I spent the loneliest year of my life and after being at [the university] for six months I tendered my resignation. I returned to my previous position [in psychological services]; in this position I had a system of supports and colleagues that were both a social and a professional support system.

Upon assuming a position at a university, it became difficult to maintain a work-life balance: "I spent all of my time teaching or in my office, overwhelmed with the task of preparing three courses I had never taught before, and spending so much time asking questions. . ." For many participants, "Establishing my research agenda was a huge challenge!" One participant said, "The stress and long work hours that have been part of my pre-tenure years have at times made me question my decision to pursue an academic career. The experience has left me feeling inadequate as both an employee and as a mother."

Participants encountered many difficulties as they moved into a new form of work:

> Becoming an academic was not an easy transition for me. Coming from practice where I had been [in psychological services] for over 20 years to a new environment where the expectations were very different was difficult. Being in a position where I would constantly be evaluated was also difficult. I completed my doctoral program in 2003 and had been removed from research and writing since that time, so the establishment of a research program proved very challenging. On top of that, I was not teacher trained and therefore even my teaching duties required considerable effort to develop competency.

Other participants discussed the stressors around tenure, with one participant saying,

> I found the transition from being considered an expert in my health-based job to being a novice in the academy somewhat difficult ... I felt that I had established some credibility and seniority [in psychological services], whereas at the university, I was the one who needed help and guidance to get me where I needed to be. The tenure process did nothing to help with any of this! I had left a permanent position in health where I was considered competent in my work and was now facing the prospect of proving to my peers and the administrators that I was capable and worth keeping. Add this to the mystery that surrounds what it means to have proved you deserve tenure and you have a recipe guaranteed to produce migraines, sleepless nights, and stomach ulcers in anyone.

Need to understand expectations

Participants felt overwhelmed by their limited understanding of the expectations associated with obtaining tenure. One individual said,

> You could say that I spent six years preparing to become an academic. I took on numerous research assistantships, was involved with various forms of knowledge mobilization, audited courses which I wanted to teach, and instructed pre-service education courses, yet when I was hired while my PhD was all but defended I still felt lost.

This individual highlighted the need for support in order to better understand workload expectations.

> In response to an administrator's request, I took on additional online course development, but was course development valued when you would primarily be evaluated on your peer-reviewed publications?... I took on book chapter publications, but was this the right decision when I had manuscripts that only required minimal work before sending them off to a peer-reviewed journal? In order to appear collegial, I provided teaching development workshops for faculty, and in order to obtain recognition in the field and keep up with the recent literature, I became an associate editor of an international journal; however, I often wonder if I should spend time supporting the teaching and writing of other faculty, when it is another activity which takes away from my own time for writing.

Individuals called for formal job orientation.

> Unlike when I started my job in the hospital setting, there was no orientation or anyone to tell me what I was supposed to do on my first day or in my new position.... The first weeks of my academic career were spent trying to figure out exactly how an academic should spend their days. There appeared to be no firm guidelines for a lot of things.... Not knowing if I was doing the right thing caused me some stress during those first days and even now, four years later, I still find that I have questions as to how things work, and these questions do not seem to have concrete answers.

Participants also asked for support in understanding the organizational structure of the university.

> My introduction to life as an academic has been a steep learning curve. I know little of the organizational structure, work culture, or expectations of the institution, and I sometimes do not even know what questions to ask or whom to ask.... An added challenge for me is participating in the work to develop a new program when I am new to academia and completely unaware of the university governance system. Having the process more clearly defined at the beginning of the work would have been helpful in facilitating the work.

This individual continued to say,

> I am, however, continuing to thrive because of colleagues who have simply stepped in to support me.... They have offered advice on negotiating the politics of the faculty and pitfalls to avoid, shared with me their own experiences of being new to the academy, and offered to provide support or answer questions.

Need for supportive colleagues

Supportive colleagues helped new faculty transition into their role in academia: "I think a huge part of coping was having some friendly faces to work with. I felt I had established connections and trust with some colleagues and could discuss my teaching and research with them." Participants noted they especially benefited from informal time spent with colleagues:

> Moments of connection, of shared experience and hospitality, pooled together to form a nest from which I have been able to perform differing roles, create further meaning and purpose, and build a moderately comfortable safe haven in the rigorous, chilly, isolating territory of academia.

Participants found it helpful to have colleagues who were also new to academia:

> There was a group of individuals living the same experience of not knowing what was expected of them, or where to find answers, while trying to embrace the transition from a successful career outside the university to one inside. As a group with a shared experience, we have been able to learn from each other and have supported each other both work-wise and emotionally. The knowledge that I was not the only person going through this process has been very reassuring and has helped to reduce my stress and increase my sense of belonging.

Relationships with colleagues were perceived as invaluable in regards to supporting the transition into academia and managing the demands of the job: "It is primarily my relationships that are helping me in my transition to academia." Participants noted the importance of having colleagues who could act as a support system because "as my relationships with colleagues and staff grew stronger other aspects of the work became more manageable."

Need for respected mentors

At the recommendation of the promotion and tenure committee, three participants were assigned mentors. Other participants independently sought mentors within and outside of the faculty. Participants felt mentors were instrumental in supporting their journey towards tenure:

> I was fortunate enough to be assigned a mentor who helped me become familiar with how the university worked. She helped me establish short- and long-term goals that were needed in order to reach tenure. She also supported me in preparation of my work for publication.

Participants expressed gratitude for the mentorship they received:

> I am thankful for several faculty who have taken on the role of mentor either formally or informally. It is good to have a few people of whom I can ask the mundane and the complex questions relating to academia.

Participants discussed the role of mentors both within and outside of their faculty:

> One informal mentor, an older colleague in another discipline, has played a significant role in me being able to settle in and cope. We work on projects together and just watching how she organizes funding and people has been really helpful.... She is a successful female role model for me and when things get difficult I say to myself, "She did it—then so can I."

Need for faculty writing groups

Participants articulated that they "recognize that building a solid record of publication will be key to landing [and securing] a tenure-track position." However, they experienced difficulty finding the time to publish and noted that they had "been slow to submit papers for publication, primarily paralyzed by fear of rejection." This individual continued to say,

> Participating in the writing group is helping me sort through all of these issues. Hearing that others, even those in tenure-track and tenured positions, struggle with finding time to write, struggle with insecurities, and struggle with negative feedback from journal reviewers has provided me with a sense of comfort in knowing that I am not alone.

Individuals appreciated being part of the writing group: "Finding a group that accepted me, and shared their successes and struggles, as well as supported me in helping normalize my struggles was amazing." Participants expressed that the writing group provided the needed sense of belonging:

> The writing group proved to be a tremendous source of support as the academy can be a lonely place. The writing group helped me to develop connections with other faculty who were in a similar position ... trying to cope! The writing group became a place of safety, a place where one could discuss not only goals, but also our feelings about our new roles.

The relationships that developed within the writing group provided needed support for new faculty:

> My writing group colleagues have been a real source of support. Any question I need an answer for, or even just to talk about things going on at home, I know that I just need to pop into someone's office and they will be there for me…. It makes such a difference having supportive colleagues who are willing to share knowledge and ideas. I have loved publishing papers with the writing group—a real highlight of my career.

Another participant said,

> Through the writing group I have found a space where I can be me, feel accepted for all my insecurities, and have colleagues that I can turn to to share successes and frustrations. The wide range of expertise that exists amongst this group of us has really nurtured my understanding of community in the context of work. I am forever grateful for the cohesiveness that has developed through our common need to write…. I am also grateful for how we model for each other new ways, new ideas, new approaches as it is clearly not competitive, but cooperative. To me it is the closest reality I have of what I tell my students when I ask them to share with each other … share, listen, critique, not to tear each other down, but to make each other's work stronger. That is what I feel is happening in this context.

Need to be patient with yourself

Participants articulated the importance of being patient with themselves: "Reflecting on my path to becoming an academic, I realize I could probably be a little more patient with myself and patient with time." A second participant agreed that it was important to "not beat yourself up." She continued to say,

> As I have come to work in academia I am slowly learning to leave my perfectionism behind. After all, I don't think there are enough hours in a day to complete all of the service activities you would like, spend all of the time you would like prepping for a perfectly delivered course, and obtain two publications per year in top-tier journals. As a new academic, the writing group is helping me learn that this is okay. We meet every Friday to discuss issues associated with our writing, but in the process we

> do a lot more. We support each other, provide the opportunity to expose our vulnerabilities, and have a safe space to discuss any difficulties we may be experiencing.

Although participants encountered difficulties as they transitioned into the role of an academic, they were glad they put themselves up for the challenge.

> While there were personal costs involved in taking on an academic career in my forties, there have been many benefits.... Each day presents the opportunity to explore something new, either through my teaching or my research. I also feel that my co-workers and I have formed an "academic family" and that being part of this family means that we will be there for each other as we struggle to form our new identities as academics.

Educational Importance of the Study

Transitioning into a faculty position can provide stress, uncertainty, and emotional upheaval. Negotiating academic and institutional cultures along with varied expectations from administration and colleagues is difficult for any newcomer, but can be particularly challenging for women (Grant & Knowles, 2000). Many of the participants in this study followed a non-linear path to academia and experienced difficulty becoming familiar with and adjusting to the norms and expectations of their new academic careers. According to LaRocco and Bruns (2006), new academics face a steep learning curve as they come to understand the structures of the university, adopt the language and culture of academia, and define themselves as researchers. Universities must provide faculty with information regarding the university's policy and culture, tenure and promotion systems, and effective mechanisms for structuring faculty collaboration (Savage, Karp, & Logue, 2004).

Mentorship can be defined as a relationship between two individuals, in which one person, usually of superior rank and outstanding achievement, guides the development of an entry-level individual without providing formal evaluation (Leslie, Lingard, & Whyte, 2005; Savage et al., 2004). Mentors play an important role in the success and trajectory of pre-tenured faculty (Driscoll et al., 2009; Greene et al.,

2008; Leslie et al., 2005), and mentors as well as mentees can benefit from participating in a mentor-protégé program (Wilson, Brannan, & White, 2010; Zeind et al., 2005). In the absence of formal mentoring, an informal mentoring partnership may assist new faculty in becoming adjusted and more productive in their scholarship (Barrett & Brown, 2014). Sharing academic knowledge and expertise supports academic growth, and an informal co-mentorship can foster feelings of safety and support, which is key to institutional resocialization (Barrett & Brown, 2014). In addition, informal mentorships can help junior faculty choose which activities to prioritize and determine when it is okay to say no (Leslie et al., 2005). While there appears to be little evidence of formal support for the academic development of members of education faculty (Wimmer & da Costa, 2007), academic institutions should consider how they could lay the groundwork to foster mentoring relationships. Institutions should consider how they can develop mentorship programs, for while assigned formal relationships show less success than unassigned relationships, if a mentor is not assigned, some faculty may miss out on the opportunity to benefit from the needed guidance (Law et al., 2014; Leslie et al., 2005).

Research literature points to the value of writing groups as support mechanisms for individuals who are new to academia (Galligan et al., 2003; Lee & Boud, 2003; Morss & Murray, 2001). Writing groups help new faculty develop confidence and a sense of identity (Gillespie et al., 2005; Pasternak, Longwell-Grice, Shea, & Hanson, 2009). This is especially true for female academics (Grant & Knowles, 2000), and was the experience for members of our group. For the authors and participants of this study, faculty writing groups, supportive colleagues, and respected mentors provided necessary support as they entered into, and became comfortable in, the realm of academia. As authors and participants of this study, we recommend that institutions consider how writing groups, as well as formal and informal forms of mentorship, can be used to support faculty who may experience instances of isolation or loneliness upon transitioning into a new position and who would benefit from support in understanding and meeting the expectations of the academic work milieu.

Authorship

Memorial's Education Writing Group is:

Young, G., Penney, S., Anderson, J., Badenhorst, C., Dawe, N., Hesson, J., Joy, R., Li, X., McLeod, H., Moore, S., Pelech, S., Pickett, S., Stordy, M., and Vaandering, D.

The first two individuals are the primary authors of the study, and the remaining authors are listed alphabetically.

References

Barrett, J., & Brown, H. (2014). From leaning comes meaning: Informal comentorship and the second-career academic in education. *The Qualitative Report, 37*, 1–15. Retrieved from http://www.nova.edu/ssss/QR/QR19/barrett73.pdf.

Crane, B., O'Hern, B., & Lawler, P. (2009). Second career professionals: Transitioning to a faculty role. *Journal of Faculty Development, 23*(1), 24–29.

Driscoll, L. G., Parkes, K. A., Tilley-Lubbs, G. A., Brill, J. M., & Pitts Bannister, V. R. (2009). Navigating the lonely sea: Peer mentoring and collaboration among aspiring women scholars. *Mentoring & Tutoring: Partnership in Learning, 17*(1), 5–21. doi:10.1080/13611260802699532.

Fogg, P. (2002). Moving to a different world: What happens when politicians and business leaders become professors. *Chronicle of Higher Education, 48*(26), A10–A12.

Galligan, L., Cretchley, P., George, L., McDonald, K. M., McDonald, J., & Rankin, J. (2003). Evolution and emerging trends of university writing groups. *Queensland Journal of Educational Research, 19*(1), 28–41. Retrieved from http://www.iier.org.au/qjer/qjer19/galligan.html.

Gillespie, D., Dolsak, N., Kochis, B., Krabill, R., Lerum, K., Peterson, A., & Thomas, E. (2005). Research circles: Supporting the scholarship of junior faculty. *Innovative Higher Education, 30*(3), 149-162. doi:10.1007/s10755-005-6300-9.

Grant, B., & Knowles, S. (2000). Flights of imagination: Academic women be(com)ing writers. *International Journal for Academic Development, 5*(1), 6–19.

Greene, H. C., O'Connor, K. A., Good, A. J., Ledford, C. C., Peel, B. B., & Zhang, G. (2008). Building a support system toward tenure: Challenges and needs of tenure-track faculty in colleges of education. *Mentoring & Tutoring: Partnership in Learning, 16*(4), 429–447. doi:10.1080/13611260802433791.

Kane, M., & Trochim, W. M. K. (2007). *Concept mapping for planning and evaluation*. Thousand Oaks, CA: Sage Publications.

LaRocco, D. J., & Bruns, D. A. (2006). Practitioner to professor: An examination of second career academics' entry into academia. *Education, 126*(4), 626–639.

Law, A. V., Bottenberg, M. M., Brozick, A. H., Currie, J. D., DiVall, M. V., Haines, S. T., Yablonski, E., et al. (2014). A checklist for the development of faculty mentorship programs. *American Journal of Pharmaceutical Education, 78*(5), 98-108. doi:10.5688/ajpe78598.

Lee, A., & Boud, D. (2003). Writing groups, change and academic identity: Research development as local practice. *Studies in Higher Education, 28*(2), 187–200. doi:10.1080/0307507032000058109.

Leslie, K., Lingard, L., & Whyte, S. (2005). Junior faculty experiences with informal mentoring. *Medical Teacher, 27*(8), 693–698.

Morss, K., & Murray, R. (2001). Researching academic writing within a structured programme: Insights and outcomes. *Studies in Higher Education, 26*(1), 35–52. doi:10.1080/03075070020030706.

Pasternak, D. L., Longwell-Grice, H., Shea, K. A., & Hanson, K. L. (2009). Alien environments or supportive writing communities? Pursuing writing groups in academe. *Arts & Humanities in Higher Education, 8*(3), 355-367. doi:10.1177/1474022209339958.

Richardson, L., & St. Pierre, E. A. (2008). Writing: A method of inquiry. In N. K. Denzin and Y. S. Lincoln (Eds.), *Collecting and interpreting qualitative materials* (3rd edition) (pp. 959–978). Thousand Oaks, CA: Sage Publications.

Savage, H. E., Karp, R. S., & Logue, R. (2004). Faculty mentorship at colleges and universities. *College Teaching, 52*(1), 21–24. doi:10.3200/CTCH.52.1.21-24.

Wilson, C. B., Brannan, J., & White, A. (2010). A mentor-protégé program for new faculty, Part II: Stories of mentors. *The Journal of Nursing Education, 49*(12), 665–671. doi:10.3928/01484834-20100730-08.

Wimmer, R., & da Costa, J. (2007). The academic development of education faculty: Looking back, looking ahead. *Alberta Journal of Educational Research, 53*(1), 77–86.

Zeind, C. S., Zdanowicz, M., MacDonald, K., Parkhurst, C., King, C., & Wizwer, P. (2005). Developing a sustainable faculty mentoring program. *American Journal of Pharmaceutical Education, 69*(5), 1–13.

CHAPTER 7

I Think You Are Ambivalent: The Realities of Indigenous Scholarship in Mainstream Universities

Onowa McIvor, María del Carmen Rodríguez de France,
and Trish Rosborough
Faculty of Education, University of Victoria

Introduction

Indigenous academics have been increasingly engaged in mainstream universities over the past 25 years, and in the last 10 years a growing number of these academics have begun writing about these experiences. Within these stories and reflections, across disciplines, commonalities emerge. For example, Plains Cree/Saulteaux scholar Margaret Kovach (2009) begins her piece about "being Indigenous within the academy" saying, "I trust I am not alone" (p. 51).

Indigenous scholars are commonly understood to carry dual duty. We are members of the academy accompanied by a set of rules, expectations, within departments, schools, and faculties—and—we are members of Indigenous communities, near and far. This dual duty manifests as we balance our responsibilities to teaching, research, and service with our responsibilities and expectations to membership in Indigenous communities—a concept described by Opaskwayak Cree scholar Shawn Wilson (2008) as relational accountability. Yet the two spaces—academy and community—do not always coincide, thereby creating a dual duty of expectations, roles, and standards to uphold.

Traditionally, these two spheres—academia and Indigenous communities—had little regard or respect for one another. This reality left first-generation Indigenous scholars walking in the much-described "two worlds" (Henze & Vanett, 1993). While these two worlds are gaining spaces of overlap, the span of the two still creates a wide gulf to cover and reach.

Indigenous scholars such as Eileen Antone (Onyota'a:ka of the Oneida Nation) teaches us that making space in the academy for Indigenous worldviews need not be seen as a remedial exercise but rather as a possibility for contributions that expand the walls of the academy in similar ways that we each seek to expand the canon of knowledge within and across our various disciplines (Antone & Dawson, 2014). Sami scholar Rauna Kuokkanen (2007, p. 20) calls the inclusion of Indigenous worldviews in the academy "the gift of indigenous epistemes."

We are three pre-tenured Indigenous scholars working together in a small and organizationally undefined Indigenous academic unit in a mid-sized, research-intensive university. We began our tenure-track positions within three years of each other and therefore are sharing the journey of striving for tenure, offering each other collegial support along the way. We each hold childrearing responsibilities and have large extended families and multiple community memberships, from local, to urban, to homelands far away. It is common for Indigenous academics to have large and intergenerational families (raising grandchildren or other related children), making for higher levels of family and community responsibilities. Each author came to academia at a different stage of life, with a previous career and life experiences, which inevitably influenced the experience of transitioning from graduate school into our tenure-track positions.

Indigenous scholars are often called to lead and coordinate Indigenization efforts and build and implement Indigenous programs, thereby attracting Indigenous students who are typically underrepresented at universities (Mihesuah & Wilson, 2004; Pidgeon, Archibald, & Hawkey, 2014)—and yet, little recognition is given to the internal organizational-building work we are called to do. This is considered as part of our service, which until recently has been deemed as part of the job that carries little relevance to the rest of an academic's life, especially as it pertains to reappointment, tenure, and promotion. Therefore, service expectations are higher than many of our non-Indigenous colleagues; consequently, maintaining balance is critical, yet difficult to achieve.

Here we hope to add our story to this chorus of voices, as three female Indigenous education faculty members. The next three sections, which begin with an expression in an Indigenous language, are individual perspectives of each of the authors. Subsequent to this is a section looking at the common themes that emerge from the collective experiences.

"Ik'us giga̱ 'o⫶nukwus k̠a k̠wax̱ a̱ 'nakwa̱ la lo⫶" (Your Parents Raised You Right)

While many people in our age group are downsizing, my husband and I recently bought a larger home near the university. The house has a constant flow of family and friends. The openness of the home was new to my husband when we married 40 years ago, but it's been my life experience. I grew up with relatives, family friends, and foster children coming and going. The space for family gatherings—to house a family member in transition, or to host graduate students who have come from their home communities for study—is important to me. A recent guest, who had come to Victoria to be with family when a community Elder passed away, spoke to me in Kwak'wala, saying, "Ik'us giga̱ 'o⫶nukwus k̠a k̠wax̱ a̱ 'nakwa̱ la lo⫶"—your parents raised you right.

The open home isn't just a peculiarity to my family; it is our way of being as an Indigenous family. I am a woman of mixed heritage; my ancestry is Kwakwa̱ ka̱ 'wakw and European. I identify as an Indigenous woman and am tied strongly to my family, my community, and my nation. The way I walk in this world and the way I approach my scholarship and career are not separate. I carry with me the responsibilities and teachings that I was born into. I carry a strong awareness that my behaviour reflects on my relations, past, present, and future.

I came to the role of assistant professor in Indigenous education late in my career. Like many Indigenous women, I began my post-secondary education as a mature adult. When my youngest child began kindergarten, I went back to school to get a BA and then an MA. I did this while raising my young family and working as an educator, in various capacities, in my community. My work brought me to Victoria, British Columbia's capital city, and to a job in Aboriginal education with the provincial government. My plan was to stay for two years and then head back to my home community in the northern part of Vancouver Island. My heart lives in T'sax̱ is, the

Kwakiutl community where my mother grew up and where I raised my babies. Fourteen years later, I still have not moved home.

After more than a decade of providing leadership in Aboriginal education for the British Columbia (B.C.) provincial government and a year after completing my doctorate in education, I moved into my role as assistant professor in Indigenous education. I feel fortunate to be in a position that aligns with my passion. I have the privilege of teaching, researching, and contributing as a community-engaged scholar in an area I care about deeply—Indigenous education and language revitalization. At least I have that privilege for now. This is a reappointment year for me. If I am successful, I will have another three years to prove myself worthy of tenure. Today I think I am on track. There are other days when I fear I am on a path to early retirement.

I am on a steep learning path. Transitioning from a position where I had designated authority to a position as a junior faculty member means I am negotiating and navigating the bounds of my role. I made the transition at a time when we were taking down the walls (literally) in government offices to create more collaborative working processes. I was surprised to find how isolating and individualistic the university environment feels. The physical environment of row after row of closed offices and few open gathering spaces is a metaphor for the division between the work of individuals within the organization. Of course, I could be doing more to break down those metaphorical walls, but as new faculty, my time is dominated by figuring out how to be a good teacher, develop a research agenda, and contribute through service.

I joined the university excited in particular to teach "EŁ TELNIWT and Indigenous Education." This course is a requirement for all Bachelor of Education (BEd) students at the University of Victoria and focuses on Indigenous content and instructional practices that are aligned with Indigenous culture. In my years as a policy maker in Aboriginal education, I saw such courses develop in response to direction from the Aboriginal education community. It has been widely acknowledged in B.C. that all pre-service teacher programs should include at least one course in Indigenous education. In 2012, the Teachers' Regulation Branch (TRB) made First Nations content mandatory to the equivalent of a one-semester-long course. Yet, the responsibility I feel is to the community who has put such hope in the systemic outcomes of this required content inclusion.

Perhaps because of this, I take marking for this course very seriously. For me, it is a critical opportunity to engage with students—future teachers—who are wrestling with issues of Indigenous-settler relations, particularly forms of racism and altruism that reproduce dangerous understandings of and behaviors toward Indigenous children and youth. I feel committed in my role to helping my students learn and develop respectful ways to be in relationship with Indigenous peoples.

A joy of my role in Indigenous education is working with our community-based partnership programs. I have the privilege of teaching and learning with Indigenous communities who are committed to the revitalization of their languages. Teaching in these programs requires a commitment beyond preparing a good syllabus, building lesson plans, and staying current in the relevant literature. To do this work in a good way requires showing up and building connections, along with co-teaching, participating in events, and maintaining relationships with students outside of course time. Yet, these activities are given little acknowledgement in reappointment and tenure processes. I have found that teaching takes as much time as one is willing to give it, and in my first year, I allowed teaching responsibilities to dominate. However, that is only one part of my job.

The other two components of my role as an assistant professor are research and service. Like teaching, I find great privilege, opportunity, and responsibility in both research and dissemination, and in wider service. As an assistant professor in Indigenous education, I have the opportunity to build a research agenda that is fueled by my passion for Indigenous language revitalization. It is research and practice that I hope will support my community and other Indigenous communities in the work to revitalize languages. I have come to this at a time when others have opened doors, creating physical, conceptual, and intellectual spaces for Indigenous language work. I am grateful to them, and carry the responsibility to continue to open such spaces for others. Like teaching, research could easily take up the whole of my time. Certainly, service on campus requires much more than the officially expected 20% of my workload. As Indigenous faculty, the call to sit on committees and to participate in events is high. It is challenging to know what is okay to say no to, particularly when requests come from senior people, the department chair, the dean, and the provost's office.

Finding some balance is necessary, in a large part because of the way I will be evaluated as an employee for reappointment and, later, tenure. There is a constant tension between the formal and informal requirements of my job, and also the responsibilities and relationships I carry with me as a Kwakiutl person, an Indigenous woman, and an educator. Preparing my yearly salary and merit package and soon my reappointment package is a challenging process. I am asked to represent myself as an individual, when my journey is collective. Like my home, I aim for my practice to align with my cultural teachings about relationships and community responsibility.

Kepiihcihi—Thank You

The late Zapotec writer Andrés Henestrosa (1997) said that one can speak twenty languages but the mother tongue is the one in which one dreams, thinks, cries, and prays. My arrival to the territory of the Lekwungen-speaking people (which includes Victoria) almost two decades ago has been a journey full of adventure, experience, learning, trial, and success. As a person of Indigenous Kickapoo heritage from México, my first language is Spanish, thus living constantly in a second language is not easy, even though I am considered to be proficient and competent in English. Transitioning from being an international student to pursuing a career in the same university where I completed my degree has required the development of new skills and new ways of thinking and being; and it has also required learning new languages—the language of the academic world and, most importantly, the languages of the Indigenous communities for whom I work and with whom I have established relational accountability. In other words, the work has required meeting the responsibility that a scholar/researcher has, to establish a relationship with the world around her in order to be accountable to all her relations. This has not been easy; it has taken me a few years to be recognized by some leaders in communities, to be acknowledged as a person who is worthy of trust and even friendship, as someone who is committed to developing partnerships, collaboration, and networks of support. Elders now welcome me and invite me to their homes—an honour, and a privilege that has developed over time.

"Where are you from?" was the first question Elder George asked when we first met in Vancouver on Musqueam traditional territory. I introduced myself and acknowledged the territory and the fact that I was a visitor to the land. George greeted me in Kwak'wala, saying "Gila'kasla," and acknowledged he was a visitor to that territory too. This is part of the protocol I have learned as I navigate and learn about the complexities of geographical and historical occurrences, political disruptions, and present realities that permeate Indigenous communities and Canadian society. In tandem, I am also learning to move about in the academic world, where protocol and expectations about service, teaching, and research are considered separate from each other but held by common threads only every once in a while, depending on where the research is done, how it is done, and what is obtained from it. However, in the case of Indigenous scholars, these three dimensions are forever interwoven, requiring a commitment to people and their communities, to one's research, and to the larger society. As an outsider, learning what it means to be accountable to "all my relations" has been a constant learning exercise, a trial-and-error practice where there is no room for assumptions. I have learned that trust is established in different ways at different times, and I sometimes wonder how much my dark skin has helped me in the process and how much it has mired opportunities.

I was fortunate to gain some knowledge working with diverse communities in various capacities prior to my tenure-track appointment at a university. One of my early experiences was as part of a team facilitating healing circles, and designing learning opportunities for survivors of residential schools; this allowed me to learn first-hand about people's histories and stories, about their lives, their ways of being, and their aspirations for the future. It was in these circles that I learned the ethic of non-interference, the importance of local protocol, the relationships among families, and the accountability that is necessary when one is a member of a group, which was not very different from my own teachings and family dynamics; and yet, I needed to remember that in each group or community of Indigenous people there are commonalities and differences. The shared aspects of my worldview and my view of the world as I understood it from being an international Indigenous scholar intersected in the axiology, the ontology, and the epistemology—in other words, in the values, the ways of being, and the ways of knowing between my heritage and the customs of this land.

As a way to learn more, I have engaged with local communities in various capacities: as an instructor, as a researcher, and as a support person for programs where student teachers are involved. Since one of my duties is facilitating courses for mostly non-Indigenous pre-service teachers, I feel a strong sense of responsibility, not only to create awareness about the historical wrongdoings and the political abuses and exploitations that Indigenous people have experienced but also to create spaces where social change is the aspiration of future teachers. Consequently, I am involved in projects, networks, research, and teaching courses beyond the faculty of education; I am unable to fathom an academic life isolated from peers, from other content areas, and from learning opportunities in diverse contexts. However, devoting oneself with unbridled passion to an academic life presents risks of various kinds. One such risk is dedicating a large portion of time and energy to service, which until recently has been deemed as part of the job that carries little relevance to the rest of an academic's life, especially as it pertains to reappointment, tenure, and promotion. Fortunately for us, this university is starting to acknowledge service as beneficial and necessary to scholarship and research. This is especially true given the recognition by post-secondary institutions of the need to engage in community collaborations through centers of community-based research or community-engaged scholarship. As Indigenous scholars, however, this recognition has always existed, and it is acknowledged at an individual and at a community level; it is understood that when one works in community one also works holistically.

One year ago I was given a three-ring binder to start collecting my documents to apply for tenure; this process has been a reflexive exercise, for it has allowed me to pay attention to who I am on paper, and to imagine who I want to become. Beyond the practical representation of a holder of my being, these three rings represent my life as a scholar: One ring represents research; another ring represents teaching; and one last ring relates to the most important aspect of my life: service. These rings are also reminders of who I am outside of the academic world: I am a mother of three pre-adolescent children who, like me, are on the cusp of transition towards "becoming." Not very different from who they are right now, and yet close to exploring new life dimensions, emotions, and experiences.

The Indigenous education unit at this university is still growing and expanding; we have non-Indigenous colleagues who are respectful allies and a support to the three of us—Indigenous academics who continue to navigate the complexities of an institution rooted in Eurocentric conservative values that are often in conflict with Indigenous worldviews. However, it is my hope that with the unwavering support from my Indigenous colleagues, my journey towards learning the language of the academy will be a rewarding experience. It is also my hope that with help from the people of the various communities in which I work, my journey towards learning their languages will be a reciprocal one where, through participating in our language-revitalization programs, I will be able to help them dream, think, and pray in their mother tongue. For the continued opportunity to work with communities in a reciprocal relationship, I am thankful.

miyoskamin (Springtime)

In the mid-2000s, it was not uncommon for Indigenous doctoral students to be hired into faculty positions and supported to complete their PhDs. It was also not unusual for these same Indigenous scholars to be hired into leadership positions within the academy, to assist with building Indigenous programs (and therefore attract more Indigenous students) within those faculties that were often largely void of both Indigenous faculty and Indigenous students (Mihesuah & Wilson, 2004). By these standards, I guess my life experience has not been unusual, and yet by the norms of the academy it is an uncommon trajectory.

I spent my first four years in the academy as a senior lecturer and Director of Indigenous Education while completing my doctoral degree. When I began the position, I had not yet completed my course work. Once my degree was completed I was reclassified as an assistant professor and continued to hold the directorship position. This marked the official start to my tenure clock. I have just completed a reappointment process that renews the tenure-track position. I am now working hard at the final stages of preparing for tenure, which looks to be about a year into the horizon. My current plan is to apply for tenure a year early, but it actually feels more like several years late, given my early start as senior lecturer.

I grew up in northern Saskatchewan where the boreal forest meets the prairie. It is equal parts bush country and agricultural. This part of the world has four very distinct seasons: Long cold winters, hopeful springs, rejuvenating summers, and contemplative falls. Experiencing these seasons through my life has shaped my worldview. If I am so blessed as to have a long life as an academic, I may have the opportunity to experience all four seasons. My early engagement in the academy and (continued) road to tenure has felt like springtime. I have been there seven years, and it has been a time of hope, exerting invigorating robust energy—breaking down barriers like the ice flow when the rivers open up. I have had tremendous opportunities to collaborate in new program development, new course development, Indigenous community-university partnership development, grant writing, and new research endeavors. This is not to say that these new experiences will not be available to me again, but rather that this has been a very particular time—shaped by newness.

My tenure-track experience has been strongly influenced by coming into the academy in a leadership role. Elders often describe our life's intention as a calling. I was called to assist with building up Indigenous education in a largely non-Indigenous faculty, and while my teaching responsibilities were reduced, the expectations around research and scholarship were not. Of course, my early years were spent focused on completing my doctorate, although I did some publishing during that time as well. Yet, my development as a scholar was continuously interrupted by my leadership and administrative duties; but then, was it? This is the tricky thing about scholarship. What counts? Universities have created a difficult pattern of hiring pre-doctoral Indigenous faculty to build their Indigenous presence and programs, while holding them to the same standards as all other faculty members who do not have these aims or responsibilities but are then reluctant to recognize program development as scholarship. Increasingly we are seeing examples of change to recognize these kinds of scholarly contributions, for example, the recent addition of "Community-Engaged Scholarship" to our home department's tenure and promotion policies.

I received a wide variety of advice in my early days as an academic. Some would say, "Head down; write, write, write; repeat-teach the same course all year if you can to reduce your preparation time, and pave your way to tenure—nothing else matters until you have that." Other advice I received was, "Do not worry about tenure, if you are doing everything that you are supposed to, it will come." I was also told, at the time, that nothing that I did as a senior lecturer mattered for tenure, so worry about it once you complete your PhD. Others would say, "No, it is your lifetime of work that matters, so never slack!" More recently I have received the advice that I have "got to get out of leadership in order to develop myself more completely as a [real] scholar." The message was: The academic unit and the programs and courses that I have been collaboratively involved in building, and that are beginning to fill the void of Indigenous students and faculty in the academy, are meaningless on the road to tenure. Leave leadership and become a "real" scholar. When I pushed back and tried to explain my understanding of Indigenous scholarship, of collaboration, of innovation, of responsibility to community for both research and academic partnerships, I was told, "I think you are ambivalent ... about being a scholar"—a major blow for someone who has spent the last fifteen years working towards this moment. However, I came to understand this experience as a clash of worldviews, and my Elders have long since taught me that all those who arrive in your life are there to teach you something.

Academia is a culture like any other, its origins over a thousand years old, rooted in northern Europe, with an all-male, all-white cast. Fast forward a thousand years on a new continent colonized by the same crowd, ban Indigenous peoples from institutions of higher learning until the 1960s, slowly welcoming us and later inviting us to help fill the void they created. Often this inside crowd thinks itself to be beyond policies of assimilation but continues to insist we become just like them. They want us to dress like them, think like them, talk like them, write like them, and teach like them. And if we don't ... we are invited to leave under the auspices of a tenure process. This may seem like a cynical view, but the systems we operate within are structural and slow to change, and we (Indigenous and non-Indigenous alike) are still right here in it. In this moment, we are still growing and learning together, we are still opening our eyes to the ways that universities work (intentionally or unintentionally) toward the assimilation of Indigenous people through hierarchical structures of almost all positions of power, held by non-Indigenous peoples who cannot separate themselves from their own worldview. Additionally, they (or the institution) refuse to create parallel positions of power specifically for Indigenous contributions to governance or structures within the universities, such as independent academic units or Indigenous-specific faculties as safe havens for Indigenous scholarship to grow unencumbered of worldview gatekeeping.

So where does this leave us? Where do we go from here? One challenge is the collective mentalities of Indigenous people offer a double-shock (cultural and organizational) to an environment where individualism is rewarded and encouraged. So the crossroads is that we continue to work with our communities and with one another on the road to tenure—yet, the actual road to tenure we must walk alone. We will eventually stand alone before a jury of our peers to determine if our scholarship and our contributions are enough, the right kind, and worthy of support to be invited to stay.

We are all striving, Indigenous peoples and our allies, to better understand the world, to make a difference in our lifetime, to work with students to build them up and help them along their journey in any way we can. Despite the current challenges and historical hurts, we *are* making progress together as more social-justice-minded leaders make space and more Indigenous peoples take up leadership positions and battle the front lines to make it better for the next generations to come.

Now, the last energetic push towards tenure, the final breaking of the ice before the sweet sun of a rejuvenating summer not far off onto the horizon—not to lazily bask—but rather to watch the seeds begin to sprout, to see the buds unfold into leaves, and to feel the warm summer breeze blow like a deep exhale.

Common Threads

While our stories are personal and unique to each of us, common threads weave throughout. There are commonalities with other pre-tenured faculty making career transitions, and there are commonalities shared between us and with other Indigenous scholars who have paved the way in their institutions, and who now serve as role models for the generations of emerging Indigenous scholars to come.

As pre-tenured academics needing to represent our unit in various committees, initiatives, and projects in the faculty, there are times when we have felt limited in our actions or in what we can say because we have less authority than our more senior and tenured colleagues. While this may be similar for non-Indigenous colleagues, there is a feeling of being chastised and not being allowed to be authentic or act with integrity in some of these instances. Onondaga scholar Keith James (2004) labels this as finding ourselves "in the 'out' group in the dynamics of departments and academic institutions, as well as at the bottom of the academic hierarchy" (p. 50). As we move through the system and learn how to hold our ground, we are repeatedly reminded that the institution is founded upon a culture that is not ours, surrounded by a system that rewards individualism and independent work. However, as Indigenous scholars we are measured outside of the academy by our dedication and practice of collaboration.

Our very presence is political. We embody both the tensions and possibilities that exist in Indigenous-settler relations. Institutions of higher education are often thought to be above racism, above social inequities, but the reality is universities are made up of humans who all bring their cultures, life experiences, family histories, and biases. Universities are simply reflections of greater society. For Indigenous scholars, being in adversarial spaces and pushed into survival mode moves us away from our natural cultural way of being in the world: that of being generous with our time and resources, bringing a natural spirit of giving, and a collective and supportive spirit to our work with allied others. We are reminded of our natural way of being when given the incredible opportunity to work in our communities—it reminds us of how incredibly disruptive the university environment is to the development and nourishment of Indigenous spirit. In "community" (a colloquial phrase commonly used amongst Indigenous people to describe time we spend in an Indigenous community), we can relax and be ourselves. We are valued and appreciated for the knowledge and collaborative spirit that we bring. That is not to say there are never difficulties working in community, or that lateral violence does not exist there—it does—but we also have processes and ways of being that can work through these difficulties in natural ways that bring healing and new levels of connection and understanding.

Beyond this continuous experience of cultural incongruence, we are also constantly reminded of being outnumbered. Very few institutions have a proportional (or higher) number of Indigenous scholars, and so it makes it difficult to work with or be measured by others more like us. Turner (2008) concurs: "At this time in our development as an intellectual culture (as part of mainstream intellectual culture), our numbers are small ... which means that we must make our intellectual labor count" (p. 10). This reality amplifies our responsibility to make our work meaningful and create change for our communities. While the three of us have experience working with and for communities, the experience necessary to develop skills, knowledge, and academic acumen has been limited by the lack of an Indigenous mentor from whom we could have learned. Some of us were assigned a mentor at the beginning of our tenure-track appointment, but these mentors were non-Indigenous, and often times our differing worldviews prevented us from engaging with them in meaningful ways to support our academic growth. This was a big challenge to surmount, and it illustrates the under-representation of Indigenous scholars in the academy.

Despite being under-represented, we acknowledge we have a role to play in decolonizing education and teaching practice, and in turn, to contribute to institutional and systemic change. Alfred (2004) asserts:

> Like all Indigenous people, if we are accountable to our nations and truly cognizant and respectful of cultures, we have as a responsibility to do what we can where we are to ensure the survival of our culture and our nations. Being in the university, we as Indigenous academics have the responsibility to work to defeat the operation of colonialism within the university and to reorder academe. (p. 89)

One way in which this can be achieved is by creating spaces for dialogue, or what Willie Ermine (2007) describes as "ethical spaces," the space where "two societies, with disparate worldviews, are poised to engage each other" (p. 193). Dialogue and relationship building guide this process, which acknowledges the complexities needed to establish equity and leadership in respectful ways as well as the place of emotion, uncertainty, and possibility leading to change and transformation.

This change also needs to be done in collaboration with communities, for it is the communities who inform and guide the work we do; therefore, we have the professional and ethical responsibility to be accountable to them. This represents another clash of worldviews; as articulated by Kovach (2009), "[R]ules are established and decisions are made as to what counts as knowledge and how that knowledge is generated" (p. 55). There is tension between what matters for the success of programs and what matters for tenure; there is also tension generated when thinking about what matters to the individual versus what matters to the collective.

In this regard, we are also aware that we need to embrace our allies, those who contribute to our Indigenous programs, to the betterment of our communities, to our professional development, and to imagining a future where we all promote and participate in social change. This requires that we foster and nurture those relationships. However, establishing and nurturing these relationships requires more investment in service that takes additional time and energy.

Closing Words

In contrast to Alfred's (2004) words about a responsibility to "reorder academe," James (2004) warns Indigenous scholars to be "realistic about their perceptions of academia" (p. 62) as they often hold an idealized view of what academic institutions stand for and how they function. Further, Cherokee Daniel Heath Justice (2004) questions the whole enterprise of "Indigenizing the academy" pondering, "Should we even do so?" (p. 101). He then softens his approach admitting that "[t]he academy can also be a site of significant cultural recovery work, a place where all people who are disconnected from their histories can begin their journeys homeward" (p. 101). We can certainly attest to the latter, as we have all witnessed and experienced this healing, cultural connection, and "returning home" that can occur for Indigenous scholars and students alike in higher-education settings. A post-secondary education can be a healing journey, a time and place to make sense of the intergenerational trauma experienced by our people worldwide, and providing empowerment through education to transform the future. Alfred (2004) affirms, "Indigenous academics can serve an important role: as teachers of an empowering and truthful sense of the past and who we are, and as visionaries of a dignified alternative to the indignity of cultural assimilation and political surrender" (p. 95). As Indigenous scholars we continue to walk in two worlds, and interpret such worlds with "two-eyed seeing" (Bartlett, Marshall, & Marshall, 2010), where the strengths of the Indigenous and the non-Indigenous contexts contribute to reciprocal relationships, responsibilities to our communities, and mutual accountability. It is only in this way that we will create a shared future where we can walk this academic path not with ambivalence, but with strength, beauty, and gifts to offer.

References

Alfred, T. (2004). Warrior scholarship: Seeing the university as a ground of contention. In D. Mihesuah, & A. W. Wilson (Eds.), *Indigenizing the academy: Transforming scholarship and empowering communities*, pp. 88–99. Lincoln, NE: University of Nebraska Press.

Antone, E., & Dawson, T. (2014). "But how do I put this dream catcher into my teaching dossier?" Learnings and teachings from one faculty member's tenure experience of documenting community-based teaching and learning. In C. Etmanski, B. L. Hall, & T. Dawson (Eds.), *Learning and teaching community-based research: Linking pedagogy to practice*, pp. 287–387. Toronto, ON: University of Toronto Press.

Bartlett, C., Marshall, M., & Marshall, A. (2010). "Integrative science: Enabling concepts within a journey guided by trees holding hands and two-eyed seeing." In Two-eyed seeing knowledge sharing series, manuscript No. 1. Institute for Integrative Science and Health, Cape Breton University, Sydney, NS. Unpublished manuscript. Available from http://www.integrativescience.ca/uploads/articles/2007-Bartlett-Marshall-Integrative- Science-Two-Eyed-Seeing-Aboriginal-co-learning-trees-holding-hands.pdf.

Ermine, W. (2007). The ethical space of engagement. *Indigenous Law Journal*, 6(1), 193–203.

Henestrosa, A. (1997). *Los Hombres que Dispersó la Danza*. México, D. F.: Editorial Porrúa.

Henze, R. C., & Vanett, L. (1993). To walk in two worlds: Or more? Challenging a common metaphor of native education. *Anthropology and Education Quarterly*, 24(2), 116–134.

James, K. (2004). Corrupt state university: The organizational psychology of native experience in higher education. In D. Mihesuah, & A. W. Wilson (Eds.), *Indigenizing the academy: Transforming scholarship and empowering communities*, pp. 48–68. Lincoln, NE: University of Nebraska Press.

Justice, D. H. (2004). Seeing (and reading) red: Indian outlaws in the ivory tower. In D. Mihesuah, & A. W. Wilson (Eds.), *Indigenizing the academy: Transforming scholarship and empowering communities*, pp. 100–123. Lincoln, NE: University of Nebraska Press.

Kovach, M. (2009). Being Indigenous in the academy: Creating space for Indigenous scholars. In A. M. Timpson (Ed.), *First Nations, first thoughts: The impacts of Indigenous thought in Canada*, pp. 51–73. Vancouver, B.C.: UBC Press.

Kuokkanen, R. (2007). *Reshaping the university: Responsibility, Indigenous epistemes, and the logic of the gift*. Vancouver, B.C.: UBC Press.

Mihesuah, D., & Wilson, A. W. (2004). *Indigenizing the academy: Transforming scholarship and empowering communities* Lincoln, NE: University of Nebraska Press.

Pidgeon, M., Archibald, J., & Hawkey, C. (2014). Relationships matter: Supporting Aboriginal graduate students in British Columbia, Canada. *The Canadian Journal of Higher Education, 44*(1), 1–21.

Turner, D. (2008). *This is not a peace pipe: Towards a critical Indigenous philosophy.* Toronto, ON: University of Toronto Press.

Wilson, S. (2008). *Research is ceremony: Indigenous research methods.* Black Point, NS: Fernwood Publishing.

CHAPTER 8

A Dynamic Duet: Fluid Mentorship and Holistic Co-Teaching

Manu Sharma and Cam Cobb
Faculty of Education, University of Windsor

First Lessons

Cam, September 20, 2010

It was Monday, September 20, 2010. Up to the previous week I had been teaching with the Toronto District School Board (TDSB). Three months after graduating with my PhD, I was hired as a tenure-track professor at the University of Windsor. It was a whole new career.

The path from my nearly empty office to my first class in the auditorium was a short one. To get to the auditorium, I had to make my way down two flights of stairs and cross a wide lobby. The lobby would be bustling by late morning, but at 7:30 a.m. on Monday it was eerily silent. Class was beginning in less than an hour. Standing by my desk, I grasped a memory stick. It contained a PowerPoint presentation that was to guide my first lesson at the university.

In countdown mode, I mentally went over reasons why I shouldn't be nervous. For one, I had international experience teaching adults and children in South Korea. I had taught six different grades in eleven years with the TDSB. Besides, this was a course on differentiated instruction, and I had spent three years teaching special education, and in that time I developed over 50 individual education plans (IEP) and participated in over 75 identification, placement, and review committees (IPRC). Yet this was different. In 45 minutes I was to teach a large post-secondary class of nearly 200 students.

Feeling somewhat apprehensive, I briskly made my way downstairs, and strolled into the auditorium. I marched to the technology station located near the stage at the front of the room. Having tested this technology station earlier, I was familiar with the process of setting up the computer and data projector. Something was wrong. The projector wasn't working, and I didn't know how to fix it. Glancing at my watch in desperation I noticed that I had 40 minutes to my first lesson ...

Manu, September 13, 2013

Deep in my heart and soul I have always been an educator. I worked as an educator for ten years with the City of Toronto, serving the needs of inner-city communities. From the various people I met there, I learned about their daily challenges and what they valued. As we established bonds of trust, they shared their stories, and this helped me understand the perspectives of inner-city children. These were important insights at the beginning of my teaching career. At the same time, I taught with the TDSB for six years in five different inner-city schools, where I was able to connect with the students, as I had relations with their community outside of the school itself. My leadership positions in the local community center grounded my teaching experiences and gave rise to a passion to create change. In particular, I was committed to making transformative spaces of change in public education, because I felt and observed a lot of the underserved communities were being overlooked. Sometimes students were pushed into the cracks of the system. I was honoured to be at these schools and emotionally moved by the students, often because of all of their hard work to break the constant stereotypes that were ascribed and prescribed to their communities, often by people who never worked with their community before.

This was a sharp contrast to having worked for the student center at the University of Toronto as a program intern promoting health, wellness, and extracurricular programming; here I saw how access to good programming and healthy eating was easy for post-secondary students. In addition, as I completed my undergraduate degree I had opportunities to travel and teach in Japan, Antigua and Barbuda, and Germany; many of these experiences also contrasted starkly with my experiences working with marginalized communities in Canada.

I was thrilled to graduate with the warmth of sunshine in June 2013. I had already started applying for post-secondary positions because, with the aforementioned educator experiences, I knew it was what I wanted to do! I was lucky to be invited to teach in a limited term position as the Experiential Learning Specialist at the University of Windsor. In the interview, I asked to teach an extra course or two. My reason for asking to teach a few more courses and to take on more initiatives in the Faculty of Education was a way to create a stronger portfolio and become a tenure-track streamed professor in the near future. I have had a love to teach post-secondary students ever since I first taught at the University of Toronto as a graduate student. I loved to engage and go deep in critical discussion with educators. Thus, the university offered me the opportunity to teach one full-year optional course that was within my job description, and then any other courses I wanted to teach were viewed as overload. I jumped at the opportunity to teach three half-year courses that came up on the overload-course teaching list throughout the year. As a result, I taught four courses within my first full-time post-secondary employment opportunity.

Reflecting back upon my first day of teaching my course on Language and Cultural Engagement, I remember having organized a welcoming and insightful lesson! By 7:30 a.m. on September 13, 2013, I had breakfast treats laid out on the front table, I put on some relaxing Spanish guitar music, and had "get to know you" sheets out on my horse-shoe table layout. I was excited but nervous about my optional course, as I was unsure if students would come and, moreover, if they would stay. I felt the stakes were high as they trickled in, looking a bit tired and unsure about this optional course. There were only nine students and I was ready for 40! I was ready to do a diagnostic check-in about the critical issues and teaching concerns they had, as they were beginning their teacher journey, and it was my personal mission to address their concerns and issues throughout our course together. My first assigned reading was about open-mindedness, and the students shared that most of them had not read it. With so much preparation and many things to do, I had to alter the tentative plans for the first class ...

The Path to Co-Teaching

The preceding vignettes recount the stories of how two beginning professors experienced their respective initial lessons at the University of Windsor. Both Cam and Manu had taught children and adults in Canada and abroad. They both had worked with the TDSB and recently obtained their PhDs. While the two were excited to teach in a post-secondary setting, both were also excitedly nervous. Anticipating the sort of rich dialogue that can be fostered in adult classrooms, they felt enthusiastic. Reflecting on the idea of teaching large classes of 40–200 students, they felt apprehensive. Such conflicting feelings are not atypical for new professors.

Starting a new career in academia is at once exciting and daunting—even if one is starting out with years of varied educational experiences. In fact, beginning *and* experienced professors struggle with such tasks as organizing courses and assignments, assessing student work and providing feedback, and managing large classes (Gedalof, 2004; Piccinin, 2003).

The days and weeks following Manu and Cam's initial lessons quickly passed. In their first few months at the faculty, both professors had the pleasure of working with energetic teacher candidates, thoughtful graduate students, and supportive colleagues. Cam took courses at the university's Centre of Teaching and Learning, focusing on such topics as learner-centered teaching, constructive alignment, and authentic assessment. Manu connected with previous and current colleagues to assist her through teaching and learning challenges. Both professors had support networks, but nevertheless there were challenges becoming a post-secondary educator, a current and creative researcher, and a helpful team contributor to the faculty and the university.

While each professor approached these challenges individually, they were both intrigued by the possibility of collaborating through co-teaching a course. In recent years, a number of researchers have articulated a rich view of co-teaching, where educators collaboratively (1) set expectations and plan activities and assignments, (2) facilitate activities, and (3) reflect on teaching and assessing student work (Conderman, 2011; Embury & Kroeger, 2012; Enfield & Stasz, 2011). Drawing from these thinkers, Cam and Manu envisioned co-teaching in a holistic sense—an ongoing collaboration that involves co-planning, co-delivery, and co-assessment and reflection on the whole process. Thus, when they decided to co-teach, they saw it as an opportunity for support, growth, and adventure. They were successful in attaining permission to co-teach a graduate-level course, scheduled from January to April 2014.

Narratives and Reflections

This chapter has been designed to share narratives from the lone beginning-educator experience in juxtaposition to the story of two collaborating educators' experiences while further into the beginning years of their professorships. It demonstrates the story of two beginning professors unfolding with a focus on how they used a co-teaching model as a way of experimenting with and strengthening practice. Initially, Cam presents a vignette and subsequently reflects on the experience of co-developing and co-teaching a Master of Education course in the winter semester of 2014 with Manu. Cam discusses how he and Manu mutually benefitted in terms of pedagogy and indicates how the experience led both to embark on collaborative research during the spring and summer. Subsequently, Manu shares a narrative and reflection based on her experience in collaborating with Cam on a Bachelor of Education course in the fall of 2014. She discusses how holistic co-teaching led her and Cam to continue to grow as educators, and to collaborate on further research as well as ongoing service work. Crafting these narratives was a multi-step process. Initially, Cam and Manu each drew from their own memories of shared lived experiences to draft their stories. They subsequently dialogued with one another to revise their narratives for accuracy, wording, and tone. This process led both professors to ensure their vignettes captured the spirit and collaborative nature of the experiences at hand. In the concluding segment of this chapter, the two retrospectively consider the benefits and challenges associated with co-teaching as a way of supporting the work and growth of being early career professors. Because their co-teaching adventure was full of supportive and challenging experiences, and because it led to exciting research and meaningful university service, it played out like a dynamic duet!

A Casual Conversation (Cam, February 10, 2014)

Manu stood at the computer station at the front of the small classroom. She was in the process of logging off the computer and shutting down the data projector. As she did this, I organized my notes, which covered one of the tables in the classroom. After putting everything into my backpack, I stepped over to clear the chalkboard.

"How do you think it went?" Manu asked.

"I think it went well," I replied.

"Do you think they're comfortable with the curriculum theory graphic-organizer project?"

"They're more comfortable than before today's lesson. I think the mind-map analysis activity really helped everyone understand the parameters of the project."

"What would you change in the activity?"

"I don't know that I would change anything. I think it went well. You reviewed the assignment parameters through dialogue. You guided the class through developing a small-group activity. Each group devised a mind-map (visual organizer) representing Chapter 2 of Freire's Pedagogy of the Oppressed. *I noticed that while we were circulating around the room and conferencing with the groups everyone seemed to be excited."*

"Do you think it was too rushed? It went by really quickly," Manu reflected.

"I don't think that's a bad thing necessarily," I responded.

"Right. But this activity could've easily been extended into next week's lesson—"

"—I agree. But the activity achieved what we set out to achieve."

"That's true. I think everyone's clearer on the graphic organizer project. They've all made exemplars and they've formed their groups for the project."

"And it isn't due for another two months."

Manu paused for a moment. *"Let's give them some class time to conference with us and with their group mates during the next few lessons,"* she suggested.

"I think that's a good idea."

Context of the Vignettes

The above vignette depicts a casual conversation Manu and Cam had while tidying up the classroom after a lesson. While the conversation was casual, it was reflective in nature, as the two co-teachers discussed how a co-developed and co-facilitated activity turned out. They had been teaching the curriculum-theory course for just over a month. *Fundamentals of Curriculum Theory and Development* is a semester-long graduate course. It is foundational—and indeed required—for all students in the curriculum concentration of the Master of Education program, whether they are in the thesis stream, the major research-paper stream, or the course-based stream. The classes are held once a week, and are each three hours long.

An Appreciation of Educators' Lived Experiences

In submitting an application to co-teach the curriculum course in the fall of 2013, Cam and Manu saw multiple benefits to collaborating. For Manu, it presented an opportunity to teach her first graduate course, working with another beginning professor (one who had taught the course before). She would be able to observe Cam's teaching, collaborate on devising a new syllabus, and work together to refine learning outcomes, course assignments, and activities. For Cam, collaborating presented an opportunity to closely observe how another beginning professor would approach the interlocking nature of curriculum theory and social-justice learning in leading discussions and guiding students through meaningful assignments. He would also benefit from co-teaching with an energetic educator who brought a different approach to fostering student engagement.

After their application was approved, the two mapped out a set of learning outcomes with four student-centered assessments, including an online and in-class series of reflections, a critique presentation, a final paper, and (as mentioned above) a visual organizer. After mapping out the course assignments, the two selected a set of readings that would lead students to examine the evolutionary nature of curriculum and discourse (including such thinkers as John Dewey, Henry Giroux, and Nel Noddings). The set of readings was carefully sequenced, and on occasion lessons were designed with two readings presented as provocative pairings (e.g. Ralph W. Tyler was paired with Christine Sleeter and Jamy Stillman). The two professors scaffolded activities that would not only lead the class to explore the readings (both inside and outside of class), but also prepare, step-by-step, for the four course assessments.

Building Trust

After their first lesson, the two had their first post-lesson reflective conversation, chatting about how their strategies and activities worked out in terms of fostering dialogue and engagement with and among the students. They also talked about how they might adjust things for the following week's lesson. While their first conversation was honest, Manu and Cam were, to a degree, guarded. After all, they had just met one another a few months earlier. The two beginning professors knew one another as colleagues, but they were still getting to know one another as co-educators.

Yet as the course unfolded, Cam and Manu continued to dialogue before and after lessons to consider how things went, plan new activities, and assess students' work. As beginning professors, they wrestled with a variety of questions, including

What is a suitable amount of readings to discuss each week?
How much time should be devoted to whole-class work and how much should be devoted to small-group work?
How should the delivery of verbal instructions be paced?
What can be done to ensure verbal instructions are clear?
How directly should students be called upon in class discussions?
How far should students be pushed to deepen their verbal contributions to dialogue and discussions?
How much time, energy, and guidance should be spent preparing students for course assignments?

There are no easy answers to these questions. Yet continuously providing, and receiving, rich feedback led both professors to refine their practice during the wintertime. Ultimately, as they became more comfortable with one another, the feedback was less guarded, and as a result Manu and Cam approached their co-teaching, as well as the course itself, as a continuing work in progress.

Path to Research

As previously mentioned, Manu and Cam utilized a variety of co-teaching strategies in the classroom. Some of these strategies included mentor modeling; one teach, one assist; station teaching; and synchronous teaching (see Cook & Friend, 1995; Friend & Bursuck, 2011; Friend & Cook, 2000; Friend, Reising, & Cook, 1993). While they applied these collaborative practices to foster analytic thinking and scholarship in/among students, they also endeavored to foster rich experiences rooted in social-justice learning. For the two beginning professors, it was important to convey a critical view of curriculum as both an evolving idea and as a product of power relations in an ever-changing political landscape (Burbules & Burk, 1999).

As time passed and both professors reflected on their collaborative practice, they gathered and examined a variety of articles written about co-teaching. It was an ongoing learning experience, and as the course neared its end date, Cam and Manu decided to collaborate on a systematic literature review (Boote & Beile, 2005; Randolph, 2009). Specifically, they aimed to carefully gather, code, and analyze a pool of research articles to determine what current research had to say about co-teaching focused on social justice. After selecting keywords and search engines, an initial search yielded over 130 peer-reviewed articles. An abstract-by-abstract survey led the two researchers to narrow their article pool to 19 research studies, which focused on the intersection between social justice and co-teaching. Initiating the literature-review process during the intersession/summertime not only presented Cam and Manu with a research opportunity but it also saw them connect their practice with their ongoing curiosity—and for both, social-justice-focused co-teaching represented an exciting new area of research and publication to pursue. As beginning professors, Manu and Cam were also well aware of the importance of conducting meaningful research and publishing research findings.

A Responsive Conversation (Manu, September 23, 2014)

Context of Course Development

In the summer semester there was an opportunity advertised to teach a Contemporary Social Issues course to teacher candidates in the fall semester. Immediately, Cam and Manu jumped at this opportunity and applied to co-teach it, despite it being advertised for one instructor. The two were made aware that they would be splitting the salary of one instructor taking on an overload course. Cam and Manu both already had full teaching loads according to their job descriptions, but they desired to teach this course together because (1) they wanted to try a non-traditional pedagogical approach to teaching at the university level, and (2) the course focused on social-justice issues and it would be best presented in a way that modeled multiple perspectives, lived experiences, and shared power in the classroom. Thus, when the application was approved, over the course of the summer Manu and Cam met to plan and envision their syllabus and goals for the Contemporary Issues in Education course. This course was mandatory for all Bachelor of Education teachers. Manu and Cam were given the opportunity to teach it for 50 minutes a week to 40 junior and intermediate teacher candidates. Like Manu, Cam had taught this course before, and as a result they drew upon their previously independently taught courses on social-justice issues in education to create and design a new and more enhanced syllabus for their co-taught course in Windsor.

Cam explained his past experiences of teaching the course with Manu, and she brought her past teaching experiences and enthusiasm to developing a model of co-teaching to the course, with a vision of social justice. She was excited to see how this would have an interactive effect on the students in the class and break the traditional course-delivery model, as it required a sharing of power. The dialogue about revision, redesign, and new ways to engage students in class was more open, and not as reserved as during the first course, due to the past experience of co-teaching and getting to know each other as colleagues.

Contemporary Social Issues in Education Narrative

One particular story that comes to mind was, on Tuesday, September 23, 2014. During the third lesson of the school year Manu and Cam were to help teacher candidates begin brainstorming and planning for their end of term assignment—a unit plan. It was decided that Cam, who had done this unit-plan activity before and had exemplars, would lead the class and Manu would assist by adding critical questions and responding to students' questions. Cam defined one part of social-justice pedagogy as responsive. He shared that the unit plan required students/groups to outline a school-classroom context as well as a social issue within that context. Cam explained that the way the group addresses the issue in their unit plan would indicate how they are able to identify issues and then address them in their teaching practice. While Manu was attentively listening to Cam's instructions and explanations to the class, she found herself wanting to interject and suggest looking at critical social issues in education with a proactive lens and not only through a responsive lens. However, out of respect and professionalism Manu reserved her thoughts on this matter until after the class.

Manu recalled an office conversation after class where she shared what she thought was missed out in the class lesson that day. Cam was very receptive and thanked her for bringing it up, and then they dialogued about how they could re-approach the unit-planning assignment by adding a proactive lens. After talking about this concern, they both agreed it was important, and decided to speak with the class about proactive pedagogy in the following lesson, on September 30.

Multiple Perspectives: Encouraging Divergent Thinking

One of the insights Manu and Cam gained from this narrative is that co-teaching allowed both to recognize the value and importance of multiple perspectives. Both professors realized that their own lived experience shaped their individual way of thinking. Manu had a social-justice perspective, and that is something she had consciously been trying to bring into all her educational and teaching spaces. The fact that Cam provided a space that was inviting and attentive to hearing Manu's perspective allowed for growth and expansion in how they co-taught. Manu was glad that she was able to chime in to extend an invitation to see another perspective, as Cam had provided her with so much guidance throughout the past terms.

As collaborators who were comfortable being constructive and open with one another (e.g. about things that worked well, as well as things that did not), Cam and Manu were better positioned to pinpoint areas to improve upon in their practice (Cobb & Sharma, 2015). In the case of the above narrative, Manu helped Cam to identify how there was an alternative perspective missing, and then they devised a plan to address this possible perspective. This open and critical reflection is a key benefit of the co-teaching dynamic (in this case, in the frameworks: one teach, one assist and one teach, one observe) (Conderman as cited in Cobb & Sharma, 2015). It is important to note that when reflecting with a critical lens, both professors were exercising a principle of social justice—recognizing the nuances and silences in dialogue (Cobb & Sharma, 2015).

This analysis also provides a critical insight as it demonstrates how sometimes, despite Manu and Cam's best intentions and considerations, they may not have included more perspectives on any given topic. This was important for Cam and Manu's teacher candidates to recognize, as often they are seen to be the authorities and experts in the classroom. To show diversity in perspectives is to demonstrate how there can be more than one way to understand any given topic, and this encourages elementary- and high-school students to be open to seeking out multiple perspectives instead of a sole answer.

Fluidity in Class and Instructor Learning: Modeling Flexibility

It was refreshing to come back to the class on September 30, 2014, with openness about rethinking the nature of social justice and equity in the unit-plan assignment. Manu and Cam were open to sharing with the class how social justice and equity work can be understood and used to promote understanding in a proactive way. Both professors were able to be flexible to change the content of the lesson because they agreed about the importance of the sharing their reflective dialogue from the last class with the students.

On Tuesday, September 30, Manu and Cam co-led a discussion that very briefly reviewed the unit-plan assignment, and gave the class an opportunity to explore the importance of both proactive and responsive social justice. They co-facilitated a conversation with the class that drew attention to the difference between proactive and responsive social-justice pedagogy. This distinction then helped create a consciousness about thinking in both proactive and responsive ways to social-justice issues.

The students acknowledged that while this course assignment focused on the responsive approach to social-justice issues, both were essential to social-justice-informed pedagogy itself. Because the students were able to draw this conclusion through discussion, Cam and Manu were both satisfied about how they implemented their critical reflection based on their discussions on September 23, in this class (Cobb & Sharma, 2015).

Tenure-Track Responsibilities Shared: Co-Teaching, Co-Research, and Co-Publishing

As Manu and Cam taught more class lessons together, they became more comfortable in sharing pedagogical strategies and providing constructive feedback on the lesson and learning happening in class. The co-teaching allowed for multiple perspectives to be brought forth in developing class goals and expectations. Moreover, the ongoing dialogue of emergent narratives from class gave rise to wonderful opportunities to co-research new concepts and ideas.

The co-researching was enriching as it allowed them to use scholarly articles to gain more insight on concepts such as social justice and co-teaching. They were able to conduct literature reviews on topics which arose from classes and then use this information as a background framework for integrating their vignettes. The beginning professors were excited to see the theory enhance and deepen their reflections on their co-teaching practice. The research opportunities were timely, and their collaborative teaching and co-research led to co-publishing.

The co-publishing has been an exercise to revise and make concrete Cam and Manu's learning to various audiences and areas of scholarship in education. They have worked on three pieces of scholarship thus far: one was a conceptual literature review on co-teaching models; another is based on narrative-inquiry cases from their teaching; and finally this wonderful chapter. Each of these co-publishing projects have been insightful on what the process of publishing is like for two authors submitting together, how to interpret feedback, and how to develop smooth transitions in writing styles that allow for both authors' voices to be heard and understood. It has become a work of art that is emergent and yet revised constantly to make space for new ideas and interpretations.

As a result of the co-teaching, co-researching, and co-publishing together, Manu's potential opportunity for tenure-track positions has increased, and Cam's tenure process has launched more smoothly with a positive, collegial support system. It has been amazing to see how collegiality and working through some shared tenure responsibilities and expectations make the process more accessible and inviting. The authors encourage this unique model of co-teaching, co-researching, and co-publishing to other scholars on their tenure-track path. They would welcome and embrace new challenges in co-teaching opportunities whether it is in teaching courses, research initiatives, and/or publishing. Manu and Cam deeply believe the more work done in co-partnerships the more responsive educators are to one another and the students they serve.

Conclusion

This chapter tells the story of two beginning professors' fluid mentorship and holistic co-teaching. For Manu and Cam, the fluid mentorship lay in this duet co-teaching performance in which both were able to support and help facilitate each other's growth and learning at different times. The holistic co-teaching—co-planning, co-delivering, and co-assessing while having ongoing reflections on the teaching experiences—served as the cornerstone of this dynamic duet. Cam and Manu learned to deepen their appreciation of different lived experiences as educators and built trust by lowering power dynamics. They also encouraged understanding by maintaining an open disposition to multiple perspectives in the classroom, and by embracing the fluidity necessary when engaging in holistic co-teaching to meet the diverse needs of students.

In addition, because of their experiences in co-teaching they were able to develop a strong trust and network system that extended into their research agendas and university service. Having support in their early phases of becoming professors was an irreplaceable adventure that has strengthened and supported their journey. Holistic co-teaching represents an engaging way to help beginning professors to foster fluid mentorship as they navigate the unfamiliar waters of their new role. The richness and critical insights Cam and Manu had while co-teaching helped to shape their learning trajectory and influence one another's academic journey—a promising and fruitful experience!

Manu and Cam hope that other early career professors also take up this model of fluid mentorship and holistic co-teaching, as the benefits are beyond foreseeable. On a larger scale, when universities support such mentorship and holistic co-teaching, they emulate the value of collaboration, and learning spurts. When students see and engage with educators who value collaboration and have space to always learn and grow from one another, they are influenced to take a chance and co-teach. Parallel to an early faculty member's learning trajectory is a teacher candidate's trajectory. In the field of teacher education, co-teaching during practicum placements can also help teacher candidates overcome some of their early fears or anxieties about teaching. Moreover, if their holistic co-teaching experiences are full of growth in a supportive environment, perhaps when they become classroom teachers, they will continue to strive building fluid mentorship for incoming teacher candidates. Thus, the cycle of fluid mentorship and holistic co-teaching would be influential in providing a support network and transition to all beginning educators.

References

Boote, D. N., & Beile, P. (2005). Scholars before researchers: On the centrality of the dissertation literature review in research preparation. *Educational Researcher, 34*(6), 3–15.

Burbules, N. C., & Berk, R. (1999). Critical thinking and critical pedagogy: Relations, differences, and limits. In T. S. Popkewitz & L. Fendler (Eds.), *Critical theories in education* (pp. 45–66). New York, NY: Routledge.

Cobb, C., & Sharma, M. (2015). I've got you covered: Adventures in social justice-informed co-teaching. *Journal of the Scholarship Teaching and Learning, 15*(4), 41–57.

Conderman, G. (2011). Middle school co-teaching: Effective practices and student reflections. *Middle School Journal, 42*(4), 24–31.

Cook, L., & Friend, M. (1995). Co-teaching: Guidelines for creating effective practices. *Focus on Exceptional Children, 28*(3), 1–16.

Embury, D. C., & Kroeger, S. D. (2012). Let's ask the kids: Consumer constructions of co-teaching. *International Journal of Special Education, 27*(2), 102–112.

Enfield, M., & Stasz, B. (2011). Presence without being present: Reflection and action in a community of practice. *Journal of the Scholarship of Teaching and Learning, 11*(1), 108–118.

Friend, M., & Bursuck, W. M. (2011). *Including students with special needs: A practical guide for classroom teachers* (6th ed.). Boston, MA: Pearson.

Friend, M., & Cook, L. (2000). *Interactions: Collaborative skills for school professionals.* Boston, MA: Allyn and Bacon.

Friend, M., Reising, M., & Cook. L. (1993). Co-teaching: An overview of the past, a glimpse at the present, and considerations for the future. *Preventing School Failure, 37*(4), 6–10.

Gedalof, A. J. (2004). *Teaching large classes.* Halifax, NS: Society for Teaching and Learning in Higher Education.

Piccinin, S. J. (2003). *Feedback: Key to learning.* Halifax, NS: Society for Teaching and Learning in Higher Education.

Randolph, J. J. (2009). A guide to writing the dissertation literature review. *Practical Assessment, Research and Evaluation, 14*(13), 1–13.

SECTION III

EDITORS' PREFACE

Mid-Tenure-Track

The mid-tenure-track section includes authors who are beyond their first year of tenure-track but have less than two years of experience. As such, they are becoming familiar with institutional norms but have not yet applied for tenure. Even though the application for tenure is one or more years away, it is a focus for these authors.

The authors, as we will also see in the early tenure-track section, talk about the transition into higher education. Practical issues, such as moving, are mentioned. There is some focus on children and spouses, and the impact the transition may have had for these important individuals. There is considerable reference to previously "worthy" scholarship, which has uncertain value in applying for tenure. These authors are identifying that their previous expertise, which got them the tenure-track position, is going to be valued differently, if at all, when applying for tenure. The focus of these issues is from within the position and, in this sense, reality seems to be settling in. They have moved beyond the initial stage of the tenure-track.

In this stage the authors are reflecting on the dizzying first few months and remembering coming to terms with organizational factors: navigating the campus and faculty building, teaching loads, forming relationships in professional organizations, and the like. They are "remembering when," but like reminiscing over most things, they are also beginning to acquire different sorts of knowledge, and their perspective is changing. The writing focuses on the institutional move as a whole and has less emphasis on discrete components. Tenure-track faculty members at this stage are more aware and are becoming engaged in university governance. They are building their understanding of the institution, how it functions and its politics, through their involvement with faculty council, senate, committee work, and other elements of university life. This is developing "social acceptance" with their colleagues (Ponjuan, Conley, & Trower, 2011).

They are also identifying issues related to funding of research, conducting of research, rejection or acceptance of submissions to journals, and research partnerships. Research is clearly present, and in increasingly detailed descriptions. The authors use explicit frameworks to organize their writing. These authors cite their own research. However, the evidence in table 1 suggests this occurs with half of the chapters in every section, and it is not actually unique to this stage. That said, there seemed to be greater care with strategic elements in their writing, perhaps indicative of the notions of value and credit that will arise in the inevitable application for tenure. It is in the mid-tenure-track section that we, the editors of this book, are cited—suggesting an elevated recognition of the academic requirements of style, or perhaps the politics of being accepted for a publication. The authors in this section tend to cite more references on average than any other section. It may be that this is a result of having had time to engage in reading the literature prior to the workload additions that engagement in governance and the larger academic community entails. The reader is left to judge whether references and self-citations, summarized in table 1, are being used in the same manner as in other sections.

Table 1. Incidence of Citation Use and Self-Citation by Tenure-Track Stage.

Category	Number of citations (authors)			
	Early (4)	Mid (4)	Late (5)	Group (3)
Average number of overall citations	13	22	12	17
Citation count by order of authors in sections of book	5, 9, 24, 13	8, 15, 26, 37	11, 12, 19, 20, 0	20, 13, 13
Citing own publications by order of authors in sections of book	0, 1, 0, 4	1, 0, 6, 0	0, 1, 2, 0, 0	0, 0, 1

In terms of the editors communicating with these authors during the process of developing the book, one word comes to mind: catharsis. The process gave an opportunity for reflection on the lived experience that they have been immersed in. It is therapeutic (Ellis, Adams, & Bochner, 2011), perhaps related to the writing process or simply a widely lived experience that applies to all tenure-track faculty members. It is clear that mid-tenure-track authors have had time to see more of academia, consider their growing concerns about the meaning of tenure, and time to adapt, while recognizing the absence of a clear path for adaptation. At the same time, they have had some successes and are finding they are making progress, even if it has been done with less clarity than they may have wished for.

The authors are beginning to strike the balance—one of conformity to, but voiced within the demands of the academy. Meeting deadlines and responses to questions were addressed in a timely manner that assisted with editorial needs. They seemed to be working in an orderly manner. In short, the mid-tenure-track individuals seem to be looking briefly in the rear-view mirror and remembering their beginnings; but they are also focused on what comes next. They are identifying the steps they will have to take to achieve tenure, and taking them in a conscious manner.

Tim Sibbald's chapter is the first to appear in this section, as he has the longest term of experience within the range that we called "mid." His use of technical roles, professional roles, and personal roles as a vehicle for sense-making illuminates many issues of the mid-tenure-track assistant professor. Tim provides a very helpful to-do list that many will use as a great starting point when organizing their own beginnings.

Margarida Romero emigrated from Spain to begin a tenure-track position at Laval. Her chapter highlights a challenging start to academia in Europe. She describes some of the struggles moving to Canada, including unexpected financial issues. She also began a family, and offers some thoughts about this.

Lloyd Kornelsen has an unusual tenure-track position, as he was offered tenure but has been required to apply for promotion within four years. What is unusual is that the school he taught at and the faculty are affiliated by the same overall governance structure—he may have tenure, but there is an ambiguity of whether it is with the faculty, the school, or the overall organization. His chapter describes a sense of "outsiderness," an experience many other authors articulate. Lloyd's storytelling methodology makes this chapter highly readable and may inspire some solid reflection among readers.

Peter Milley is the author with the least amount of academic experience in the mid-tenure-track section of the book. He moved from a role in the Canadian civil service to his position in education leadership, offering some perspectives regarding this transition. Peter offers two figures to illustrate the issues of adaptation, resilience, and achievement.

References

Ellis, C., Adams, T. E., & Bochner, A. P. (2011). Autoethnography: An overview. *Forum: Qualitative Social Research, 12*(1), Art. 10.

Ponjuan, L., Conley, V. M., & Trower, C. (2011). Career stage differences in pre-tenure track faculty perceptions of professional and personal relationships with colleagues. *The Journal of Higher Education, 82*(3), 319–346.

CHAPTER 9

Practitioner to Academic: A Composition of Transitions

Timothy M. Sibbald
Schulich School of Education, Nipissing University

I was a professional high-school math teacher. Perfectly comfortable and established in my role, although not without occasionally bemoaning having lived in the same city for twenty years and, perhaps, being fed up with it. The search for an academic role also followed the growth of children and an imminent stage with an empty nest (Sibbald, 2017). Within that teaching role, the decision to move to academia was sought and ultimately led to a move of 600 km to work in a faculty of education. The role in the faculty was preparation of pre-service teacher candidates to teach mathematics in schools, combined with research and service—a role that has significant differences from high-school teaching (Tzur, 2001).

While the transition was complex with numerous interwoven details (both serious and humorous), a framework that is useful in comprehending the change entails using three separate components or "roles": technical roles, professional roles, and personal roles. This is similar to Bridges and Mitchel (2000), who consider organizational and personal roles, but there are differences when looking within the organizational aspect because the technical and professional roles that are used here are tailored to the particular context.

The technical roles are tasks necessary to fulfill the duties of the job but are lacking personal control in terms of defining the way that the tasks are done. For example, regardless of whether one is teaching in a school or a university there are meetings, but the format of the meetings and structural elements of the meetings are not something that I had influence over in either role. The professional roles are the duties that have an element of personal control. Choices are made in terms of how one enacts some elements of their role, and those choices reflect a professionalism that one brings to the role. An example is the planning of how a lesson is conducted within a school or university, and the professional role entails deciding, among other things, the instructional methodology. Finally, personal roles are confined to the recognized intersection of career and daily living elements (Heppner, Fuller, & Multon, 1998), where the latter can be independent of the workplace, but in the intersection are influenced by it. For example, flexible hours may provide a Wednesday with no classes, and that can lead to a choice about grocery shopping on Wednesday and performing academic work on Saturday to avoid crowded stores; the change in personal time is part of the personal role. Note that these three components are a framework for examining the transition and do not represent the full individual. In particular, the personal roles are being confined in a manner that ignores any elements of life that are independent of career.

A second consideration for structuring elements of the analysis is the representation of time. While events have a certain chronology, it is more important to consider the affiliation of events in terms of the impact they have on the process. Several frameworks exist that distinguish different periods in transitions that loosely correspond to time but can have significant overlaps. The approach that is used here was informed by existing frameworks but has an emergent characteristic that necessitates interpretation for comparison with existing frameworks. The approach will be described, followed by how it relates, and differs, from existing frameworks.

The time dimension is characterized in terms of stages, which were observed to run more slowly than anticipated (Bridges and Mitchell, 2000; Schlossberg, 2011). The stages are called *initiation*, *episodic*, *lingering*, and *resolution*. The first, initiation, is the earliest stage prior to actually joining the new organization. It includes, but is not limited to, the completion of the preceding role. It is interpreted as including any gap between the initial role and the new role. Therefore, a month transition period between the two roles is allocated to the initial stage. The episodic stage is characterized by short-term events that represent adjustment to the new environment and processes. It may include events that are a significant portion of the entire transition process, but typically is represented by shorter elements. The lingering stage is for longer-term processes and events that cannot be resolved in short time spans and are likely to take significant portions of the transition time to reach a resolution. To draw the distinction, consider how teaching courses allows refinement along the way and provides a progression of feedback that breaks it into episodic periods. However, progress in academic publishing requires research to be conducted, papers to be written, and finally acceptance and publication—a process that, from beginning to end, may take several years. Finally, the resolution stage is the completion of the transition. If it is a successful transition and tenure is achieved, then it will be a return to job security. That success is not guaranteed and it is possible that resolution will not see tenure. (It is notable that this uncertainty about the outcome was a requirement of the call for chapters in this book!)

Bridges and Mitchell (2000) use a similar model to the one used here. They call their time stages *saying goodbye, neutral zone,* and *moving forward*. They note that the neutral zone can last six months to two years and suggest that it has a characteristic of adapting to new ways of doing things. The model used here is similar but breaks the neutral zone into shorter- and longer-term components that characterize a professor's role. Another similar model is Nicholson (1984), who considers how personal development and role development interact as stages labelled *replication, absorption, determination,* and *exploration*. While this model has considerable value for the current study, with absorption and determination paralleling the episodic and lingering stages, an important consideration that needs to be stressed in the current work is that they occur simultaneously with the proportion slowly changing from the former to the latter. That is to say, those episodic elements dominate early in the transition, while lingering dominates the later transition. During the course of the transition both occur because new and routinized aspects of the new role coexist.

Young and Lockhart (1995) draw a distinction between change and transition and provide a confidence model for the latter. In this chapter the movement between school and university is the change, the transition is the consequential psychological effects. While the model appears to fit with my particular instance, it does not provide much distinction within each stage. By comparing three types of roles with four time stages, better acuity of details is feasible. Similar comments apply to Schlossberg (2011) who suggests an analysis of resources to assess the transition consequences of a change. Heppner, Fuller, and Multon (1998) examined personality factors using a factor analysis through involuntary transitions. While components are doubtlessly applicable, it does not inform about the specific voluntary role transition.

The rest of the chapter is broken into the four stages and within each stage the three roles are detailed. Each section demonstrates the interplay between the roles that led, in the early stages, to my referring to myself being "out of balance." The progression through the stages shows the evolution of the transition and how skills were modified or developed to fit the new circumstance. The choice of the two frameworks, roles and stages, provides a view of the transition as requiring a rebuilding, in spite of existing skills, to regain the capacity that one had prior to the transition.

Initial Stage

The initial stage was a welling of emotions from the impending departure from the current workplace and colleagues. There were various concerns, such as missing the youthful high-school students and their remarkable knack for challenging me with new ideas. I wondered about the new organization I would be joining. I did not believe I was in denial assessing my prior and new workplaces—the proverbial grass being equally green on both sides of the fence. However, I was excited about the prospect of a transition after a decade teaching in the same secondary school and an additional decade living in the town where that school was located.

Professionally, there was a hiatus. I continued to teach, but I was essentially coasting to the end of the role with energy focused on the transition rather than on innovations. Pragmatic issues, of a personal nature, such as where to live in the new town and buying a second vehicle, used considerable time. At the same time, initial thinking about how to tackle the research component took place. I wrote a to-do list, with ideas for articles, workshops, and directions for research—perhaps just to put my mind at ease that this new role requirement could be addressed. In hindsight this effort was unrealistic, but I am glad I constructed the lists as I continue to feel it will ultimately be useful.

An important event that is relevant to this chapter had occurred in the summer. As a director of a provincial organization, I had set about scanning 28 years of the association's journal. During this process I noticed that the high school I had attended had won an award for cooperative effort amongst the members of the department. This caused me to wonder about nominating the department I was in, because it was also highly cooperative. The private-sector workplace I had worked in, prior to being employed as a teacher, had also been cooperative and, even a decade later, I remain in touch with that employer. In my new role, I found the organization environment was not the same, and while I could not identify the new type of organizational environment, I was cognizant of it being different and needing to be addressed in my adjustment strategy (Nicholson, 1984).

The personal role was the primary concern in this stage. Much as my spouse had been agreeable to my efforts to pursue a university role, it had taken so long to find a position that it seemed unlikely to actually occur. In fact, I recall saying this was the last one I was applying for, having spent approximately three years monitoring postings. Having made the decision, which was a joint decision between my spouse and me, there was a lingering concern that the move was only for my benefit and, much as my spouse agreed, I wondered if she was as enthusiastic about the lifestyle change that was evident with the move.

Our youngest daughter had one semester of school left in the city, which was also of great personal concern. How would that be managed? What were the longer-term implications of potentially using home, in the new city, as a place to look for summer employment?

Episodic Stage

Episodic events in the technical role revolved primarily around adjusting to the new workplace. I had, in preparation for the original interview, read the collective agreement and also read the contractual letter of appointment for the tenure-track role. Since I had a background in the private sector, I followed the details of the contractual letter and arrived at the university on August 1. Subsequently, it became apparent that most of the new tenure-track faculty arrived much later, regardless of their contract. This was the first sign that I did not fully understand the organizational environment—specifically the flexibility that the role allows. Arriving a month before classes started did facilitate attention with many small tasks, such as learning how to change the voicemail message on the phone in my office and making sure I had appropriate keys and a parking pass. During the first weeks of September, there was an orientation for new faculty and I was able to supply a list of 24 tasks that I had done in preparation for the role. Others were aghast at the number of things they needed to do while preparing for the classes that began in days. This may have been the first time I reflected on the role of personal discipline in responding to the new-found flexibility—the thought reflected established academics I knew who certainly showed that discipline, but I do not feel I have mastered it.

The New-Faculty To-Do List:

1. Get identification card
2. Get parking pass
3. Get keys to office
4. Find out where your mailbox is
5. Set up telephone message
6. Get updated in the online environment
7. Fill out form for classroom keys
8. Pick up classroom keys
9. Find and get a planner
10. Get supplied office materials
11. Get complimentary copy of textbook
12. Check whether human-resources details are accurate
13. Apply for online teaching web space if desired
14. Use your ID card at library
15. Apply for professional website space (if you want it)
16. New-faculty orientation (if provided)
17. Complete tri-council policy statement online tutorial
18. Develop course outlines
19. Acquire any computer/software equipment

20. Learn how to use any unfamiliar items from 19.
21. Check that you can get projectors/SmartBoards in your classroom to work (some require special access or procedures)
22. Get website picture taken
23. Make a SSHRC CV
24. Begin developing ideas for any initial institutional funding (startup research grant)

The professional role was essentially stagnant. This shocked me, personally, and I stressed about not achieving as much as I wanted to on the professional front. I did in fact achieve quite a bit, but there was nothing significant to show for the effort that went into it. A lot of readiness tasks were completed, and I familiarized myself with tools for seeking funding. I also read two colleagues' applications for tenure. While these tasks are necessary and prepare one to engage academia, they do not achieve results in the short term. As a result, there was little in the short term. Discussions with new faculty and building relationships were as much an emotional juncture as a serious professional proposition. There was a recognition that one could collaborate, but also a lingering reality that the broad scope of such collaborative notions was essentially founded in a social need to build relationships, rather than realistic collaboration. There was an initial effort to find out which professionals did what in the new city. This was hindered by a multitude of factors, but primarily dominated by flexible schedules resulting in no professional colleagues at the university prior to September and, when they did arrive, being very busy addressing course needs.

Early attempts at conference presentations met with limited success. This appears to have been due to personal wrestling with the distinction between practitioner and academic. It was also influenced by constraining the professional money I had available to places where I could present rather than simply attend. In hindsight, the presentations I offered up had a teacher lens and did not properly reflect the academic lens required. These issues caused discordance since I did not, and perhaps still don't, understand why academia is separated from the practitioner's realm.

The personal role was challenging in an unclear manner. However, while attending an MEd defense (as a spectator), the student's use of Maslow's hierarchy of needs led to a self-reflection regarding how I had moved from a self-actualized high-school teacher into a new role, with issues of esteem and belonging. My spouse and daughter had remained in the old town, so the move saw me living alone, with periodic trips back to the old town. Living on my own revealed that, behaviours from 24 years earlier, prior to marriage, remained and I found myself reliving bachelor behaviours around cooking, cleaning, and the hours I kept. I have always maintained that my spouse keeps me on an even keel, and it was evident how true this continues to be.

One particular episode that was noteworthy was an unexpected case of appendicitis. Reflecting upon the experience in the hospital, I naturally considered the cause but rapidly discovered that it was an impossible task. Those bachelor behaviours had seen everything from beer and spicy snacks through to testing the edibility of lichens after watching a survival show. In short, there were so many possibly contributing agents that I realized I would be unable to determine if any particular thing had caused the appendicitis. I later made a research argument suggesting that diathesis stress (Dozois & Ouimet, 2010) should be considered as a possible outcome of transitions! Similarly, I have wondered if it might also have represented a low point on my journey as seen through the lens of Maslow's hierarchy of needs.

Lingering Stage

As much as all tasks started in an episodic manner, with familiarization being required, some of those tasks became routine. Faculty council meetings have a structure that is significantly different than high-school staff meetings. In the episodic stage, I had a "blind following" view, not sure what was going on or how the structural form of the meetings was designed with certain needs in mind. For example, an agenda is established and sent out a week in advance—it was unclear why it was so far in advance when that had never been necessary in any other workplace. The routines began to take form and, while I grew to follow what was going on and to recognize key faculty participants, that was the extent of my understanding.

However, in the lingering stage, new opportunities arose, and I started to meet people who could explain different facets of the university environment. Seeing the senate meetings helped in understanding what is going on at faculty council meetings. Discussion with division chairs clarified how different elements of the organization work. As time has gone by, I have an increasing range of experiences with the different elements of the organization and growing comfort in knowing who can steer me to the proper person for most issues that might arise.

The professional role saw me teaching a variety of courses with a large preparation requirement. I had taught a lot of the material before, but different elements of the schedule, equipment, and resources provided a need for revamping. In some cases, since the schedule was set before I was hired, there were courses I had not taught and they required substantial preparation. Through this period, I was managing the course components but feeling increasingly stressed that I was not addressing the needs of the research component of my role.

The email system highlighted the many activities and opportunities that seemed to be available. There is much to distract oneself within the university environment, and in the early days a certain degree of engagement did allow learning about the community. One of the first opportunities I did take on was a call for chapter proposals. This was not in my immediate area of study but nevertheless involved a topic that I could relevantly write about. The call required a framework, which led to a struggle developing a framework for a topic area I was not so familiar with. It served me well, though, because, while I struggled, it also pushed my thinking about the element of intention in research designs. That idea was later embedded into a professional-development workshop.

During a relative high point of the lingering stage, I decided to terminate a contractual option that could have allowed me to return to my former employer. I had maintained the option for six months, but could have maintained it for up to two years. This was an important non-event in the sense that it was a symbolic boundary (Bridges & Mitchell, 2000) but actually had no consequence in terms of performance. It did periodically make me wonder why I had given up job security, but also gave me pause to consider the principled approach I was taking.

Resolution Stage

The resolution of technical roles is by no means an understanding of all the structures or details of the organization. However, it is experience with all of the key components and some degree of awareness of the variety that might exist beyond. I have now participated in convocation and the installing of a new president for the university. So, while I have not seen a new chancellor installed, I have some understanding of what this means in terms of the process that is now underway. Similarly, I have gained some awareness of most components of the organization that have an impact on my ability to perform my role.

As I become more comfortable with the position, in terms of the technical role, I am able to use it to take on larger tasks. Organizing a one-day conference, for example, was a new experience, but I knew how to find out the details necessary. In fact, it surpassed expectations because it was video-linked, at the eleventh hour, to a site 150 km away. That this could be achieved was a demonstration of professional relationships with both a student who assisted and members of the teaching community of the region.

This leads to the professional role, where a provincial organization proved to be a mechanism for meeting colleagues in the region I had moved to. While there was potential for a power imbalance because I was on the provincial executive, by being active and being supportive, I was welcomed into the new region. At the same time, funding proposals were written, workshops presented, and the first pieces of unfunded research began to take shape. It was also this period that led to the idea for this particular book. In the absence of a clear research direction, one applies scholarship where they can, and self-examination of our critical experiences definitively fits the circumstances of being tenure-track. In some respects, the leadership to drive the initiative of this book was my own effort to fulfill an element of a personal vision of the role.

The personal role has had a curious response to the new circumstances. The flexible hours of professors allowed my spouse and me to take a three-week vacation in March. While I was concerned at missing key time in the school year, she was right that we needed it, and it was an excellent way to celebrate our impending twenty-fifth anniversary. That vacation, however, was also a signal that we have arrived in our new location. That we felt that we could leave our new house, spend the money, and work around the requirements of the new work environment is as indicative of having come to terms with the new reality as anything else.

We continue to develop the personal side of the role. As I write, I am at a two-day conference and my spouse has travelled with me to visit our daughter. On the return trip home we will visit more of the family. However, the fact that I am writing in this circumstance points to flexible hours also taking the role in new directions. At times, I wonder if a tenure decision will lead to a reconsideration of work-life balance, or is it a case that I am highly engaged because I am doing what I enjoy doing?

Conclusion

Looking forward, I can see a need to review the details of the tenure and promotion process. I have heard a lot and should verify what I have heard. However, the reality is that in my second year I focused on attending conferences and an increasing role in a provincial organization. As a result, I have willingly entered a bottleneck of a conference season knowing that I will be excessively busy. Perhaps in June I will find time to read what tenure entails.

One of the most important aspects of my move to academia has been the examination of the process itself. I have long been interested in a framework known as the *teacher as researcher* stance. It is a concept that interested me from the first time I learned of it in graduate school. Having been a practitioner and made the transition to academia, I have found myself able to speak to both sides of this divide. My practitioner feelings suggested that the practitioner-academic divide was ill-founded, and I have presented that case in a research conference. However, an analysis of the transition demonstrates that a significant restructuring of personal approaches is necessary in order to succeed, illustrating that there genuinely is a practitioner-academic divide. The practitioner role and the academic role are different. What remains uncertain is whether this is fundamentally due to organizational structures or much more deeply rooted in different rational processes used to address two distinct points of view—a grassroots view that may interpret the implications of other places for what they imply about the viewer's classroom, or a panoramic view of education that examines what is theoretically possible and examines the constraints and conditions that define where it may have utility.

More frequently than not, the resolution of tenure-track is a dismissive view of the process. I am too busy engaging the role to worry about the detail of explaining what I am doing—for now. That busyness is focused, productive, and, while there are some areas that need attention, I am able to address the key elements that need more support for the tenure process. In some senses, I have all but arrived…. However, I will hold off celebrating until I have fulfilled the requirements and received word that it is official.

References

Bridges, W., & Mitchell, S. (2000). Leading transition: A new model for change. *Leader to Leader, 16*(3), 30–36.

Dozois, D. J. A., & Ouimet, A. J. (2010). Theoretical perspectives on abnormal behavior. In D. J. A. Dozois & P. Firestone (Eds.), *Abnormal psychology perspectives* (4th edition)(pp. 22–43).

Heppner, M. J., Fuller, B. E., & Multon, K. D. (1998). Adults in involuntary career transition: An analysis of the relationship between the psychological and career domains. *Journal of Career Assessment, 6*(3), 329–346.

Nicholson, N. (1984). A theory of work role transitions. *Administrative Science Quarterly, 29*(2), 172–191.

Schlossberg, N. K. (2011). The challenge of change: the transition model and its applications. *Journal of Employment Counseling, 48*, 159–162.

Sibbald, T. M. (2017). Engaging academia as the nest empties. In C. DeRoche and E. Berger (Eds.), *The parent-track: Timing, balance and choice within academia*. Waterloo, ON: Wilfred Laurier University Press.

Tzur, R. (2001). Becoming a mathematics teacher-educator: conceptualizing the terrain through self-reflective analysis. *Journal of Mathematics Teacher Education, 4*(4), 259–283.

Young, A., & Lockhart, T. (1995). *A cycle of change: The transition curve.* Cranfield University School of Management. Retrieved from http://www.ucd.ie/t4cms/Transition%20Curve%20Cranfield%20Article.pdf.

CHAPTER 10

Surviving and Thriving in the First Years of Tenure-Track: A Journey Through France, Spain, and Québec

Margarida Romero
Faculty of Education, Université Laval

Introduction

This chapter is a personal journey of my early years of tenure-track. It has had both good and difficult episodes; such is (academic) life! The first years of my academic life have been a roller coaster, where the best and worst have often overlapped. My journey started in 2003, when I decided to devote myself to research, with the objective of reducing inequality through education. Having a personal mission statement helped me to overcome the challenges through my research journey in France, Spain, and Québec. At the bottom of the roller coaster my pretentious mission statement helped me see beyond the immediate difficulties and work hard to climb the proverbial hill. At rock bottom I even considered quitting academia. Today, I'm tenure-track, which ensures my survival if I do my job correctly. I'm grateful to have the opportunity to contribute to the educational sciences through my research and satisfied with all that I learned during the ups and downs of my journey.

The chapter is organized chronologically, from the decision to join academia, to the first years of professorship in Barcelona, and finally, to the move to Québec.

Academia in Mind

Becoming a researcher takes time and a conscious decision. You cannot become a full researcher overnight. In Europe, a doctorate (PhD) is required before joining academia as a professor and, more often, one or more years of international postdoctoral studies after the doctorate (Dillon, 2003). My decision to (try to) become a researcher came from a long-term career reflection. I was lucky to meet incredible teachers that made me develop a great appreciation of the teaching profession and educational sciences. I always loved to learn and my few, temporary, and partial certitudes come from research studies. This is what I considered through slow decision-making (Kahneman, 2011), and then the gut-based decision (Gigerenzer, 2007) was made. It was based on the frustration of having been invited to unplug the critical thinking mode while working in low- and medium-qualified jobs. I always had the vital need to be allowed to think outside the box and the desire to help reduce inequality through education. Working since the age of 16 has also shown me the inequity and discourteous status of women in certain low-qualified professions, but also how high-tech companies are merciless with ageing professionals beyond 50 (Platman & Taylor, 2004). My slow decision making identified a few professions where being a woman of experience has value, and academia was among the few professions.

The lack of schooling opportunities my mother had was also a familial drive to overcome. My mom's intellectual capabilities have shown me that a reflective practitioner (Schön, 1983) with high metacognitive abilities can achieve intellectual and professional excellence without formal education. I promised myself to help people like my mother have the opportunity to develop their education. Having this educational goal in mind, I developed a pretentious but humanistic personal mission statement, which helped me to survive the different challenges in the journey of becoming a researcher: Contribute to the development of lifelong learning opportunities in a humanistic way.

PhD Hardship as a Way to Prepare for Tenure-Track Challenges

My doctoral journey was circumstantially atypical. I would love to have had a scholarship and an opportunity to be sedentary in a single research center. At the moment I started my PhD, my future husband and I were in the process of deciding where to live. The high-tech eLearning society that employed us was created in the Internet bubble of 2000, in the South of France, and it broke up in 2005. We lived in a heavenly paradise, where the only eLearning society was the one we joined in 2001. The incertitude led me to engage in a European Joint Doctorate (EJD) with two PhD directors in France and Spain. In hindsight, I see this decision as one of the best moves in my research career. I had no funding for my PhD but I was involved in two research networks, which subsequently helped to open the right doors. Not being funded forced me to be efficient, a key competence for surviving in the research-teaching-service load of the early years of the tenure-track. Having three supervisors helped me to gain perspective and develop my own epistemological path. The increased workload during the PhD, and not having a real path to follow, forced me to develop and create my own research strategic plan: I started from an early stage to create and submit international competitive research projects to the 7th Framework Programme for Research and Technology (2007–2013) of the European Commission. Since 2007, I have been involved in six international competitive research projects, a really valuable experience in terms of network development, funding opportunities, and professional growth.

Self-Abused as Self-Employed ...

Two months after starting the steps to enroll in a PhD program in France, the eLearning company where my future husband and I worked broke up. Before moving to a new location, we created a small enterprise and became self-employed. France was not the friendliest place for small enterprises; we were both overworked and overtaxed. We hardly succeeded in paying our invoices. Our activity was just insane considering the time and vital energy requirements of being your own manager, seller, worker, and accountant. We had no one to blame but ourselves. I learned to fail and recover. When working on your own, you experience how hard it is to complete all the tasks of selling, signing contracts, doing the work, and being paid. You have to invest a lot of time to ensure your customers' satisfaction and your reputation. In my case, the straw that broke my back was an economic abuse from a supposed friend. Trusting in our relationship with him, we worked two months for free, before he transferred our work to a low-cost competitor. Losing two months of work while fighting to find time for my PhD was the incident that made me realize that I needed to move to a salaried position if I was going to complete my PhD.

Moving Back to a Salaried Position

I moved to a salaried position at the end of 2007. After working hard for a Barcelona-based business school as a self-employed consultant (in our French-taxed small and medium enterprise), they offered me a permanent salaried position. I was so happy to be in a stable working pattern again! During the year I lived in Barcelona, I travelled at least one weekend per month to join my future husband in the South of France. While the business school was a very cozy space with chic people, I lived a double life, taking the Friday night bus at 2 a.m. to return to France. The European bus lines were the cheapest way to travel, but I was unsure about my travel mates. I pretended to sleep, but was really trying to be as invisible as I could—not going out of the bus during the stops, and taking a seat as close as possible to the bus driver. One night, the climate was very tense. One of the passengers urinated in the corridor and the smell was disgusting. Oh, god! Looking back at this period I realize how lucky I was for not having major incidents during the night bus travels ... I was unable to realize the hardship of the situation because my mind was absorbed in my PhD; I was a zombie.

First Steps in Academia

The end of the tunnel began to show in the summer of 2008. My Spanish PhD supervisor invited me to join the Departament de Psicologia Bàsica, Evolutiva i de l'Educació of the Universitat Autonoma de Barcelona as an assistant professor. My dream of joining academia started to take life. I really thrived. I loved being part of the academic life, and I really appreciated the opportunity to teach pre-service teachers in the Faculty of Education. Future teachers are often motivated by their appreciation of children and school. However, they were not assured to obtain a position in education, and they were aware of their limits to internationalize their career if the Catalan or Spanish education administration did not offer them an opportunity. They knew they were joining a profession with many uncertainties. There was a lot of passion, social commitment, and strong humanistic values among the students. My students were really conscious that being part of the education system in a southern European country, in a time of economic crisis, was more than vocational. Working with such high-quality persons compensated for being required to teach courses that were not in my field of expertise. Teaching out of your area was assumed to be normal for assistant professors who fill the holes in the department's teaching workload.

During my early years of professorship in Barcelona I was thriving and became a workaholic, inebriated by the pressure and the joys of the academic life. I wanted to obtain tenure, and I really took pleasure in the efforts to develop my teaching-research-service experiences. I accomplished a lot: an EJD, two research awards, a first co-edited book, an international research project as principal investigator ... But I lost my work-life balance.

Collateral Effects of the Crisis-Hit Spanish Public Universities

My position was in the process of being stabilized when, in 2011, the tenure-track process was frozen in some Catalan public universities. The debt crisis made the government not only reduce our salaries but unilaterally break the tenure-track opportunities. In this context of uncertainties, some of my colleagues migrated to northern Europe (UK, Finland, etc.), the USA, and emergent countries (Mexico, Chile, etc.). I tried to do the best I could to remain positive despite the uncertainties; but I'm probably an individual who is vulnerable to workplace stress. Stress hinders your health and is thought to be abortogenic (Arck et al., 2001). In 2012, I decided to prepare myself to quit academia after losing two pregnancies in a row.

Before Losing My Two Pregnancies ...

During my PhD and my early years of professorship I had no personal life. I was a workaholic thriving on the research-teaching-service career and doing everything at my best. I was not exceptional. In a Darwinistic context, most of my colleagues in their earliest year of the tenure-track had in mind that, in Spain, you should be almost the best to survive. It was not only a matter of publish or perish (Lussier, 2010; Parchomovsky, 2000) but to have excellent student evaluations and be remarkable in your service. Having children is not easy in that context. Some of my female colleagues were childless or had delayed child rearing to their late 30s. My maternal instinct awoke when I turned 32. My partner was not hard to convince about the idea of becoming a father. We organized my pregnancy as a project. I booked in my Google calendar the three months of maternity leave to fit into the summer break. In my head, planning a baby was nearly as easy as buying a book online and deciding on the delivery modality and date. How wrong I was ... After a year and many medical checks, I was finally pregnant. I maintained my high engagement in research, teaching, and service. I was in the second month of the pregnancy when I attended a research meeting in London. Landing at the airport, I had cramps in an unusual way. I was losing my first angel. I was in shock. This is the last thing I imagined happening to me, when I vomited before entering the taxi to the plane at the airport. I was so body-disconnected that feeling abnormally sick in the morning did not preoccupy me. I was focused on the presentation that needed finishing for the meeting, the papers in progress—everything except the most important one, my little angel. I was devastated.

During the London research meeting, I only shared my loss with one person (another workaholic childless researcher like me), and I (unconsciously) skipped the grief and took part in the three-day research meeting. I tried to stay positive and think in a probabilistic way: spontaneous abortion rates are around 10% (Lawson et al., 2012). I didn't realize how my first little angel was already a part of my life, how I loved her, and how broken I was about the loss. I realized that I was trying to live a super-woman ideal, telling myself that having a baby is something one can "manage." Three months later I was expecting again. This time I started to pay attention to my little one by taking care of myself and prioritizing in a way that allows one to achieve a work-life balance: saying no. I refused to attend evening and Saturday research meetings, declined some student supervisions, and responded to emails within 48 hours rather than immediately. These little changes showed me the pressure of students and colleagues. A senior research colleague was concerned about my "disengagement" for not answering emails within the same day and not coming to some meetings outside normal office hours. I was just beginning to realize how family unfriendly, and male-dominated, most of the organizations (academia included) were in Spain. I took time to meet colleagues that could be role models as mother-researchers. They struggled, especially when family support was not available. More sadly, they felt powerless to change the research pressure hindering their work-life balance. I learned about the European Charter for Researchers (European Commission, 2005), but most of the principles to make academia family friendly were ignored in Spain. I started to realize that quitting academia could be the best strategy to achieve some work-life balance. I was taking care of myself and doing all that was possible to have the best pregnancy. I was overly positive about the arrival of this second little one. I was doing everything right, but this did not prevent the worst.

I lost my second angel, along with my heart and my mind. I fell into the deep of a dark hole. I continued working (there is no leave for an early loss) but I was a zombie. How can you make sense of the teaching, supervision, pedagogical innovations, or research when you are in such a painful grief? I felt guilty about having had my pregnancies so late. While I was the average age of a mother in Spain (31.6 in 2012; OECD, 2014), the average age is a response to economic pressure and not the healthiest age for having children. After the late 20s, chromosomal abnormalities and all kinds of other adverse outcomes for the baby and the mother statistically increase. I was assuming the 40s was my deadline.

I was not aware of the decline in fertility rate with age before struggling to conceive. Research shows an important decline in fertility after the mid-thirties (Pal & Santoro, 2003). I felt guilty for not having been proactive and prioritizing a healthy pregnancy instead of doing a PhD. If the price to survive in academia is not having kids, then I would have loved to have made an informed choice and decided to become a mother instead of a paper-oriented academic. I felt guilty for not having done more to avoid the research pressure, guilty for not having taken more time for myself. I felt like a research ego monster failing to accompany her two little angels to life. It took me two hellish months to come back to a kind of normal mind and to stop hating myself, my life, my decisions, and (mercilessly) academia.

During these two infernal months, I was even more selective in my time, and politely declined to engage in publishing, additional supervisions, and research projects. I shared with my colleagues my double loss, and I was shocked how an early loss is disregarded. With the best intentions, everyone had a story to share about someone who knows someone who, after struggling to conceive and having (early and late) miscarriage, was able to achieve childbirth or to adopt. Research colleagues were good in reporting facts, but definitively not the empathic shoulder to cry on. Two months after my second loss, I was feeling out of the research circle. My colleagues didn't want to bother me and skipped me (with the best intentions, I guess) very quickly, following their own crazy competition to be productive in research. The accumulated assets during the previous years were not enough of a guarantee to promote my research involvement after my grief. There were so many junior positions, like me, that I even felt that being out of the race was very convenient for those wanting my teaching-research-service load and paycheque.

After some weeks, I had in mind to quit academia, but I did not share it with any of my colleagues. I needed an alternate way to pay our bills, and I decided to quit progressively, in the following academic year. I needed time to heal, to guide the students I was currently supervising, finish some reports, and develop new professional energies and strategies to work as an eLearning freelance consultant. With my partner, we decided to take the time to heal before trying to conceive again. Having in my mind that I would quit research relieved a lot of pressure. I felt a new kind of freedom that I never experienced before. I involved myself only with persons, tasks, and events that were meaningful, and I declined anything else. I learnt definitively and effectively to say no. I was amazed to observe that saying no made me more respected than before, while maximizing meaningfulness and efficiency. Three months after establishing this new mindset, I started to feel good and in a new relationship with academia, where I respected myself, while being more efficient. So why was I quitting?

An Unexpected Opportunity

Some weeks after reconnecting myself to the research-teaching-service mission, the long and sunny days of May made me feel alive and lucky for having been slow to act on my decision to quit academia during my second grief. I was out of the dark hole, and good things started occurring. As it happened, at the end of May, I got an email from a professor at the Université Laval in Québec, sending me the link for a tenure-track-position competition in educational technology. I felt honoured to receive the invitation to apply from someone with whom I wasn't in contact before. This unexpected invitation saved my faith in academia.

I cynically said to myself that the invitation was probably a strategy to justify the international competitiveness of the position, and that my tiny career as a junior researcher would be used to justify the strength of the predefined local candidate. However, a part of me wanted to believe in the honesty of the invitation. I had little to lose by applying for this position. My French PhD supervisors wrote an outstanding recommendation letter, for which I am grateful. I'm sure the recommendation was a key to overcome the first CV-based selection step. I was invited to a videoconference interview on the same day of a conference on eLearning in France, where I was invited as a keynote speaker. Should I cancel my keynote to be sure to be in a quiet place for ensuring the quality of the interview? Or should I maintain my speaking engagement and join the interview afterwards through a (possibly unstable) Wi-Fi connection? My gut-based decision was to maintain my engagement with the conference organizers and meet the expectations of the plenary session audience. After the keynote, I found a little calm corner of a table for the videoconference interview. However, after half an hour, the calm corner became the coffee-break space. I was surrounded by the conference participants and their chats. This noisy context made me think that I lost any possible tiny opportunity to be hired. A month after the interview, I received confirmation about having been selected. "Oh, my goodness, unbelievable!" When, a year later, during a lunch with my new colleagues, I discussed how messy my interview context was, a member of the selection committee revealed how the skills I had displayed to survive such a messy context made the selection committee sure that I was a resourceful person, able to teach in any circumstances. Wow! I should probably consider integrating "surviving skills in hardship contexts" in my next CV.

From Barcelona to Québec

Being hired by Université Laval was a life-changing opportunity far beyond my expectations of academia. I was so lucky to be part of a fair selection committee. I was excited about the idea of engaging in a department which showed this ethical quality in the selection process. It was like a miracle in the middle of the crisis-hit context we were experiencing in Spain.

When I read the job description and the work-life balance policies in Québec, I felt like a lottery winner. It sounded like a place where research and having a life is possible in a human way, a place where meeting the job requirements ensures you to keep your job and be tenured, without a Darwinist selection where only the best will survive the merciless research arena. That sounded so good. I was enthused after traversing the grief of my angels that we agreed to move to Québec and turn a page on our life in Barcelona. The eight months of transition were full of happy events. First, we decided to marry. The oxytocin explosion made me pregnant again, this time at an unexpected moment. That was a surprise and a life lesson.

Our happiness and hope for a better academic cocoon made us pregnant. Initially, I felt bad about how my state would be perceived by my future colleagues, but I quickly focused on my new little angel and decided that whatever happened she would come first. My bump kept growing. I was certain this time I would be able to welcome my angel. I was in a full connection with her. She was such a sweet little one in the bump, kicking and moving all along the transition period.

A Sense of Downgrading …

We sold everything in Barcelona, and we arrived with three pieces of luggage and a one-meter cube module with our most precious items. From having a very comfortable life in Barcelona, we started a new life from scratch. We did not imagine how hard the economic downgrade would be, and we continued with the lifestyle we had had in Spain. The first pay resulted in a big crisis, close to divorce. My net wage was 50% of the gross wage. Other persons working in Québec informed us that the net could be 65% of the gross. Being paid 50% of the gross wage made us seriously struggle to make ends meet. The apartment we had rented was calculated based on 65% of the new wage, and not 50%. We were required to avoid any non-essential activity involving money (from taking a hot beverage to going to the hairdresser). We strolled a lot in the park in front of our apartment, trying to concentrate on the bump, and cooking homemade food that could be achieved at a lower cost and higher quality than the supermarket. The penury led us to a healthier diet and made me embrace the "voluntary simplicity" mindset (Shama, 1985), aiming to consume less in a more respectful way, avoiding "many possessions irrelevant to the chief purpose of life" (Gregg, 1936). The voluntary simplicity approach was a first step in preparing for a maternally instinctive way of mothering and growing a baby. In hindsight, economic hardship prevented us from falling into the trap of baby consumerism.

A Short-Term Academic Downgrade, an Upgrade in the Mid-Term

Though my new position was supposed to bring me an upgrade in the mid-term, the short term was a downgrade, not only from a salary point of view, but also in terms of the seniority recognition. My three years of professorship were appreciated in the job application, but not recognized as three years of seniority in my tenure-track. I was not offered the opportunity to negotiate and I felt guilty about arriving pregnant. I accepted the contract as it was proposed. I took a 20-week maternity leave. I maintained my research engagements, the graduate supervisions in progress in Barcelona, and the new ones in Université Laval along with the preparation of my new courses. My plate was quite full, but the majority of my colleagues were parents and fully supportive about flexible arrangements. I did a lot of teleworking with my little treasure lying in the sling. I did the course preparation and videoconference-based supervisions while breastfeeding at home, feeling safe and close to my little one. I felt happy to be able to find a work-life balance during my maternity leave. I was fully present for my baby and took advantage of her sling naps to work in a gentle way.

Gender Equity and Motherhood

Despite my efforts to maintain a high engagement towards my research and teaching commitments during the maternity leave, I was not spared the experience of having an ironic critique from a senior-male researcher. This happened during the Christmas party, in front of all my colleagues, just after finishing my maternity leave. The attack occurred on the day I left my breast-fed baby for the first time. I felt so bad that my eyes blushed. My throat was trembling and I had only some seconds to hold my composure, trying to hide my tears and keep some kind of dignity. What a return! Some months after, I was more confident with a colleague, and I came back to the incident. She assured me that only a few people noticed, and that a group of female colleagues (all of them moms) blamed the discriminatory remark on my maternity leave and asked him to apologize just after the incident. I was happy to learn that. The senior-male colleague has never given any type of apology, but I'm relieved knowing that some of my colleagues supported me through this incident and continue to fight all forms of female discrimination. I admire how they faced up to the discriminatory (subtle or evident) facts in our academic lives. From my Spanish perspective, Québec women are generally assertive in a positive way; they have been educated to be respected and don't tolerate gender discrimination. The weeks passed and, little by little, I developed a warm relationship with my closest colleagues. But more importantly, despite of minor adjustments to a new academic environment, my life is happier than ever, with my baby growing healthy and happy. I'm lucky to have found a work-life balance, allowing me to experience motherhood while maintaining my research-teaching-service search for excellence.

Grateful to Work as an Education Scholar

My early years in academia have had ups and downs. Hardship made me realize how lucky I am today to be in the tenure-track process for a permanent position in one of the most wonderful jobs I know. I'm grateful of the opportunity to contribute to the educational sciences through my research, the chance to collaborate with highly inspirational colleagues worldwide, and glad to supervise very talented students. Becoming a scholar in education is an incredible opportunity. Education is one of the most powerful tools for contributing to our community and society in their well-being and development. I'm grateful for having the opportunity to be part of a faculty of education. I love to collaborate with the future teachers I have in my class, to develop their passion for education from a learner-centered perspective (Cornelius-White, 2007) for their own development as reflective practitioners. My mission as a professor in educational technologies is to help future teachers to develop critical thinking and reflective practice for their curricular integration of information and communication technologies. I'm lucky to be allowed to create a new postgraduate course on digital game-based learning and align my research interests and teaching. Every day, I feel thankful of being able to develop my research-teaching-service mission in a family-friendly place.

To conclude this chapter I would like to thank everyone who has supported me through all these years as I work toward my dream to become a scholar in education. First and foremost, my family and husband; second, most of my colleagues and students during my research journey in France, Spain, and Québec. *Gràcies, gracias, merci*, thank you!

References

Arck, P., Rose, M., Hertwig, K., Hagen, E., Hildebrandt, M., & Klapp, B. (2001). Stress and immune mediators in miscarriage. *Human Reproduction, 16*(7), 1505–1511.

Cornelius-White, J. (2007). Learner-centered teacher-student relationships are effective: A meta-analysis. *Review of Educational Research, 77*(1), 113–143.

Dillon, N. (2003). The postdoctoral system under the spotlight. *EMBO Reports, 4*(1), 2–4.

European Commission. (2005). The European Charter for Researchers: The Code of Conduct for the Recruitment of Researchers. *Euraxess.* Retrieved from http://ec.europa.eu/euraxess/index.cfm/rights/europeanCharter

Gigerenzer, G. (2007). *Gut feelings: The intelligence of the unconscious.* London, UK: Penguin.

Gregg, R. (1936). Voluntary simplicity. *Visva-Bharati Quarterly,* 36–37.

Kahneman, D. (2011). *Thinking, fast and slow.* New York, NY: Macmillan.

Lawson, C. C., Rocheleau, C. M., Whelan, E. A., Hibert, E. N. L., Grajewski, B., Spiegelman, D., & Rich-Edwards, J. W. (2012). Occupational exposures among nurses and risk of spontaneous abortion. *American Journal of Obstetrics and Gynecology, 206*(4), 327.e1–327.e8.

Lussier, R. N. (2010). *Publish don't perish: 100 tips that improve your ability to get published.* Charlotte, NC: Information Age Publishing.

OECD. (2014). *SF2.3: Age of mothers at childbirth* (pp. 1–7). OECD—Social Policy Division—Directorate of Employment, Labour and Social Affairs. Retrieved from http://www.oecd.org/els/soc/SF_2_3_Age_mothers_childbirth.pdf.

Pal, L., & Santoro, N. (2003). Age-related decline in fertility. *Endocrinology and Metabolism Clinics of North America, 32*(3), 669–688.

Parchomovsky, G. (2000). Publish or perish. *Michigan Law Review,* 926–952.

Platman, K., & Taylor, P. (2004). *Workforce Ageing in the New Economy: A Comparative Study of Information Technology Employment. A European summary report focusing on the United Kingdom, Germany & the Netherlands.* Cambridge Interdisciplinary Research Centre on Ageing. The University of Cambridge. Retrieved from http://www.mature-project.eu/materials/PlatmanTaylorSummaryReport2004.pdf.

Schön, D. A. (1983). *The reflective practitioner: How professionals think in action* (Vol. 5126). London, UK: Basic books.

Shama, A. (1985). The voluntary simplicity consumer. *Journal of Consumer Marketing, 2*(4), 57–63.

CHAPTER 11

For Academy's Sake: A Former Practitioner's Search for Scholarly Relevance

Lloyd Kornelsen
Faculty of Education, University of Winnipeg

In July 2013, six months after successfully defending my PhD dissertation, I applied for, was offered, and accepted a tenure-track position as an assistant professor in the Faculty of Education, University of Winnipeg. At the time, I was teaching at a high-school affiliated with the University of Winnipeg and had earned tenure at the high school. The university agreed to carry over my tenure status to the new position, but maintained that I would need to apply for promotion within four years.

In many ways this new position marks a culmination of 28 years of working in the field of education, as a high-school teacher, adult educator, and conflict mediator. But also, it represents a beginning—an opportunity to extend my work in different directions and through different means, often in ways I could not have imagined as a classroom teacher. I now have time to think, write, create, and collaborate in ways not possible before. This past year, for example, I have been involved in creating and coordinating international practica, sharing my work with peers globally, organizing campus and community-wide teach-ins, and doing research with former teaching colleagues in the field—and all the while writing (and getting published) about what I'm learning. In many ways, the transition from the field to the academy, from an ending to a beginning, feels seamless, as my past work life has informed, contextualized, and grounded my current work.

The first 18 months in the Faculty of Education have been an overwhelmingly positive experience. I feel fortunate to be in a position that allows for, and encourages, the pursuit of lifelong academic interests and curiosities. My new colleagues, fellow faculty members, and administrators have been supportive, inviting to me to join research and writing projects; participate in service opportunities; develop my research/teaching program, and attend conferences; they have introduced me to people working in my field and helped me navigate the service, research, teaching terrain of the academy. They have reminded me of the imperatives that drive successful promotion.

A Question of Fitting In

Even though I have mostly enjoyed the past 20 months, I have also, at times, struggled with feelings of demoralization and "outsiderness." It has little to do with the work, the people I work with, or the administrators to whom I report. It has more to do with unspoken messages from the academy that what I did before July 2013, the date of my appointment, is not considered scholarly for promotion purposes, most simply it seems because it does not fit the criteria of service/teaching/research in post-PhD and post-secondary contexts. However, what the academy is, who speaks for it, or where it exactly stands on the issue is not entirely clear. The collective agreement is not definitive; and many of my colleagues are uncertain about how and whether pre-appointment work factors into promotion. It feels, at times, a little phantasmal. However, everyone has warned of university tenure and promotion committees (TPCs) who, appealing to academic tradition and precedent, will not recognize pre-appointment work. Many colleagues acknowledge the inherent injustice of pre-appointment work not being recognized. In the end, everyone with whom I have spoken acknowledges that it will be difficult to convince TPCs that work in the field warrants promotion.

It is this that is demoralizing: the notion that service, research and teaching that was explicitly and implicitly rendered for many years in the field is seen as not contributing to, or manifesting, formal scholarship. So, while basking in new and novel work experiences this past year and a half, I have also been trying to explain—to myself and others—how and why previous work serves as a necessary and seamless function for my current scholarly endeavors; and that the work that teachers do in the field informs, advances, and nuances research, teaching, and service undertakings—often in unique and indispensable ways—and is therefore worthy of formal scholarly recognition. To that end, for the past 18 months, I have been revisiting past work experience, recalling seminal events and paradigm-shifting stories, looking to understand how they may inform matters of scholarly concern. (It is an endeavor that has been at the heart of my writing/publishing projects since my appointment. See the Kornelsen references.) It is in this spirit and with this intent that this paper retells three of those stories.

But before the retelling, several background notes: First, the act of justifying is partly a practice of reconciliation. Arguing to have past professional experience respected and recognized has meant needing to better understand the perspectives and requirements of the academy. It entails explaining one to the other, the field to the academy and the academy to the field, and serving as an interpreter for each and mediator of both—and invariably recognizing that I now inhabit both worlds (or they inhabit me?). My sense of outsider-ness, at least in part, derives from feeling as though I do not belong in either world, exclusively. So, while this paper explores why and how teacher-practitioners belong/fit in the academy, it is also necessarily speaks of a reconciliation of sorts, between field and academy.

Second, my feelings of outsider-ness also stem from a strong sense of self-doubt: Do I really know enough to profess? How can I make claims for scholarly recognition when my university colleagues are much more conversant in their fields than I feel that I am in mine? I spent years managing classrooms, grading assignments, and attending parent-teacher nights. In those years my colleagues were reading scholarly literature, writing Social Sciences and Humanities Research Council (SSHRC) grant applications, and defending research claims. How can I possibly think of myself as an equal, when in many ways I am not? It is a question that animates this paper and troubles my quest for promotion.

Third, as a way of approaching the issue, seeking scholarly legitimacy, I have been reading literature on an epistemological orientation known as embodied and connected knowing. It challenges the dominant educational paradigm of separated knowing, claiming that the trust-worthiest knowledge comes from personal experience (Saltmarsh, 1996). It is with this in mind that Huber, Caine, Huber,

& Steeves (2013), discussing the scholarly implications of teaching practice and teacher knowledge, cite Connelly and Clandinin (1988):

> [Personal practical knowledge is found] in the person's past experience, the person's present mind and body, and the person's future plans and actions. Knowledge is not only "in the mind." It is "in the body." And it is seen and found "in our practices." [Personal practical knowledge] is a particular way of reconstructing the past and the intentions for the future to deal with the exigencies of a present situation. (p. 25)

What do Connelly and Clandinin mean, exactly; and how does *embodied* practice inform or enrich scholarly perspectives and insight? As alluded to above, by way of addressing that question, I have been *reconstructing* my teaching past; and three teaching experiences have come to stand out for their seminal impact. In the upcoming section I describe these experiences and explore what they mean for my current academic pursuits. For each retold experience (story), I describe the precipitating event, examine how it affected my thinking and teaching practice, and discuss how it informs my intentions for the future. The objective is to *reconstruct the past*, with a view to understanding *embodied knowledge* and how it addresses *the exigencies of the present situation*—thereby expanding horizons in education; in short, to offer an *embodied* account for what I know and how that advances a perspective on education.

Stories from Experience

The following experiences were chosen for the influential role they played in my teaching life, and for the indelible impact they have on the questions that animate my current work. Several things should be noted at the outset. First, the descriptions are lengthy: The objective is to convey a sense of "startling unexpectedness" or cognitive dissonance that was associated with each event—experiences that education scholars like Greene (1995) and Mezirow (1995) say precipitate transformational insights—and to provide an explanatory narrative for how the experience shapes my current work and informs an education concern or contention. Second, these types of transformative experiences are not unique—they are a part of the lives of many teachers. My hope is that these stories can be illustrative of teacher experience generally and of how knowledge, acquired through practice, necessarily relates to and informs concerns with which a faculty of education has to do. My experiences are not exceptional; colleagues with whom I work share stories of equal and greater consequence, as do friends and peers still teaching in the field. Mine derive from teaching high-school social studies for 28 years.

A Newcomer's Story and the Pedagogy of Storytelling

Near the beginning of my teaching career I taught an evening class on world geography. One night we were discussing responsibilities of global citizenship, using Canada's response to the Southeast Asian refugee crisis as an example. A question came up: Should the Canadian government take the stance that Canadians owe as much to children who sift through garbage landfills in Nicaragua, say, as they do homeless children in Canada? This was position articulated in a speech by Prime Minister Pierre Elliott Trudeau many years earlier. The question led to a spirited discussion. Many students thought that Canada should look after its own problems first and not worry too much about people beyond its borders. At the break, Rami (a pseudonym for one of the students) asked whether she might say something to the rest of the class.

After the break, Rami told her story. She had come to Canada several years earlier, from a refugee camp in Thailand. Rami was born in Laos, where as a young child her family had fled the country, escaping political and economic persecution. After spending several years in a Thai refugee camp (where friends of hers died), her father became friends with a Canadian aid worker who introduced him to a Canadian consulate official who arranged for his family to come to Canada. That was four years ago; all of Rami's friends were still in the refugee camp, waiting for some country to take them in.

When she stopped talking, all was quiet; the tension that had animated the debate earlier, evaporated; strident debating positions vanished. It seemed as though people did not know what to make of Rami. She was one of us; she was gregarious, and laughed a lot. No one had thought of her as different, as a refugee from far away; and yet her story was that of a refugee, the type of person we had talked about earlier. But, even though Rami came from far away, from a country whose culture, language, and history was very different from

Canada's, she was also a Canadian and a member of our community of evening learners; her story was immersed in values and desires we all shared—security, freedom, and peace, and a love of friends and family. The world was no longer clearly divided between Canada and the rest of the world, between us and them. I doubt any of us, for a long while afterward, saw images of refugees on television without seeing Rami, one of us. (A variation of Ravi's story is recounted in a previous publication: Kornelsen (2013b).)

I think more was learned that night about global citizenship and what it means to think as one than in a whole term of classes: there was a revelation of what it means to be open to, and care for the other (the other was us), a synthesis of local and global identities, and a discovery of universal commonality amidst global diversity. It showed how all three—the cognitive, the affective, and the ethical—play a part in global citizenship: knowledge of the international refugee situation, empathy for the situation and the people affected, and struggle with the right response.

Rami's story demonstrates how storytelling may serve as a pedagogy of peace—in several ways. First, storytelling is a means of communication that is singular and non-linear—a way of conveying a truth that is impossible to grasp any other way. As I remember it, it was Rami's story that inspired the class to see her and experience her on Buber's (2006) *I-Thou* terms, "orienting ourselves to the presence of the other person" (p. 33). The story, through Rami, personified all refugees, globally; and hence, the refugee "other"—the stereotype—became humanized, a person to whom we could relate. (A subsequent reflection has led to an interpretation that suggests that Rami's storytelling created a sense of shame and coercion for others in the class—not, in fact, a reduction of distance—hence the silence. However, I think what happened was more akin to what Greene [1995] and Mezirow [1995] say presages transformational learning: a disorienting life experience that invokes a sense of cognitive dissonance.)

Second, Rami's story helped the class hold and understand a central paradox, or a contradictory impulse of world citizenship: unity amidst diversity. The story, with its universal themes and values all could identify with—love, safety, security, family, and synchronicity—elicited openness to, and recognition of, a global injustice. Yet, it was experienced and remembered by a singular person with a different culture and worldview from elsewhere.

Third, Rami showed that storytelling can be a means of establishing identity, amidst and within community. Maxine Greene (1995), philosopher of education and politics, has written widely on preparing young people for the public space. Describing individuals as containing "provinces of meaning," she says young people need to overcome their silences and release their "persons," for the sake of realizing their identity, and for the benefit of the community. The only way of doing this, she says, is through people telling and sharing their stories. Greene calls on teachers to create the space and time in classrooms where students are given the opportunity to express their meanings publicly. As they do so, individuals reveal themselves in their distinctiveness and difference in the company of others. They become aware of their unique identity and are able to imagine what it must be like to be the other, to be attentive to the stranger. Out of this "heteroglossia," as she calls it, a common concern emerges, a community. I have witnessed this in the classroom often. When students begin to share their stories and meanings, their individual identities begin to emerge and a heterogeneous community begins to develop. It helps students to imagine a similar but broader global community of distinction, difference, and common concern; and gives them an opportunity to participate, being seen as members, and having an identity within a larger community (Kornelsen, 2013b).

The years following, working as a peace educator and a conflict consultant, I learned more of the pedagogic value and mediating effectiveness of stories and storytelling. Stories can engender intersubjective awareness and mutual recognition, serving as a means of finding and giving voice to students' identity and dignity, and initiating introspection and reflexivity. Storytelling became a central part of my teaching and mediating work.

Today, as an education professor, I explore storytelling as global citizenship and peace education pedagogy with pre-service teachers and continue using it as a basic teaching methodology. Also, I am beginning to see how stories and storytelling are critical to researching lived experience—particularly as it relates to the teaching life of high-school social-studies teachers. People's stories can serve as a unique portal to human experience and phenomena, bringing meaning and conveying lived reality in ways not otherwise possible. As John Dewey contended, and as Huber, Caine, Huber, and Steeves (2013) echoed almost a hundred years later, "[E]ducation, life, and experience are one and the same" (p. 220). The challenge will be convincing my teaching colleagues that their own life experience, as represented in the stories they tell, represents real research—because many doubt their stories matter. (It is something that I witnessed in a research project with classroom teachers last year; and it has been alluded to in the education literature [Aulls and Shore, 2008].)

A Provincial Exam and the Purpose of Education

A few years after Rami told her story, the Manitoba government, through its Department of Education, mandated a standardized final exam for World Issues, a Grade 12 social-studies course. The explicit objective of the exam was to measure student and teacher performance so as to serve the needs of parents, businesses, and educational institutions to assess teaching and learning success—to help hold teachers and schools to account. The rationale was to improve learning outcomes, thereby serving the province's need for economic competitiveness—indeed a laudable goal.

However, the experience of helping students learn about issues of the world that year was not a pleasant one. It felt as though those aspects most important to teaching—developing relationships with students, helping make the course content relevant and meaningful, encouraging students to learn from themselves and each other, and motivating students to go beyond the curriculum—were jeopardized by the demands of preparing for the exam. The anxiety I felt over being judged by outside authorities and fear of my students' performance permeated class discussion, activities, and assignments. I taught earnestly, often from a "thou shalt" attitude, and with a top-down approach. In the end the students wrote the exam and scored above the provincial average. However, I am not sure how much the students actually learned about world issues—the state of the world, its problems, and their place in it. Much of the curriculum on which the students were tested was out of date: the curriculum had been written during the Cold War, which had ended many years earlier. The material we covered was barely relevant. In the end, it felt as though we had all become separated, the teacher, students and course material—diminished and instrumentalized. Based on discussions with Department of Education personnel, this was not the intent of the people who created and implemented the exam policy; however, since the policy was presented to classroom teachers as a *fait accompli*, over which they had little or no control, it had this effect.

Many years later, reading Hanna Arendt, I discovered another reason for the exam's unpleasantness. In *The Human Condition* (1958), Arendt argued that if education's primary purpose is efficiency with no transcendent end or inherent virtue other than effectiveness, it becomes meaningless.

> The perplexity of utilitarianism is that it gets caught in the unending chain of means and ends without ever arriving at some principle which could justify the category of means and ends, that is, of utility itself. The 'in order to' has become the content of the 'for the sake of'; in other words, utility established as meaning generates meaninglessness. (p. 154)

Since the government justified their standards policy as necessary for meeting Manitoba's global competitiveness needs, the exam had the effect of reducing education to a utilitarian purpose—economic competitiveness—which was really just a means to another end. However, the end that the authors of the standardized exam policy had envisioned was never clearly articulated. Nor, as I remember, was it deemed to be a concern of public education.

In the mid-1990s, then, I encountered the standards-in-education movement—its purpose economic competitiveness, and its means standardized learning and assessment. In my opinion, it was anathema to a model of good education. But it forced me to confront the question: Why do we do this? To what end should we educate, if not for economic competitiveness, and how, if not through standardized testing? If not educating *in order to*, what should we be educating *for the sake of*? I discussed it with friends, colleagues, and students, and read a book called the *Pedagogy of the Oppressed*, by Paulo Freire (1970). Freire's view of education was the antithesis of the standards-in-education movement. In a word, it was humanizing. What was the end of education? Becoming human. What were the means? Dialogue between human beings, teacher, and learners—subjects seeking collaboratively to name and live in the world. What knowledge was important? Knowledge that is constructed by teachers and learners, grounded in the reality of their lives (*conscientization*).

Paulo Freire's critical pedagogy was a godsend, a heartening response to the instrumentalist methodology of the standards approach—a pedagogy that coherently, and with integrity, articulated the thing that I had been inarticulately struggling toward in the classroom, for years. I now knew what I was doing. Ironically, it had taken a year of teaching to a standardized exam to realize that I was a critical pedagogue.

It is not easy; teaching as a critical pedagogue is perhaps not even possible. If, as Freire (2007) says, the goal of education is to help learners become human, people who can name their world and act upon it, then it follows that a teacher's primary responsibility is to help students change from being objects who are *alienated spectators* to subjects who *participant actors*. This can only be accomplished, Freire says, when education is a practice of freedom, and when teachers practice dialogue, "the encounter between two people (learner and teacher), mediated by the world in order to name the world" (p. 88). Dialogue requires that the world be unveiled (something no one can do for another). The goal is to help students be "considerers of the world" (139). It is a daunting task.

Peter Jarvis and Max Van Manen (both of whom have written extensively on the ethics of the teacher-learner relationship) say that teaching dialogically requires an ongoing openness to the call and vulnerability of the other (Van Manen, 2000), and a continual accessibility to and care for the learner (Jarvis 1997). In addition, according to Andres Vercoe (1998), a Freirean apologist, teachers must always approach the same topic afresh—relearning, recreating, and remaking the subject anew every time, with every new learner. To teach this way, with open vulnerability and fresh eyes, can be exhausting and discouraging; it is easy to fall into a habit of top-down, technique-driven teaching that objectifies and dehumanizes. Freire and others (Kornelsen, 2006) say that to teach dialogically, day in and day out, requires unflinching commitment and love.

By 1999, I felt emotionally and mentally exhausted. I knew it had something to do with my teaching, but I did not know what exactly. To make sense of it, I left teaching for a year, took a sabbatical, and enrolled in a Master of Adult Education program. The questions and issues I grappled with that year—and the ones that would eventually form the basis of my thesis research—emerged from, and were shaped by my years in the classroom. They had to do with what I most feared might end my professional teaching life, burn-out and depression, and with what most still attracted me to teaching, experiencing *flow*: forgetting about time, sensing greater inner clarity, losing an awareness of self, and experiencing heightened mindfulness.

Building on Freire's critical pedagogy, the reading and writing I did that year and several years subsequently made an indelible impression on my thinking and practice of teaching—in both high-school and adult-education contexts. I learned, along with Walck (1997), that it takes a lifetime to learn to become a true teacher—not because it takes years to master poses and techniques, but because it is an un-ending process of building a frame of mind—one of freedom and openness to all that can and will happen—and to move beyond the boundaries of the classroom to write the text of students' lives. It is exhausting work; there is no easy way.

After the year away, I returned to teaching, but with a greater sensitivity to my power and presence, and a heightened respect for the craft and vocation of teaching. Today, as a member of a faculty of education, my biggest teaching concern has to do with what it means to educate aspiring teachers; how to help them know, live, and practice their teaching position, power, and responsibility. One case in point: If we are encouraging teacher candidates to be critical thinkers and teach for critical thinking, how best can we do so? How do we navigate the terrain between teaching about critical pedagogy and teaching for critical pedagogy?

A Global Citizenship Practicum and the Role of Social-Studies Teachers

In 2003 a colleague and I took thirteen high-school students to Costa Rica for two weeks to live and work in the village of Pedrogosso. The trip represented the culmination of a course on global citizenship. On the morning of the day after we arrived, a couple of students approached us, confused and scared. They did not know what to think of a situation at their homestay. There was a man in the backyard, locked up in a cell-like structure, howling like a wolf all night long. He was their host mom's older brother who had been injured in a car accident several years earlier.

Jayne and Lily (pseudonyms) were looking for advice. Adrienne (pseudonym) and I were not sure how to respond. We needed to keep our students safe, healthy, and not overwhelmed; but we also wanted them to respect their hosts and be open to cultural difference and difficulty. What exactly were our professional responsibilities here (moral and pedagogic)? How we responded could signal either acceptance or judgment—with implications for global citizenship learning.

Did the circumstances call for critique or curiosity? Shouldn't we let Lily and Jayne interpret their own experience, or should we offer guidance and judgment?

In the end, Adrienne and I did little. We visited their home the next day and had tea with Lily, Jayne, and their host. All seemed well; no one mentioned the man in the backyard. But for a long time afterward Adrienne and I wondered whether that had been the right thing to do. Should we have done more? (A variation of the Jayne and Lily story is recounted in a previous publication, Kornelsen, 2013c.)

Eight years later, as part of a PhD research project, I revisited the Costa Rica practicum experience with the student-participants. The caged man was the first thing both Lily and Jayne talked about; it was their most enduring memory. Here is Jayne:

> *Jayne:* I'll never forget (it). I'll never forget the image of the cell because the union of love and imprisonment were and still are difficult for me to understand.
> *Lloyd:* What sense did you make of it at the time? You still remember it.
> *Jayne:* Remembering how we had been prepared that we were supposed to be very open to the places that we were going, and the cultural differences. There was always a big emphasis put on, "this is a cultural ... you're going into a different culture." And I think Lily and I both didn't really know what to do with it. So we responded in as "OK, we understand," but being pretty confused as to wanting very much to talk to you or Adrienne because we didn't know ...
> *Lloyd:* Do you think we should have done more, Adrienne and I?
> *Jayne:* No. I think that would have made us feel like it was wrong. Like it wasn't really supposed to happen that way, but that would imply an expectation or preconceived notion of this experience and we weren't supposed to have any of those ...
> *Lloyd:* I remember at the time how it bothered you, not quite knowing what to do with it yourself.
> *Jayne:* Yeah, and now when I look back on it I don't think about that part of it. And I wonder whether if that's because I feel like it was treated like it was OK. Maybe it's not OK; maybe I'm wrong. Maybe I'm still terribly confused and I'm only realizing that now. But I guess, had you guys come in and said and tried to walk us through it I think that would have been different

because we kind of had to deal with ... So, I don't know, it was our experience.
(pp. 220–221, Kornelsen, 2013a)

Jayne's recollections demonstrate how an experience that disrupts one's understanding of the world and of one's sense of right or wrong may reverberate a lifetime. But her recollections did more. In addition to illustrating a conundrum at the heart of global citizenship (reconciling a universal sense of justice and a sympathetic imagination of the different), they also speak to a challenge at the center of Freire's critical pedagogy, and point to teachers' inescapable role and responsibility at its center. It is this:

According to critical theorists like Freire, student learning is rooted in independence and autonomy. A teacher's primary responsibility is to cultivate intersubjective, dialogical relationships with their students. Dialogical theory views students and teachers in a spirit of mutuality unveiling the world together. However, there are times when teachers are called on to intervene and prescribe, for the sake of balancing the capacity and challenge for those taught (Dewey, 1997). In short, in the interests of learning, teachers sometimes need to exercise power, unilaterally. The issue becomes: how should teachers navigate their professional concerns and responsibilities within intersubjective and dialogic relationships—between respecting freedom and autonomy, and intervening and prescribing. It is a challenge in most any teaching-learning situation—most dramatically illustrated in the Jane and Lily incident. Wherein lies the balance, how can one best know for what the situation calls? Recently, in a study that looked at qualities of exemplary adult educators, I found that master teachers seem to have an instinctive sensibility for knowing when to do what, and how. It comes from experience and education, but most significantly it is rooted in an abiding care for students and a deep respect for the course material, suggesting that teachers are at their discriminating best when they are mindfully present. In sum, cultivating and navigating intersubjective student-teacher relationships requires the judgment of a teacher who is heedful of his/her whole teaching self (Kornelsen, 2014a; Kornelsen, 2014b).

As the Jayne/Lily incident showed, this conundrum is a central concern for those teaching for democratic and global citizenship—for helping students reconcile the tension at the heart of global citizenship and coming to know their agency and name their worlds

(Appiah, 2008). Since this teaching sensibility is necessarily uniquely experienced, understanding its practice could be enhanced by inquiring of teachers their ways of cultivating dialogical relationships and navigating the transecting spaces of student autonomy and teacher responsibility (Kornelsen, 2014a).

In the past several years many of my social-studies teaching friends and colleagues—master teachers—have begun to retire, taking with them rich insight into educating youth for democratic and global citizenship—knowledge and wisdom that comes from years of seeking to engage students in meaningful conversations about their world, about political responsibilities, and shared obligations. Hannah Arendt (1968) called it unveiling work. It seems a waste, scores of teachers leaving the classroom—a lifetime of energy expended and exceptional understandings acquired—without sharing their educating acumen. Therefore, before they leave, I would like to talk to social-studies teachers—those teachers charged with educating for civic engagement—and ask them about their insights into being present and balancing listening and speaking; and investigate what their reflections reveal and their stories illumine (Kornelsen, 2014b).

What the Stories Mean to Scholarly Relevance

These three accounts and the embodied knowledge they represent—what do they and their revisiting mean? What have I learned from reconstructing these experiences, the past 20 months—about how I fit into the academy and about how experience in the field informs and enriches scholarly work? What are the implications for my current work?

First, these experiences help explain the worries, perspectives, and interests I bring to a faculty of education and account for my current research, teaching, and service motivations: The story of a newcomer Canadian showing how storytelling can be critical pedagogy, and in the end leading me to see how narrative inquiry is integral to researching teacher knowledge; an encounter with a standardized exam, revealing the moral implications of teaching and how critical pedagogy is a way of coherently and morally bridging the means and ends of education; and a conversation with a student in Costa Rica, showing how teachers are integral to enlightening a conundrum at the heart of global citizenship education. These experiences have had an indelible effect on how I understand education and the questions that frame my current work.

But questions remain and continue to trouble: What is unique about these insights and motivations derived from experience? How are they scholarly? Previous experience invariably informs, motivates, and explains current practice, but how does it contribute to a body of knowledge, exactly? After looking back at 28 years of practice, trying to make sense of several influential teaching events, this is what I believe it is: I have lived questions and issues that animate education, necessarily researching them day in and day out, over many years, struggling to teach well. Sometimes getting it right, sometimes not. Today, I have a knowing and understanding that, even though it is hard to articulate, is present in all I do. I feel it whenever I walk into a classroom, design a research questionnaire, or witness an argument at a committee meeting. This is what I consider embodied knowledge to be; and it can best be articulated and understood in practice—in continuing to live the questions. But I also believe that it offers a response, perspective, or insight that cannot come from anywhere else, and which is important to the practices, questions, and services explored in faculties of education, by teachers, researchers, and committee members.

Second, because I have been rewriting these stories while working in a faculty of education (receiving feedback from colleagues and reading related literature), I have been compelled to think about those experiences more critically, interpret them more objectively, and write about them more clearly than I otherwise might. In short, I have needed to engage with past experience through a scholarly lens. Consequently, I better know my teaching life and how it fits with the teaching, research, and service endeavours in the field of education. Indeed, without the scholarly sensibilities and direction of the academy, these stories might have had little value for education beyond anecdote or vignette, which suggests a crucial responsibility for the academy: providing the guidance and support to help people in the field articulate and critique the meaning of their experiences. In my case I have many scholars to thank, including Maxime Greene for shedding light on the pedagogy of storytelling, Connelly and Clandidinin for claiming narrative inquiry as a way of accessing teacher knowledge, Max Van Manen for exploring the morality of the teacher-student relationship, and Kwame Appiah for revealing a conundrum within global citizenship education.

Third, and most importantly, my experiences are only exemplars, representative of many others, and of other teachers'. Every teacher, by virtue of living their questions and researching their practice, possesses *embodied knowledge*. Revisiting my own experience—interrogating it for scholarly merit—has given me a better understanding of my defensive reaction to the academy's ambivalence regarding the value of practitioner experience. It has not so much to do with me, but with my former teaching colleagues (many of whom leave teaching by mid-life) and with how understanding and knowledge of education is undermined and diminished when experience in the field is discounted or marginalized. As critical theorists, Kincheloe, McLaren, and Steinberg (2011) point out:

> In the conservative educational order of mainstream schooling, knowledge is something that is produced far away from the school by experts in an exalted domain. This must change if critical reform of schooling is to exist. Teachers must have more voice and more respect in the culture of education. Teachers must join the culture of researchers if a new level of educational rigour and quality is ever to be achieved. (p. 165)

If so, what are the implications for me, an academic, a former practitioner now working far away in *an exalted domain*, someone who is searching for ways to articulate and demonstrate practitioners' scholarly relevance, almost two years into his appointment and thinking about promotion?

Implications for Promotion

In the fall of 2013, a colleague, from the University of Manitoba, and I, on behalf of the Manitoba Education Research Network, and with support from Manitoba School Improvement Program and Manitoba Education, started bi-monthly meetings with a select group of ten Grade 12 teachers from across the province to talk about the new social-studies course: Global Issues: Citizenship and Sustainability. The objective was to research the challenges of teaching and implementing this new course, the only inquiry-based course in the Manitoba K-12 social-studies curriculum. After the first meeting, it became apparent that the participants were as interested in simply meeting with their teaching colleagues and having open, free-wheeling discussions, sharing stories and anecdotes, from past and present, about teaching issues, challenges, and learnings. In the end, eight months later, participants agreed that the richest research findings were those that derived from group discussions, when the meeting agenda—crafted by the two university professors in the room—was loosened, and the group went where it needed to go. At the culminating public forum—attended by university professors, school administrators, and Manitoba Education consultants—where the teachers' shared their findings, the audience expressed enthusiastic approval and support for the scholarly value of this type of teacher-led discussion along with a story-based research component. Funding was granted for another year; the project was lauded in a national education publication (*Education Canada*, Spring 2015). However, several challenges have recently presented: Accessing funding for 2015–2016 (funding from government sources is diminishing due to changes in research priorities); finding ways to broaden the scope of the research group/s to involve more teachers and disciplines; continuing to ascertain the merit, scholarly and otherwise, of this type of teacher-led, experientially based research; negotiating what each, the academics and practitioners, can and need to offer the other; and seeking broader public engagement and support. Working with the program has demonstrated to a colleague (a former practitioner who also worries about *teachers joining the culture of researchers*) and me that we have a fitting responsibility in addressing these challenges—so that that teachers' lived experience can continue to be accessed, publicized, and valued.

Second, I think I have a responsibility to both field and academy to use my pursuit for promotion as a way of normalizing/equalizing their relationship. For, if people working in the field have lived the things about which faculties of education teach, do research, and offer service, then we in the academy need to find ways to include their scholarly sensibilities and honour their embodied experience— for teachers' sake and for the sake of the academy. Working in a faculty of education the past 18 months has helped me to understand why. The question for me now, is how: How might practitioners' sensibilities be included, their embodied knowledge honored; and what has it to do with me, now? Conceivably I can use my situation, as someone seeking scholarly recognition through promotion—in the face of his own doubts about whether he is scholarly enough—as an opportunity to navigate a "how"—to find a way of presenting his past experience as scholarly. One of the most important things I have learned so far is this: Just as teacher experience may offer indispensable knowledge and perspective to faculties of education, faculties of education can be vital and necessary in helping teachers articulate and know their experience. If so, as I get ready to apply for promotion I need to: (1) Read more. Sages, philosophers, and pedagogues have for a long time thought about those issues that have animated my teaching life, such as the meaning of stories, the nature of teacher-student relationships, or the practices of citizenship. What they have written helps extend, enlighten, nuance, and clarify the meaning of my teaching life. (2) Continue to re-search past experience for how it enlightens and extends what has been written. (3) Have confidence in the scholarly potential that rests in experience, and present it as such; but seek perspective, insight, and advice from colleagues in the academy on how to so do. In other words, continue to reconcile past and present, academy and field, Plato and Aristotle, and theory and practice. If I succeed, then this approach might be one answer to the question of how, posited above.

References

Appiah, K. A. (2008). Education for global citizenship. In D. L. Coulter & J. R. Weins (Eds.), *Why do we educate? Renewing the conversation* (pp. 83–99). Malden, MA: National Society for the Study of Education.

Arendt, H. (1958). *The human condition*. Chicago, IL: University of Chicago Press.

Arendt, H. (1968). *Between past and future*. New York, NY: Penguin Books.

Aulls, M. W., & Shore B. M. (2008). *Inquiry in education*. vol. 1. New York, NY: Routledge.

Buber, M. (2006). *Between man and man*. (R. G. Smith, Trans.). London, UK: Kegan Paul.

Connelly, F. M., & Clandinin, D. J. (1988). *Teachers as curriculum planners: Narratives of experience*. New York, NY: Teachers College Press.

Dewey, J. (1997). *Experience and education*. New York, NY: Simon and Schuster.

Freire, P. (1970). *Pedagogy of the oppressed*. New York, NY: Herder and Herder.

Freire, P. (2007). *Pedagogy of the oppressed* (30th anniversary edition). New York, NY: Continuum.

Greene, M. (1996). Plurality, diversity and the public space. In A. Oldenquis (Ed.), *Can democracy be taught?* (pp. 27–44). Bloomington, IN: Phi Delta Kappa Educational Foundation.

Greene, M. (1995). *Releasing the imagination: Essays on education, the arts and social change*. San Francisco, CA: Jossey-Bass.

Huber, J., Caine, V., Huber, M., & Steeves, P. (2013). Narrative inquiry as pedagogy in education: The extraordinary potential of living, telling, retelling, and reliving stories of experience. *Review of Research in Education, 37*(1), 212–242.

Hunter, H. (2015). The Manitoba Education Research Network: Teacher research to enhance engagement and equity in education. *Education Canada, 55*(1). 49–51.

Jarvis, P. (1995). Teachers and learners in adult education: Transaction or moral interaction? *Studies in the Education of Adults, 27*(1), 24–35.

Kincheloe, J. L., McLaren, P., & Steinberg, S. R. (2011). Critical pedagogy and qualitative research. In N. K. Denzen & Y. S. Lincoln (Eds.), *The Sage handbook of qualitative research* (pp. 163–177). Thousand Oaks, CA: Sage.

Kornelsen, L. (2006). Teaching with presence. In P. Cranton (Ed.), *Authenticity in teaching* (pp. 73–82). San Francisco, CA: Jossey-Bass.

Kornelsen, L. (2013a). "Remembering Costa Rica 2003: Exploring the influence of a high school global citizenship practicum through the memories, meanings, and lives of its participants eight years later" (unpublished doctoral dissertation). University of Manitoba, Winnipeg, MB.

Kornelsen, L. (2013b). The role of storytelling at the intersection of transformative conflict resolutions and peace education. *Storytelling, Self, Society: An Interdisciplinary Journal of Storytelling Studies, 9*(2), 237–260.

Kornelsen, L. (2013c). Educating for global citizenship: An elusive quest, *The Manitoba Education Research Network [MERN] Journal, 6*, 27–32.

Kornelsen, L. (2014a). *Stories of transformation: Memories of a global citizenship practicum*. Ulm, Germany: The International Center for Innovation in Education.

Kornelsen, L. (2014b). "The grade 12 inquiry project: A facilitator's impressions." *Manitoba Education Research Network [MERN] Journal, 9*, 37–42.

Mezirow, J. (1995). Transformative theory of adult learning. In M. R. Welton (Ed), *Defence of the lifeworld* (pp. 39–70). New York, NY: Sunny Press.

Saltmarsh, J. (1996). Education for critical citizenship: John Dewey's contribution to the pedagogy of community service learning. *Michigan Journal of Community Service Learning, 3*(1), 13–21.

Van Manen, M. (2000). Moral language and pedagogical experience. *Journal of Curriculum Studies, 32*(2), 315–327.

Vercoe, A. (1998). The student-teacher relationship in Freire's pedagogy: The art of giving and receiving. *New Zealand Journal of Adult Learning, 26*(1), 56–73.

Walck, C. L. (1997). A teaching life. *Journal of Management Education, 21*(4), 473–482.

CHAPTER 12

Transitioning to the Academic Tenure-Track at Mid-Career: Exploring Adaptive and Maladaptive Responses to Challenges and Adversity

Peter Milley
Faculty of Education, University of Ottawa

From outside the academy, the job of a professor looks rewarding and privileged. Few other occupations offer similar levels of autonomy, incentives for deep inquiry, occasions for interacting with people who are deeply committed to their work, and opportunities for facilitating the growth of others. With this image in mind, I could not believe my good fortune, when, in the winter of 2013, I was offered (at mid-career) a position as assistant professor of organizational studies in the Faculty of Education at the University of Ottawa.

My contract started in July 2013, but I arranged to be on campus several weeks beforehand. I arrived under the blue sky of an early summer morning and strolled across campus with a sense of accomplishment. Being there represented the attainment of a goal that had simmered for more than a decade while I pursued an alternative career in executive leadership development and policy research in the Canadian federal public service. The campus was calm and quiet. Administrative personnel in the faculty were happy to see me and eager to help. When I opened the door to my office for the first time, a faculty-branded satchel and coffee mug, new laptop computer, and big window with a view of the campus greeted me. These details created an immediate sense of belonging after having lived through the deterioration of working conditions in the public service over the preceding years (Public Service Alliance of Canada,

2015), and reaffirmed the appropriateness of resigning from a permanent government job to become an academic.

The first several weeks were idyllic. I became acquainted with colleagues who were on campus at that time of year, including one who had kindly agreed to be a mentor. I created a work plan, familiarized myself with various systems, hired a graduate student, and began drafting a funding proposal. I designed my first course and learned how to program the on-line platform to support its delivery. In August, I met with a senior colleague with whom I would be team-teaching in the undergraduate teacher-education program, a helpful arrangement that was part of my induction to the faculty, as I came with a background that did not include primary and secondary (i.e., K-12) education. Around this time, two colleagues kindly invited me into their projects—a research-grant proposal and a funding application to develop a massive open online course (MOOC). It felt like progress was being made.

As August drew to a close, students suddenly started filling the hallways, last-minute program-planning meetings took place, and reality set in. The year was beginning in earnest. Teaching materials needed to be finalized, deadlines loomed, and colleagues started asking about my progress and offering advice about making tenure. I started feeling seriously anxious. Some of this consisted of the familiar nervousness that would support good performance. But it was also tinged with a murky sense of dread. I began questioning the priorities I had pursued over the summer. Only eight weeks had passed and I felt weeks behind. Similar to novice faculty in other settings (Hellsten, Martin, McIntyre, & Kinzel, 2011), my idealistic sentiments about academic life started to recede. I would soon come to learn that setting a course for tenure at mid-life and mid-career was going to be a voyage more turbulent than anticipated. As others had observed (Hellsten, Martin, & McIntyre, 2010), it would be a test of resilience.

Research Goals and Methodology

This chapter presents a personal narrative about challenges that have arisen in a transition at mid-life and mid-career to the tenure-track, along with their destabilizing influences. Using concepts about resilience drawn from ecology (Holling, 2001) and developmental psychology (Masten & O'Dougherty Wright, 2010), I provide an assessment of my responses in terms of whether they have supported or thwarted a functional, healthy transition. It is hoped this narrative will help readers with an "experience of the uncertainty that the [writer] is experiencing" (Sibbald & Handford, 2014) in the first 18 months of a transition and that the supporting analysis will provide insights about gauging the adaptive potential of responses to adversity on the tenure-track. Following the spirit of auto-ethnography, the chapter seeks to communicate personal experience as a means of deepening understanding of the broader cultural experience (Ellis & Bochner, 2000) of becoming an academic through the ritual of the tenure process. Data sources consisted of my planning records, artifacts (e.g., draft and final course syllabi, instructional and assessment materials, research proposals, manuscripts), personal correspondence (my side of the exchanges only), and records from a self-interview conducted for the creation of this chapter. This interview was conducted 16 months into the tenure-track journey, based on three questions: What have you been doing and experiencing in the transition, especially with respect to tenure? What are your successes and challenges, and how are these related to your sense of well-being? What responses seem to alleviate or exacerbate problems?

On Resilience: Theoretical Concepts from Ecology and Psychology

As foreshadowed above and detailed in what follows, I have experienced some struggles during my first 18 months on the tenure-track. Dynamics in the organizational context and my inner lifeworld have surprised me—not always in positive ways. More frequently than desired, I have felt unwell, a response that seems to be common for novice faculty (Hellsten et al., 2011). I thus decided to apply concepts about resilience to portray my experiences, with a view to identifying strategies for a healthier journey that may resonate with others in similar circumstances.

The study of resilience includes work in ecology and developmental psychology. An ecological perspective emphasizes how complex adaptive systems absorb disturbances and reorganize in light of them while continuing to retain essentially the same function and identity (Holling & Gunderson, 2002; Walker, Holling, Carpenter, & Kinzig, 2004). Similarly, a developmental-psychology perspective on resilience focuses on the "processes or patterns of positive adaptation" in the context of adversity (Masten & O'Dougherty Wright, 2010, p. 215). In these two perspectives there is also a concern about what happens when there is a lack of resilience. In the case of ecology, the focus is on the amount of disturbance a system can endure before it reaches a threshold and flips to a different state of affairs, such that it no longer retains its original functions or identity (Holling & Gunderson, 2002). In the case of psychology, the lack or absence of resilience is associated with a decline in adaptive functioning (Masten & Obradovic, 2008).

I draw on two specific research-based models of resilience: The adaptive cycle from Holling's (2001) and Holling and Gunderson's (2002) ecological theory, and Masten's (2001) concept of "protective systems" (p. 235). These models are complementary, with the former emphasizing how resilience is affected by cycles of change precipitated by disturbances, and the latter focusing on the psychological and social conditions that promote resilience in light of disturbances.

The Adaptive Cycle

The adaptive cycle provides a heuristic model for analyzing adaptive and maladaptive dynamics associated with change, including in social contexts and with respect to individuals (Patton, 2011; Walker et al., 2004). Figure 1 represents the adaptive cycle as consisting of four phases of change in an infinity loop. The phases include

Figure 1. The adaptive cycle. Moving through its phases and the potential maladaptive traps along the way.

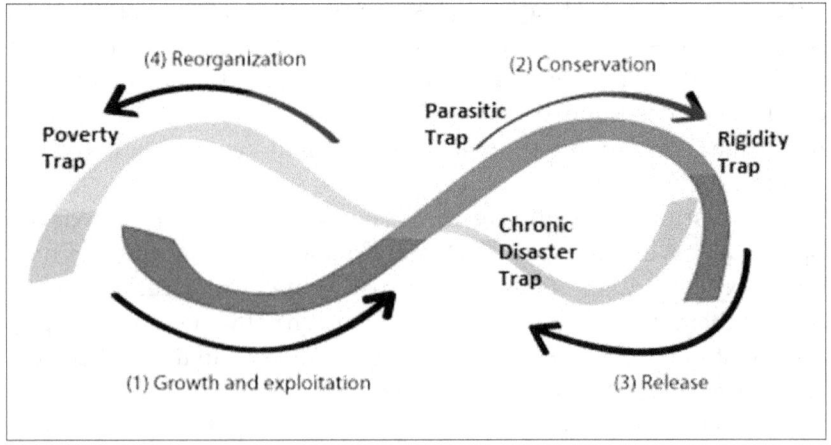

(1) growth and exploitation, (2) conservation, (3) release, and (4) reorganization. The transition from (1) to (2) consists of a relatively slow, incremental process of growth and accumulation of "capital" (e.g., the consolidation of intellectual, social, and reputational capital over the course of a career) (Holling & Gunderson, 2002, p. 35). The transition from (2) to (4) usually begins with a disturbance (e.g., an abrupt career change), creating the need for rapid response and change.

The cycle highlights two complementary modes: growth and stability (i.e., phases 1 and 2), and flux and change (i.e., phases 3 and 4). If someone lacks anticipative capacities (e.g., foresight, access to information, planning) or adaptive capacities (e.g., learning and innovation capabilities, support networks), the transition from (2) to (4) may not result in renewal. Instead, that person may experience a regime shift (e.g., a decline in health status), the outcome of which is unpredictable. There are four types of traps that can make any journey through a cycle of change dysfunctional or maladaptive:

a) Rigidity traps can develop during the conservation phase (phase 2) if too much emphasis is placed on control and stability (i.e., doing the same old things), which can smother inventiveness and initiative (Holling, 2001);
b) Chronic disasters can arise during the release phase (phase 3) if too much emphasis is placed on short-term crisis management without a sense of overall direction (Patton, 2011);
c) Poverty traps can appear during the reorganization phase (phase 4) if diversity (e.g., in ideas, skills and networks) has been diminished (Holling, 2001)—without access to diverse resources, one's capacity to generate novel insights and options to support renewal is reduced (Denhardt & Denhardt, 2010);
d) Parasitic traps can emerge during the growth and conservation phases (phases 1 and 2) that eat away at the capital accumulated through a cycle of renewal in such a way that it reduces the capacity to deal with other pressures for change (Patton, 2011).

Multiple adaptive cycles exist simultaneously in different aspects of one's experience (e.g., adapting to research, teaching and service roles). These cycles operate at small scales (e.g., teaching a new course) and large scales (e.g., transitioning to a new institutional context or career). The journey through each cycle takes place at a different rate (e.g., quickly adapting to teaching a new course, more slowing adapting to academic culture). Each cycle is interlinked such that cycles at smaller scales provide inputs (e.g., innovations, lessons learned) to support change in cycles at larger scales. Cycles at larger scales tend to move more slowly and, ideally, have a stabilizing influence on conditions at smaller scales; however, adaptive problems arising at larger scales create cascading effects that can disrupt and destabilize adaptive functioning at smaller scales (Holling, 2001).

Developmental Theories of Resilience From Psychology

From the perspective of developmental psychology, resilience is not a personality trait, as evidenced by the fact that individuals may show maladaptive functioning at one time and then prove resilient later on, or vice versa. Masten (2001) has identified some protective systems that encompass individual capabilities, social supports, and safeguards of resilience rooted in communities and cultural systems. These include

a) close relationships that provide for emotional security, cognitive growth, and positive socialization;
b) intelligence—i.e., "a human brain in 'good working order' and access to knowledge about what is happening, what to expect and what to do";
c) motivational systems that promote agency and mastery and through which people develop a sense of competence and self-efficacy;
d) self-regulation skills that allow for the control over attention, impulses, emotion, stress reactivity, behaviour, and action in the definition and pursuit of goals; and
e) meaning-making processes that allow for faith, hope, and optimism, and the realistic appraisal of events, experiences, and future possibilities (Masten & O'Dougherty Wright, pp. 225–228).

Individual resilience can be promoted by restoring or mobilizing these protective systems (Masten, 2001).

Personal Narrative

Research shows different groups of novice faculty experience the journey towards tenure differently, with some confronting practices that discriminate against them (Hellsten et al., 2011; Mason, Wolfinger, & Goulden, 2013). As a white male of middle-class origins who, by mid-life, has had significant opportunities to develop professional and cultural capital, my tenure journey started from a position of privilege (McIntosh, 2012). It would be disingenuous, however, not to admit that the first 18 months of my odyssey have been destabilizing. The tenure process, which generally takes place over four to six years, is about attaining a permanent post and gaining the recognition of colleagues, peers, and the institution. With the basic needs of security and acceptance at stake (for the first time in many years, at least professionally), my move from a permanent job with performance goals negotiated on an annual basis to an initial three-year contract with renewal based on "established but vague standards" (Hellsten et al., 2011, p. 271), along with the shift in my identity from a competent senior public servant to junior academic, has generated an unexpected amount of emotional turmoil. Other novice faculty making a transition from another career have reported similar struggles (e.g. Aitken, 2010). The process of leaving behind longstanding working relationships and trying to form meaningful new ones has precipitated a sense of loss and isolation—feelings also reported by other new professors (Hellsten et al., 2011).

Various learning curves related to my new role have also posed challenges, the most surprising of which has been on the research front. An immediate sign of difficulty appeared when I had to communicate my background with the government in the curriculum vitae format mandated by the Ontario Council of Graduate Schools (Faculty of Graduate and Postdoctoral Studies, University of Ottawa, 2015). This template featured categories and requirements entirely (and appropriately) geared to an academic career; but I found myself, for example, unable to list technical papers and publications I had written because policies in government had prohibited named authorship. This issue turned out to be the tip of an iceberg, as the methods, vocabulary, and rhetorical strategies I used to succeed in government did not transfer as readily as expected. As pointed out to me during my first year, I needed to talk and write less like a public servant and more like a scholar. This problem with transferring my capital stemmed, in part, from the peripheral nature of the relationship I established with academic culture by working full time outside the university while completing my doctoral program in educational administration (1999 to 2005). I was not just rusty at scholarly discourse; I was also a virtual stranger to the culture.

In the decade that had passed since completing my doctorate and being disconnected from university life, a number of changes happened to universities that made working in them somewhat daunting for experienced and novice faculty alike. They grew in scale and came under resource pressures (Association of Universities and Colleges of Canada, 2011). From 2001 to 2011 in Ontario, for example, there was a reported increase of 50% in the number of degrees granted. In the same period, operating revenues only increased by 10% and student-to-faculty ratios became the highest in Canada (Ontario Council of Academic Vice Presidents, 2014, p. 3). Universities also adopted more business-like practices (Giroux, 2014), with reputation becoming an important concern in light of international competition and attention paid to rankings (e.g., QS Top Universities, 2014; Times Higher Education, 2015). Similar to other professions, the professoriate was subjected to an intensification of workload and performance measurement (Archer, 2008; Hibbert et al., 2010; Pente & Adams, 2010) to increase productivity, outcomes, and impacts.

The University of Ottawa reflects these broader trends. From 2003 to 2013, aggregate student enrollments increased by 51% (67% at the graduate level) (Chamberlain, 2013). In the Faculty of Education, from 2005 to 2012, enrollments increased 24% (43% at the graduate level). The university is considered a research-intensive institution (Maclean's, 2013) with aspirations to be among the top five in Canada (University of Ottawa, 2015a). It also emphasizes the quality of teaching and learning, promising "stimulating programs provided by professors who excel at teaching and research" (University of Ottawa, 2015a, p. 3). Its strategic plan aims to bring student-to-faculty ratios down by 2020 (University of Ottawa, 2015b), perhaps to offset the fact that hiring of full-time professors from 2003–2013 lagged enrollment growth by 9% (Chamberlain, 2013). The Faculty of Education's strategic plan (2015) resonates with these priorities. In light of its core focus, education, there is a strong commitment to teaching and the importance of research productivity and developing reputational capital are palpable features of the culture (e.g., the strategic plan targets the mobilization of professors' research expertise to enhance the organization's profile).

Similar to experiences reported by novice faculty members in other universities (Brown & Sherry, 2010; Hill, 2004; Hirschkorn, 2010), my responses to pre-tenure challenges emerging from the fast-paced, results-oriented context of higher education (Pente & Adams, 2010), where globalized processes of economic restructuring and competition shape local practice (Hibbert et al., 2010), have frequently left me feeling overworked, stressed, and vulnerable. There have, of course, been rewarding moments. It is a privilege to serve, and I am appreciative of the support of the university, faculty, mentors, colleagues, and students. In mid-fall 2014 when our dean circulated the call for chapters for this book, I had been experiencing recurrent bouts of insomnia and pessimism. My pre-tenure plans and responses required scrutiny. The proposed book would provide a catalyst for reflection on how to forge a healthier adaptation process.

Adaptive Responses and Potential Maladaptive Traps

In this section, the adaptive cycle model is used as a lens to analyze my progress. My overall transition plan was to make progress on the three main roles of teaching, research, and service, while placing emphasis in year one on teaching, in year two on ramping up research, and in year three on deepening service commitments. This pattern is reflected in a recent survey of Ontario professors, which shows junior faculty doing more teaching and senior faculty doing more research (Ontario Association of Academic Vice Presidents, 2014); it was also recommended to me by a number of colleagues.

Adaptation to the teaching role
The transition to this role has gone relatively smoothly, with my experience in delivering executive leadership development programs in government and being a sessional lecturer during my doctoral studies both providing a transferable foundation. There have been three significant challenges:

   a) moving into an instructional role in a provincially accredited teacher-education program without having a background in primary or secondary (K-12) education;

b) managing the performance contradictions between *what* we teach to budding teachers and *how* we teach them in light of institutional constraints (e.g., trying to model assessment policies prescribed for schools, such as criterion referenced assessment, in an environment that still has a strong preference for norm-referenced evaluation); and

c) adjusting to class sizes (e.g., 35 students in my first graduate-level course, nearly double what I had experienced a decade earlier), the volume of assessment (e.g., 792 assignments to evaluate in the first semester) and the micro-politics arising from the pronounced "grade economy" (Wells, 2013, p. 62) in higher education.

To deal with the first problem, I conducted background research, sought advice from colleagues and friends who are, or have been, schoolteachers, and gathered formative feedback from students. To cope with the second and third issues, I invested heavily in design and preparation. I also provided descriptive feedback in evaluations, set clearer priorities, established expectations early on, and designed tools for making communication and feedback processes more transparent and efficient.

Now having taught nine sections of five new courses, each time making incremental gains by learning through experimentation, I consider my transition into the teaching role as moving into a conservation phase of an adaptive cycle. Patterns in my approach suggest there are two maladaptive traps I need to avoid in the future. First, in building confidence to teach in new areas I have a tendency to try to incorporate and master too much material. Ironically, this can lead to a sense of chronic disaster in terms of confidence (i.e., awareness that I have a broad but superficial understanding). Second, I gravitate to the teaching role because of the success and sense of meaning I find in it. This pattern risks leading me into a parasitic trap in which it eats away at other important parts of the job. As I was reminded at one point, the teaching role is only 40% of the work, and it is imperative to fit the task to the time. To address this challenge, one strategy frequently applied in education is to use teaching as a site inquiry to support the research role. I intend on pursuing this approach.

Adaptation to the research role

The transition to this crucial role has proved difficult. Arriving from a government setting largely unrelated to education (in terms of the disciplinary emphasis towards the K-12 system) and with an untapped doctoral dissertation that was almost a decade old, I was essentially starting from scratch on a research agenda. In terms of creating a research track record, I have pursued a strategy of multiple strategies:

a) harvesting parts of my doctoral dissertation that do not have a best-before date;
b) undertaking projects with mentors and colleagues;
c) drawing my expertise from government;
d) giving conference papers to force the production of research;
e) selectively responding to calls for manuscripts; and
f) launching a pilot project to generate a longer-term research program.

Some of these strategies yielded publications, others have created a small hopper of projects with potential, and some are on hold. In one case, a hard lesson was learned in spending an inordinate amount of time on a manuscript only to have it rejected for publication. Although this is considered a normal part of the process, it threw me into a tailspin because of the lost effort. Subsequent lessons from a writing course offered by the Center for Academic Leadership at the university has now provided strategies for reducing the likelihood of such rejections, including early scoping of project viability.

This pattern of research activity suggests I am in the early stages of the reorganization phase of an adaptive cycle related to the role. There appear to be two maladaptive traps that potentially lie ahead. In generating too many one-off research and publication opportunities I may fall into a state of chronic disaster in which there are too many projects, too little time available for each, and a lack of long-term direction. There is also a risk of falling into a poverty trap, not for a loss of diversity of ideas but for the inability to exploit them to create coherent, viable, longer-term programs of research along with the associated funding and networks.

Adaptation to service role

The plan was to ease incrementally into this role, and contributions so far include, for example, serving as an academic advisor for graduate programs and a member of the faculty council. This pattern of activity suggests I am still in the early stages of a release phase of an adaptive cycle and am conserving skills from my background in administration and policy that could be exploited more fully. It is worth considering whether my adherence to a fixed roll-out plan, for this aspect of the job, represents a rigidity trap. It is also worth pondering whether the relationships and networks that could be established by taking on a more robust service role could improve my adaptive processes in the research and teaching roles.

Overall adaptation to the tenure-track

Figure 2 illustrates the relationships between the adaptive cycles related to my teaching, research, and service roles, and the overall cycle of my adaptation to the tenure-track. The dynamics indicate I am still largely reorganizing in terms of this career transition and should expect (and embrace) further flux and change while taking action to avoid the maladaptive traps that lie ahead. Any real sense of certainty and stability is still a ways off.

Figure 2. My current state of overall adaptation to the tenure-track.

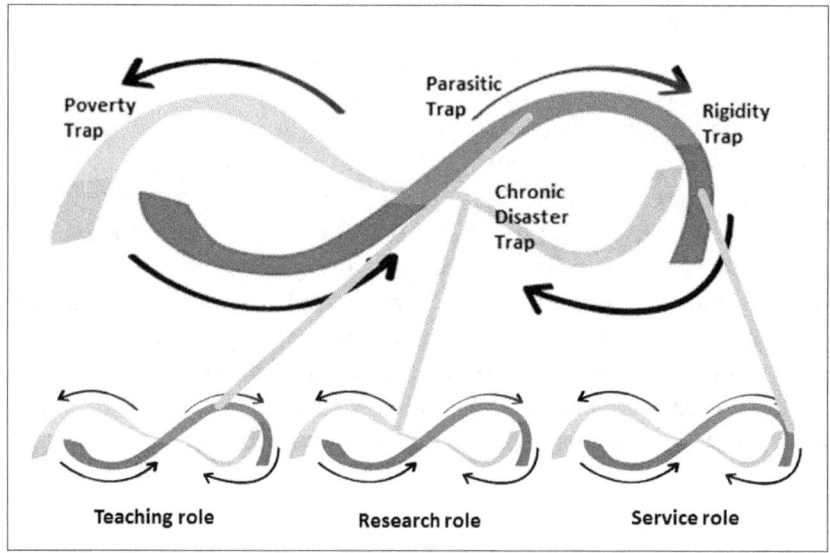

"Protective Systems" and the Tenure-Track Experience

In this section, I focus on the status of various protective systems in and around me and how they might be strengthened. I also draw on findings, from positive psychology, which suggest resilience is promoted by focusing on positive goals, resources, emotions, influences, and outcomes (Masten & O'Dougherty Wright, 2010).

Close relationships
Similar to the experiences of other novice faculty (e.g., Kawalilak & Groen, 2010), having ties with formal and informal mentors and a small circle of colleagues has provided indispensable support to my cognitive growth (e.g., through research collaborations) and professional socialization (e.g., by opening up professional networks). I am appreciative of their generosity. In a results-oriented culture, it can be a challenge to establish emotional connections and to find sources of emotional support. Letting colleagues see negative emotions led to feelings of guilt (for burdening them), remorse (for displaying weakness) and fear (the word will get out that I am not coping). Beatty (2007) would call this internalization of expectations of judgment and censure a form of "emotional absolutism" (p. 334) that culturally conditions right and wrong feelings. I could foster a more "resilient emotional reality" (ibid.) by focusing on relationships that promote the emergence of authentically positive emotions and provide safe venues for talking through negative feelings.

Intelligence
Generally, this protective system seems to be in reasonable condition, although in moments of potential chronic disaster, such as an intense period of self-doubt and insomnia that I experienced at the start of my second year of teaching and that lasted for nearly two months, I have experienced temporary issues with executive functioning skills such as "deciding what to do with longer-term objectives in mind" (Masten & O'Dougherty Wright, 2010, p. 225) (e.g., impulsively thinking about quitting) and regulating negative emotions (e.g., prefacing advice-seeking questions to colleagues with the phrase "I am struggling") and self-talk. Part of this dynamic is related to the process of figuring out how things work and what to expect, suggesting this protective system could be strengthened by gathering more information about standards and processes related

to tenure to provide a reality check and help set priorities. Over the past year, I explored this terrain by reading relevant sections in the collective agreement that governs the employment relationship between faculty members and the university, attending a workshop offered by the Association of Professors of the University of Ottawa, and asking recently tenured colleagues about their experiences. These efforts yielded some general direction and an assortment of stories, but did not provide a satisfactory sense of clarity. Although it will be worthwhile to continue seeking more comprehensive and concrete guidance, it will also be important to recognize that the process may be inherently vague (Baugher, 2015; Hellsten et al., 2011) and to approach it as a probabilistic as well as standards-based exercise.

Motivational systems

The institution promotes agency by providing significant autonomy and control to professors over the content and form of our work. It also promotes mastery in that faculty are encouraged to "excel at teaching and research" (University of Ottawa, 2015a). I have found engaging with these motivational systems works best when approached with a positive mindset and emotional state. A negative outlook dredges up the worst emotion—fear (of failure)—that can contribute to a sense of paralysis instead of agency and ineffectiveness instead of mastery. This protective system could be reinforced by recognizing and celebrating incremental gains and positive outcomes. It could also benefit from identifying and working in specific contexts that promote a positive outlook, efficacy and affirmation, such as constructive research collaborations.

Self-regulation. Being goal directed and exercising self-discipline are crucial dispositions, given the high level of expectations and degree of autonomy associated with the professorial role. The main challenge has been to pursue priorities while being pulled in many directions, especially during semesters of teaching. It has also been a test to remain focused on positive goals (what to do) instead of negative ones (what to stop doing as a result of critical lessons learned). Stress management has also been an area of concern. As a protective system for resilience, my self-regulation could be buttressed by continuing to improve basic planning and management systems, upholding boundaries with students (e.g., having clearly defined windows of time and channels for communication), and not letting work get in the way of effective stress reducers such as physical exercise.

Meaning making. Optimism, and the belief that life (and work) has meaning, helps people weather adversity. By middle age, hardships and disappointments over the course of one's life can erode these protections. The cognitive restructuring involved in re-establishing faith, hope and meaning "requires considerable capacity for reflection" (Masten & O'Dougherty Wright, 2010, p. 228). Regarding their journey towards tenure, Pente and Adams (2010) observe how finding time to take "slow breaths" (i.e., to reflect) helped to "shift the instrumental demands of productivity" (p. 117) and (re)create meaning. This approach, along with maintaining sources of meaning (family, friends, outside interests) that bring coherence and balance to life, could strengthen my resilience. The risk is to focus so much on making tenure that connections become severed with the people and experiences that matter most in the long run, a pattern that is common in academia (Mason, Wolfinger, & Goulden, 2013).

Concluding Thoughts: (Re)Establishing a Resilient Pathway to Tenure?

Resilience manifests over time and tends to follow one of four pathways: Resistance (reasonably steady, positive adaptation), recovery (an initial decline in adaptive function followed by a return to a positive level), normalization (starting in a bad spot but with changes in conditions accelerating towards normal functioning), and transformation (functioning improves after adversity) (Masten & O'Dougherty Wright, 2010). Based on the foregoing narrative and analysis, my transition to the tenure-track appears to be following a recovery pattern with respect to resilience. From a phenomenological perspective my adaptive functioning declined through the first year of the tenure-track; but it appears to be rebounding, as evidenced by successful passage through several adaptive cycles at small scales. Time will tell what type of pathway consolidates as I go through the reorganizing phase of my overall transition. Perhaps it will be transformational, which was my aspiration at the outset of the tenure process. I suspect other new professors in education share similar hopes for their own journeys; after all, the desire for positive growth and transformation is at the heart of the educational endeavour. Through the process of researching and writing this chapter, personal insights of therapeutic and strategic value have emerged, contributing to an improved sense of self-efficacy and optimism. I hope some of what has been conveyed will be of similar value to those who find themselves in parallel circumstances.

References

Aitken, A. (2010). Becoming an academic: Professional identity on the road to tenure. *Journal of Educational Thought, 44*(1), 55–68.

Archer, L. (2008). Younger academics' constructions of "authenticity," "success," and professional identity. *Studies in Higher Education, 33*(4), 385–403.

Association of Universities and Colleges of Canada. (2011). Trends in higher education. Retrieved from http://www.aucc.ca.

Baugher, J. F. (2015). Thoughts on academic tenure [web log comment, February 15]. Retrieved from http://www.joebaugher.com/Tenure.htm.

Beatty, B. (2007). Going through the emotions: Leadership that gets at the heart of school renewal. *Australian Journal of Education, 51*(3): 328–340.

Brown, W. I., & Sherry, J. G. (2010). When the tenure road is rocky: Toward integrated selves and institutions. *Journal of Educational Thought, 44*(1), 147–161.

Chamberlain, T. (2013). Primer on workloads at the University of Ottawa. Retrieved from http://www.apuo.ca/collective-agreement/workload.

Denhardt, J., & Denhardt, R. (2010). Building organizational resilience and adaptive management. In J. W. Reich, A. J. Zautra, & J. S. Hall (Eds.), *Handbook of adult resilience* (pp. 333–349). New York, NY: Guildford Press.

Ellis, C., & Bochner, A. P. (2000). Autoethnography, personal narrative, reflexivity. In N. K. Denzin & Y. S. Lincoln (Eds.), *Handbook of qualitative research* (2nd ed.) (pp. 733–768). Thousand Oaks, CA: Sage.

Faculty of Education, University of Ottawa (2015). Strategic plan: Vision 2015. Retrieved from http://education.uottawa.ca/en/about/governance/strategic-plan.

Faculty of Graduate and Postdoctoral Studies, University of Ottawa. (2015). Membership in the Faculty of Graduate Studies. Retrieved from http://www.grad.uottawa.ca/Default.aspx?tabid=1883.

Giroux, H. (2014). *Neoliberalism's war on higher education*. Chicago, IL: Haymarket.

Hellsten, L. M., Martin, S., & McIntyre, L. J. (2010). Navigating the potholes and speed bumps: Three female perspectives on tenure and promotion. *Journal of Educational Thought, 44*(1), 99–115.

Hellsten, L. M., Martin, S. L., McIntyre, L. J., & Kinzel, A. L. (2011). Women on the academic tenure track: An autoethnographic inquiry. *International Journal for Cross-Disciplinary Subjects in Education, 2*(1), 271–275.

Hibbert, K. M., Stooke, R., Pollock, K., Namukasa, I., Faez, F., & O'Sullivan, J. (2010). The "Ten-Year Road:" Joys and challenges on the road to tenure. *Journal of Educational Thought, 44*(1), 69–83.

Hill, N. R. (2004). The challenges experienced by untenured faculty members in counsellor education: A wellness perspective. *Counsellor Education and Supervision, 44*, 135–146.

Hirschkorn, M. (2010). How vulnerable am I? An experiential discussion of tenure rhetoric for new faculty. *Journal of Educational Thought, 44*(1), 41–54.

Holling, C. S. (2001). Understanding the complexity of economic, ecological, and social systems. *Ecosystems, 4*(5): 390–405.

Holling, C. S., & Gunderson, L. H. (2002). Resilience and adaptive cycles. In L. H. Gunderson & C. S. Holling (Eds.), *Panarchy: Understanding transformations in human and natural systems* (pp. 25–62). Washington, DC: Island Press.

Kawalilak, C., & Groen, J. (2010). Illuminating the tenure-track pathway: A "new" faculty perspective. *Journal of Educational Thought, 44*(1), 131–146.

Maclean's. (2013). 2013 university rankings. Retrieved from http://www.macleans.ca/tag/2013-university-rankings/.

Mason, M. A., Wolfinger, N. H., & Goulden, M. (2013). *Do babies matter? Gender and family in the ivory tower.* New Brunswick, NJ: Rutgers Press.

Masten, A. S. (2001). Ordinary magic: Resilience processes in development. *American Psychologist, 56*(3), 227–238.

Masten, A. S., & Obradovic, J. (2008). Disaster preparation and recovery: Lessons from research on resilience in human development. *Ecology and Society, 13*(1). Retrieved from http://www.ecologyandsociety.org/vol13/iss1/art3/.

Masten, A. S., & O'Dougherty Wright, M. (2010). Resilience over the lifespan: Developmental perspectives on resistance, recovery, and transformation. In J. W. Reich, A. J. Zautra, & J. S. Hall (Eds.), *Handbook of adult resilience* (pp. 213–237). New York, NY: The Guildford Press.

McIntosh, P. (2012). Reflections and future directions for privilege studies. *Journal of Social Issues, 68*(1), 194–206.

Ontario Council of Academic Vice Presidents. (2014). Faculty at work: A preliminary report on faculty work at Ontario universities 2010–2012. Retrieved from http://cou.on.ca/publications/reports.

Patton, M. Q. (2011). *Developmental evaluation: Applying complexity concepts to enhance innovation and use.* New York, London: Guildford Press.

Pente, P., & Adams, C. (2010). The slow breath to tenure: Unwinding the university. *Journal of Educational Thought, 44*(1), 117–129.

Public Service Alliance of Canada. (2015). Government employee survey shows harassment, impact of job cuts. Retrieved from http://psacunion.ca/government-employee-survey-shows-harassment-impact.

QS Top Universities. (2014). QS World University Rankings. Retrieved from: http://www.topuniversities.com/university-rankings.

Sibbald, T., & Handford, V. (2014). Call for chapter proposals: The first years of tenure track in education.

Times Higher Education. (2015). The world university rankings. Retrieved from http://www.timeshighereducation.co.uk/world-university-rankings/.

University of Ottawa. (2015a). Destination 2020: The University of Ottawa's Strategic Plan. Retrieved from http://www.uottawa.ca/about/vision.

University of Ottawa. (2015b). Destination 2020 scorecard. Retrieved from http://www.uottawa.ca/about/vision.

Walker, B., Holling, C. S., Carpenter, S. R., & Kinzig, A. (2004). Resilience, adaptability and transformability in social–ecological systems. *Ecology and Society, 9*(2): 5. Retrieved from http://www.ecologyandsociety.org/vol9/iss2/art5/.

Wells, G. (2013). Taking responsibility for learning: CHAT in a large undergraduate class. In G. Wells & A. Edwards (Eds.), *Pedagogy in higher education* (pp. 60–72). New York, NY: Cambridge University Press.

SECTION IV

EDITORS' PREFACE

Early Tenure-Track

The early years of tenure-track are a phase where prior experiences are fresh and still inform approaches to the new role and circumstances; it is common to rely on formerly effective strategies for sorting out what will work in the new situation. In view of this, it may not be surprising when one finds connections to experiences that led to tenure-track. Terminologies that are common usage among educational practitioners but uncommon among academics arise more frequently in this section. This reflects the recent-practitioner voice that is becoming an academic voice. While practitioners and academics may share similar experiences, such as teaching in their respective environments, the expressions used and reference points may be slightly different.

The variety of backgrounds that lead into tenure-track roles is the precursor to the experience that is being recounted. In some cases there is the trauma of moving, while in others it is an effort to find some sense of balance between life and work. This variety begins, for all academics, by passing through the tenure-track gate, but it is not diminished as they move along the tenure-track. What may be different during the early tenure-track experience is the amount of control each individual feels they can exercise. Comparisons with other stages suggest that during the tenure-track process one gains some sense of agency, but in the early stages that has not happened yet. The urgency in this section is focused on survival.

Early tenure-track voices tend to speak about a collection of discrete components of the role. It may be that daily demands and getting to the next task are so onerous that strategies for survival consist of focusing on the short term rather than a longer-term perspective. Alternatively, it may be that the executive function of sense-making has not been reconciled with the new circumstances. In other words, they may be actively looking for sense-making strategies that fit the new role (and will ultimately support a longer-term perspective). This fits with the conceptual notion of "role clarity" (Ponjuan, Conley, & Trower, 2011). In general, theoretical frameworks, for instance, are less utilized in this group (which verifies the editors' concern about imposing a framework requirement mentioned in the introduction).

Each of the authors in this section had less than a year in a tenure-track university position when they submitted the first draft of their chapter. As such, the voices are new in terms of academia. As editors, we wrestled with how to strike the balance between editing and interfering, especially as we saw the chapters evolve over a couple of months. When someone has been in a position less than a year, a couple of months is significant in the evolution of the academic voice! We tried to maintain the early voice, using some editorial polish, but not so much that it would obscure the writing or other struggles these authors are working through. For example, there were more violations of the specified style format (APA) among the chapters of this section than other sections (though errors occurred in all sections)—these we fixed. They may reflect less experience with the academic writing style commonly used in education; alternatively they may reflect how overwhelmed these authors are in getting through their daily tasks. Editorially, we focused on the conveyance of meaning and did not necessarily recommend changes that might improve smoothness. We did do some editing, most of which was enthusiastically embraced.

It is notable that we received feedback from one of these authors indicating they learned from the close editorial work. Suffice it to say, this particular section did require more editorial work than other sections; the editors had more discussions about these chapters and how to move forward with minimal interference. However, our sense, and it may be more reflective of the communication process than the chapters themselves, is that the preparation of the chapters and, more generally, this stage of the tenure-track, seemed to be characterized by development of personal self-efficacy.

This collection of observations is likely to reflect the larger experience of early tenure-track. Since these authors typically required more time editing their manuscripts, it is likely they require more time for other task-specific aspects of the tenure-track role. If this is the case, then one would expect to see evidence of reduced productivity when compared to the larger community of academics. This might be mitigated by mentorship or collaborative efforts that have been written about elsewhere in this book. However, reduction in productivity can contribute to work-life balance issues, lower confidence, and many other stressors.

These observations suggest that role clarity, self-efficacy, and social acceptance (Ponjuan, Conley, & Trower, 2011) may develop in different ways and become more pronounced at different stages of the tenure-track experience. In terms of the sections of this book, self-efficacy seems most closely associated with the early-tenure section, role clarity with the mid-tenure one, and social acceptance with the late-tenure section.

Having made these observations, the editors would like to acknowledge the efforts of all of the authors in this section for persevering and having faith in the editors. For all the observations, at the end of the day, every author in this section has met all the needs of the editors admirably and with considerable resilience—which demonstrates that they are addressing what they perceive to be the requirements to ultimately achieve tenure.

Victoria (Tory) Handford is the first author in this section. Her chapter focuses on the trials and tribulations of the move itself. It was quite literally a life-changing experience that followed a lengthy career that was firmly rooted in southern Ontario. We are pleased to report Tory is still breathing, and has begun to feel somewhat settled.

Greg Ogilvie tells the reader about his journey: the research, teaching, service, and personal journeys, each involving significant effort, despite Greg's careful planning for experience in these areas. The chapter is an interesting examination that challenges one to consider the extent to which the graduate-studies experience informs the initial phase of tenure-track.

Kathy Snow was offered a tenure-track position prior to completing her doctoral program. Her story is one of overload, as she struggles to balance the elements of being new to the role, finishing her duties as a doctoral student, and being a new mother. Kathy's chapter provides insight into the state of women, in general, in university settings, overlaid with her own experiences of solving the home-work balance.

Finally, Lyle Hamm writes of moving across the country to a limited-term position that became tenure-track. Among the many risk-takers in this book, it is possible that Lyle is at or near the top of the pile. In addition, at the mid-point of his limited-term appointment there was a faculty strike. Lyle describes his learning in all of these situations, offering us a positive, but realistic, view of his journey.

Reference

Ponjuan, L., Conley, V. M., & Trower, C. (2011). Career stage differences in pre-tenure track faculty perceptions of professional and personal relationships with colleagues. *The Journal of Higher Education, 82*(3), 319–346.

CHAPTER 13

From There to Here

Victoria (Tory) Handford
Faculty of Human, Social, and Educational Development,
Thompson Rivers University

First year, tenure-track assistant professor ... sounds like it should be fun! I'm looking forward to the job—the learning, working with colleagues, seeing a new part of the country—to everything. Thank you for the offer. I'll get back to you about the details, but in principle, I accept.

That was the end of the phone call with the job offer. By coincidence, my thesis advisor and his spouse were sitting in my dining room with my family. I didn't tell anyone what the phone call was—perhaps an indication of my apprehension. It was the next day before I shared with my spouse and my children that I had been offered the position.

I am at the end of my first year, tenure-track. It has not been entirely positive, or all negative. It is a journey. Change involves grieving what is lost, which transitions into anger about what is lost, recognizing the new, which leads to embracing the new and, finally, incorporating both what was lost and what is new as a lived experience, transforming oneself into a new whole. Then, we begin again—perfectly described in an old folk song by Joni Mitchell (1970), whose most famous line states "We can't return, we can only look behind from where we came, and go round and round and round in the Circle Game." While this can be expressed in many ways, as reflected in the literature of different disciplines, the common theme is the story of change.

My experience of change may not be that different than a Grade 1 teacher facing a new language-arts curriculum: it's still education, but the components, strategies, and functional environment are different. We both need to gather the adaptive and technical skills in order to be successful. It is easy to forget that I was ever good at anything; I have not found much of the old in the new—yet. My first tears about this change have occurred after almost a year in the position, as I've written this chapter. Perhaps writing has helped me with understanding, possibly indicating I am taking a first step! I may need to adjust some lessons in my graduate course on change, lighting the content with some personal honesty and recent change experience. We'll see.

Leadership and effective teaching literature identifies that performance is a function of ability, motivation, and structures. Written in mathematical language the formula looks like this: $P = f(a, m, s)$ (O'Day, 1996, in Leithwood and Beatty, 2007). In order to be performing at an effective level all three of these factors need to be making a solid and simultaneous contribution. It is necessary for my improved performance to address all three: improving my ability to name and perform the task, sustaining focus until I have finished the task, and developing further enabling structures that will support the task completion as it is now understood. Improving all three elements, at the same time, is a dance.

The Background

I have a career approaching 30 years in public education, and a long and storied family history of education that is tremendously important. While not the child (or grandchild) of people who worked exclusively in education, I was part of a family where teaching was not an uncommon career path, and where achievement in a chosen discipline, whether education or some other role, was expected.

For the first seven years of my career, I was a good (to great!) language-arts and vocal-music teacher, mostly in Grades 7 and 8. During this time, due to a shortage of contract positions, I changed schools six times, but never went a day without working fulltime. The ability to adapt to the circumstances was essential. During the fourth year of teaching, and my sixth school, the elusive contract was offered. The superintendent who was losing me (he had no contract position to offer me) is known to have said in a hiring meeting "I'll take her anywhere, teaching anything. Let's make a deal." By the end of that day I had a permanent contract. I changed schools one more time and stayed put for three years. But a pattern of professional restlessness had started to take hold.

The movement from school to school had benefits. I accumulated more experience and cleaned out more clutter than is typical of early career teachers. I saw many grade levels and a wide variety of schools: big and small, rural and urban, and families of every socio-economic status in the region. I experienced many school leadership styles and observed the effects of these on the students, parents, and staff. I was making friends, being friendly, and engaging in all the teaching and related activities that I could, knowing that my contribution would be to single events (such as a choir, a musical production, a team, a fundraising campaign), but not to ongoing committees, as I wouldn't be there to see anything through. I never became part of one particular group. I could lead a great school-wide play day, but I was always a well-liked outsider. Ultimately, at a young age, compared to those already in the role, I became an elementary vice-principal.

The vice-principalship saw four schools to accommodate three extended maternity leaves. One colleague, even today, greets me with "How are you? Are you pregnant?" I laughed at the misogyny, a characteristic of many people, not just men, and arrived in my last school where I worked with the best principal I am ever likely to know. There were almost 900 students, a daycare, and a community with high expectations. It is from this colleague that I learned how to be a truly effective school principal. His many lessons, almost none of which were explicitly taught, have come to bear on every role I have had since, including my doctoral thesis—trust and school leadership.

My role as an elementary-school principal was the longest I ever performed one job description, spanning 14 years. However, for five of the 14 years I was on leave fulfilling educational roles at the provincial level. The other nine years had me working at three different schools. My performance improved, and each assignment had increasing complexity and school size. During my time as a school principal I completed a supervisory officer's program that was designed to address all three factors for improving performance. I flourished in the role of student, but felt increasingly uncertain about the role of school superintendent. I finished the supervisory officers' program and immediately enrolled in a doctoral program.

While doing coursework I accepted a seconded position to the Ministry of Education in leadership development for a year, my first leave of absence as a school principal. This altered my world view, though it is difficult to provide specifics. After returning to the role of school principal, I began to teach principal qualification courses and worked in a graduate program in education leadership, doing sessional instruction. Meanwhile I continued the dual role of doctoral student and school principal.

When the opportunity arose to join the Ontario College of Teachers, I took a position that focused on the accreditation of faculties of education pre-service (undergraduate) programs. This was a wonderful role for me. All of this was excellent preparation for my new role as a tenure-track assistant professor; or so I thought.

The Transition

When the initial offer and revisions were sorted out it was mid-June. The new role would start in mid-August, officially. It was recognized that I could not arrive until September as accepting the position required moving from Ontario to British Columbia. I began making lists of the tasks to be done in order to get from Point A to Point B. Surely making lists is one of the most deeply ingrained skills in any school leadership position! I had learned through all my changes to use my strengths from previous learning until I built the new skills needed for the new job. I knew how to make lists, I was already making the adjustments—or so I thought. There were also a number of things that didn't make the lists, and should have, had I known.

My immediate family knew about the offer the next day, and we had many discussions before I actually signed on the dotted line. It took me a large part of the ten weeks to tell people, beyond my family, that I was leaving. I waited as long as I could. It was fully six weeks later, when I had my first dumpster in the driveway and was beginning to unclutter the house we'd lived in for 25 years, before I finally "came clean." I had not anticipated that telling people would be so difficult. I'd changed jobs many times, but this time was different. I was moving across the country, truly leaving everyone and everything behind. I am not sure that I actually believed I would move until I was literally on the airplane.

The move itself was physically and emotionally exhausting. I have three sons who were in various stages of their undergraduate education. As wonderful and helpful as they are and were, I was disrupting their expectations. I needed their physical strength to clean out the house. I also needed their emotional support as their father, my husband, had been relocated to the Yukon a year earlier. He was unable to assist beyond phone and Skype discussions. In some ways his absence made things simpler—I knew it was up to me. So, I did it.

Moving is one of the most stressful activities most people endure. Having three children moving their belongings permanently to their universities simply complicated a stressful task. In addition, addressing storage needs, working with a real estate agent to rent the house (note that I was not prepared to sell the house, serving as further evidence of my uncertainty about the wisdom of this move), wrapping up the workplace, and arranging new accommodations made the situation exceedingly difficult. The myriad of small tasks made it feel like I was the thread holding the Titanic back from the iceberg—daunting and perhaps doomed to fail. I held on.

During this time the new role was also beginning. I received my teaching assignment for the fall semester, which included The History of Education in British Columbia, an undergraduate course, and The History and Philosophy of Education, a graduate course. Given everything else, the only thing I could do with a teaching load so far from my area of expertise was largely to ignore it. While I put out a few inquiries about suitable textbooks, ultimately ignoring the problem was not the right answer, and I would pay for this solution throughout the fall semester. Following this, I was asked for my course outlines. I asked for previously developed course outlines, and got quite an earful (or "emailful") about what had or had not worked in the past. This was not what I was expecting: I was going to a university environment where these things were all worked out … where I expected to be simply the beginner, surrounded by highly effective and competent colleagues. Surely they didn't hire me because they thought I could do better than the experienced people around me … I almost quit. I am still not sure that wouldn't have been the better decision.

As I said earlier, one thing I knew about change was to identify what is staying the same, as it helps make the task less overwhelming, and helps to define what actually has to be done. How many times had I stood in front of teachers and said, "Well, this and this are staying the same; we're just going to tweak this little piece of the curriculum. You don't have to change everything." I took the pre-existing course outlines and considered the very little I could use from my background for the assignments. I spoke with the coordinator and simply ordered textbooks, because I had to have something to use. Slowly, I came to terms with it being like teaching anything else the first time through—hard work! One thing was abundantly clear before arriving: I would be working at a very minimal "ability" level. The first piece of the competence function was compromised.

I did end up with a place to live, but I did not have a large enough moving budget to fly out and look at what I might rent. I was moving across the country and the moving expenses would not have covered the costs of me moving from one local town to another. In truth, I did not have time to fly out and view options anyway, and while I needed a place to sleep I did not see my needs as a priority. This may also reflect many years in school leadership—again, not necessarily a setup for success. The rent was slightly more than we had hoped to spend, but it was walking distance from campus and the Statistics Canada website indicated a low crime rate for the area. It had a den that could serve as a second bedroom for the children, when they came to visit. A colleague, whom I had never met, went over and looked at it and said it was appropriate. I rented it for a year. This was settled. Stroke it off the list. Without spending the rest of this chapter on the details of moving, let me summarize:

- I filled four large dumpsters with accumulated junk. When I had finally thrown out the 25 years' worth of stuff I wondered why we had kept it all. Every time they pulled away another dumpster I felt better. I also wanted to stay where I was! This lightening of the load was perhaps the only change I actually needed in my life. One neighbor said, "It's kind of like a clown house ... stuff keeps coming out of this small space ..." I still laugh about this. It was most definitely true;
- I packed—and packed and I cleaned. Truly, I thought it would never end;
- I went to my doctor. My health-care coverage was about to change, and I was concerned that finding a new doctor might be difficult because the issue had been in the news. I had a complete checkup and said goodbye to the one person who was not in a reciprocal relationship with me. He had been the doctor for the birth of all three of our children, and had addressed their various health needs, and mine, for years. It

was sad for me; I think it was sad for him. It had been more reciprocal than I realized;
- I sorted out a temperature-controlled storage unit as well as a storage unit in our home's basement. I had a contractor adjust the basement to accommodate the plans—and had him complete a number of other projects that would make the house more rent-worthy, including painting most of the main floor, replacing the countertops, laying new carpeting in the family room and adjoining bedroom, and installing laminate flooring in one of the main floor bedrooms.

I said the various goodbyes. It was sad. I don't think I was that excited about the future, I was just sad.

When I finally finished the closing down of the family home, I flew with my youngest son to his university, got him settled in his first student house, only to have the rental car backed into in a parking lot. My son, all of barely 19, took control of the situation. He took pictures of the damage to the vehicles as well as of the license plate and license of the other driver. He forwarded the information to my husband and then called him to explain what happened. He was pleasant to the driver, and firm that I was to be left alone. He went with me when we returned the rental vehicle, dealt with the rental company, and put my luggage on my final flight to my destination. But this entire experience compromised the motivation component of the competence function. The only piece left to compromise was the structures component.

The First Tripartite Assignment

I arrived in what is now my home away from home with no furniture, no car, no friends, and no idea what the job was, beyond course outlines that were problematic. Structures were fully compromised.

A colleague I'd never met picked me up from my motel on the morning of my first day in town. She took me to my condo, provided a faculty tour and keys to my office, and invited me to her home for dinner that evening. There are some people that know exactly how to help—she was one of them. I don't know how long I would have lasted without her welcome that first day.

The new home took a strange shape, with an air mattress, a few dishes, and a chair—it would be at least two more weeks before more familiar furniture would arrive. Truly—how did they think I was going to make this move on the tiny moving allowance provided? I settled into a routine, bought a car (I'd never bought a car on my own), and tried to remember the names of the people in my office hallway. I sorted out the details, one after the other; with each decision and additional detail I became more and more tired. I told one colleague that I was certain first-year tripartite consisted of getting a place to live, a car, and completing my forms for human resources and the Government of British Columbia. Really—could I possibly be expected to adjust to the job as well? It did all happen and, in very little time, I was focused on the new job, what I have come to think of as, to quote an old television show, "the final frontier."

The Final Frontier

As mentioned, I was given two classes to teach. They were both outside my area of expertise, which was a problem. One of the reasons teachers don't like changing teaching assignments is because their competency is brought into question as they try to learn the new material. There is what is known as "an implementation dip" in all instructional change. For me, this implementation dip was profound. I learned that while I could understand the history of education in British Columbia, and I could draw on multiple previous learnings to create interesting and thought-provoking undergraduate classes, this course was being taught on a compressed timetable. So, instead of preparing for one three-hour lecture once a week, I was preparing for two three-hour lectures each week for the first six weeks. Additionally, I was teaching a graduate course in the philosophy of education. I had not taken a philosophy course since my own Bachelor of Education, now 30 years ago. Needless to say, my first term was comprised of very little other than lecture preparation and marking.

Had anyone had the foresight to tell me this was all that I was expected to do, it would have relieved some anxiety. But I knew the position was 40% teaching, 40% research, 20% service. So, in true school-principal fashion—it was time to simply get to it. I watched for interesting committees on which to serve, and chose two that would help me understand the institution as a whole, based on reading the strategic plan of the university and listening to the gossip along my hallway. One committee I chose was work related to the international student community. My graduate class was close to half international students, and I felt spending time learning about the issues of international students would help me. It was a committee that didn't require a huge time commitment, and it was cross-faculty, so I would start to understand the university as an organizational unit. The second committee I agreed to join was a senate subcommittee looking at the budget implications of the new strategic priorities. Once again, this was a university-wide committee; the time commitment was not onerous, and it would provide me with institutional understanding. My previous 30 years of worklife had taught me that understanding the budgets of any organization helps when trying to understand the struggles of the organization. It seemed like a good place to start. I also did a number of small things within the department and the faculty, which helped me learn about this particular part of the organization and the individuals with whom I was most frequently interacting. Good. I was doing something in the 20% service.

Research was more challenging. I was barely treading water on the 40% teaching, I seemed to have achieved the 20% service, but research, what did I know about research? I attended a variety of research meetings held by the research office, and gained some awareness of the individuals who were trying to support research. I attended meetings where others described their research interests, this being an effort to promote collaboration within our university environment. I went back several times to my doctoral thesis and tried to figure out what articles could be developed for publication that had not been published from that data set. One person on my doctoral committee told me there were at least six articles in my dissertation. My advisor and I had published one. Surely there was something else that could be said in this area, but I had no idea what that something was.

The more I worried about this lack of a research agenda the more frozen I became. I decided to do exactly what I had done all my life—simply start. I applied for an internal research grant and focused the application on examining some theory to practice leadership materials. Having submitted this application I then began the process of applying for my first Social Sciences and Humanities Research Council grant (I fondly refer to this Insight Development Grant, which is designed to support beginning researchers, as the SSHRC for Beginners) and, three weeks later, had finally completed a proposal that was an extension of my doctoral work. An associate dean from another department had told me not to bother, I would not be successful, and I would be further ahead spending the application time working on an article. He may have been right, but I didn't know what to write about, and it seemed easier to learn about the SSHRC process. I continued to do the task of peer reviewing articles when I was asked, and marveled at the abilities of those around me, all the while feeling only increasingly insecure about my own research abilities.

In the winter semester, 24 hours before the course was to begin, I was asked if I could teach a graduate course in Understanding Diversity. I knew the professor assigned to teach the course was ill, and I knew they were stuck. So, I agreed to do it, but asked to teach only two of the three credits, so that I could work with someone who was more experienced, and to remove the preparation and marking related to the last 13 lecture hours. It was new material, but it connected many things I did know something about. The department agreed and I had an experienced professor to work with, even if only in email. The students were thankful, as their course was not cancelled. In addition, there were several people I could invite as guest speakers so that I did not have to perform every moment! I learned a great deal teaching this course. I had a small success.

A few things began to make sense in the winter, despite this last-minute course addition. First of all, I started teaching a leadership course that I designed and was directly focused on school-level leadership. I spent hours on preparation. I was teaching practitioners; the research I could bring to the table was going to be helpful, even if I knew my own doctoral professors would have brought acres more research, most of it their own. The students responded positively. I was also teaching an undergraduate Philosophy of Education course on a compressed schedule. By now I knew the students in this class, as I had taught them in the fall semester. I had received some feedback from them on the first-semester course, which helped me as I planned the course outline. I had taught the graduate course in philosophy—I knew slightly more than I had four months previously, although I was far from expert.

And, purely by coincidence, while attending a school-district function with my leadership class, I had a very interesting conversation with the local school-board superintendent who identified a couple of issues that were of concern for him regarding school and district leadership. I began looking more carefully at one of the issues, and started organizing some discussions about what might be productive approaches in this area. This led to multiple meetings with the Dean, the district superintendent, the assistant superintendent, and my former doctoral advisor. Here was something people wanted done. I might not know how to do it exactly, but I certainly knew how to get it started. So, I began. I was, perhaps, having another small success.

I had an email from a person leading one of the committees I was serving on, a university vice-president, asking me to clarify my thinking, and inviting me to talk with him a little more about some possibilities. It was collegial, not a threat. I must have said something that was useful!

I agreed to teach a course I had taught previously at another institution, during the spring and summer. It was material I deeply understood, it was relevant to practitioners but had a theoretical basis which would build practical skills, and the class was very small, almost all of the students being individuals I had previously taught. I relaxed, I enjoyed, and for the first time, I felt—and was—competent. Teaching was finally enjoyable. I ended my first-year five credits over on my teaching load, but I had made some real gains in teaching. It may not have been a bad thing.

I got the little internal research grant, and began the process of writing an ethics submission and organizing the study. I did two presentations at two different conferences, and then repeated the presentations locally. Presentations are not difficult for me, but presenting myself as an academic was new. The repeated practice from multiple presentations, seeing myself as within the academy, not an interloper, was a good thing. I got rejected for the SSHRC for Beginners, but rejection is progress—I never expected to get the grant, but I did want to be seen to try to get the grant. I began doing a review of literature in relation to the issue identified by the local school superintendent and, together with my doctoral advisor, we began a plan for a program that would include some research, a program that could keep me busy for years to come. Finally, I wrote this chapter and developed a book proposal with my colleague Tim—who has encouraged me to recognize the amount of change, the failures and the successes, and ultimately, to accept that beginning faculty, me included, are mere mortals.

The living structure settled. I invited two colleagues to dinner. I enjoyed preparing the meal and my home. Another small success for me, personally, and they had a good time. So, now I was actually living in my accommodation, not simply sleeping in it.

Conclusions

Some literature refers to leadership as being comprised of two skill sets: the technical and the adaptive (Fisher and Ury, 2011; Heifetz and Linksy, 2002). Both are important. Technical and adaptive skills likely apply to more than leadership. Typically, in order to see ourselves as competent we must have the technical skills to perform the task. While it is impossible for me to see the journey as anything but beginning, I do believe the technical skills required to complete the journey are beginning to be understood, and I may be acquiring some competency in certain areas. The adaptive skills are much harder for me. Andy Hargreaves (2005) identified in an article, now a decade old, that teachers are early, mid-, or late-career professionals, depending on their age and stage. The role of assistant professor involves more than teaching, just as the role of teacher involves more than teaching. I am a late-career person by age but an early-career person by actual experience in this particular role. I have a number of very well-developed skills, some of which are useful as an assistant professor. The adaptive life factors that complicate my adjustment to my role include that I am tired, I miss my family, and I miss my home. I miss the competence that I have felt in the multiple roles I have previously held. I miss the feeling of craving learning. Each day is so crammed with learning, I can easily resist even opening email, particularly if I sense there might be another "good idea" within it. But more than anything, I am not convinced that this position is going to allow me to give back to my profession. Many late-career people, according to Hargreaves, seek this exact opportunity. But I may finally have taken on a challenge of adaptation that is too big, even for me. It has been an exhausting, humbling, and a lonely year of growth.

> Without initial irresolutions, music—indeed, all art—loses much of its meaning. So does life: While we often tend to think of tension in negative terms, and are eager to eliminate it whenever it appears, it is a source of nuance and complexity that renders our lives rich ... it presents tension, not as obstructions, but as themselves vehicles to the achievement of resolution ... in other words, to enjoy music, and to enjoy life, is to enjoy tension and see it not as a boulder blocking the path to a desirable goal, but as the path itself. (Higgins in Leibovitz, 2014)

First-year tenure-track has many, many boulders. I imagine there are more rocks of varying sizes that will emerge as I travel along this road. As I gain the ability, refine my focus on that which motivates me, and improve the routines and structures that secure me, I will, in the end, recognize the dance—and enjoy it. Perfection of performance is not the goal; the goal is to dance.

References

Fisher, R., & Ury, W. (2011). *Getting to yes: Negotiating agreement without giving in.* Toronto, ON: Penguin.

Hargreaves, A. (2005). Educational change takes ages: Life, career and generational factors in teachers' emotional responses to educational change. *Teaching and Teacher Education, 21,* 967–983.

Heifetz, R., & Linsky, M. (2002). *Leadership on the Line: Staying Alive through the Dangers of Leading.* Boston, MA: Harvard Business School Press.

Leibovitz, L. (2014). *A Broken Hallelujah: Rock and Roll, Redemption, and the Life of Leonard Cohen.* New York, NY: Norton.

Leithwood, K., & Beatty, B. (2007). *Leading with Teacher Emotions in Mind.* Thousand Oaks, CA: Corwin Press.

Mitchell, J. (1970). The circle game. *On Ladies of the Canyon* [record] Los Angeles: Reprise.

CHAPTER 14

The "Ten-Year Road" to Tenure: A Personal Narrative of the Beginning Phases of the Journey

Greg Ogilvie
Faculty of Education, University of Lethbridge

Achieving tenure is one of the key landmarks in a scholar's career, as it is the pre-eminent marker of legitimacy for long-term employment by a university. In July 2014, I formally began the journey towards achieving tenure when I was hired as an assistant professor in the Faculty of Education at the University of Lethbridge. The process of starting a new job is always daunting, as it requires adaptation to working in a setting with new colleagues, new materials, new expectations, and a new institutional culture. The initiation into an academic career is further complicated by the countdown towards proving one's adequacy for long-term employment through tenure. As the application for tenure is generally expected prior to the sixth year of employment, new scholars have a finite amount of time to prove their worth, adding considerable pressure to the already stress-laden endeavour of beginning a new job.

The characterization of the life of new scholars as difficult has been echoed in the literature, which portrays the tenure-track experience as an arduous process highlighted by stress and uncertainty (Dewald & Walsh, 2009; Mason, Casey, & Betts, 2010; Hibbert et al.,

2010). Hirschkorn (2010) emphasized the uncertainty of the tenure-track experience, as tenure requirements are contextually dependent. He also expressed concern regarding the precarious position of tenure-track candidates, as there is an inherent power differential between those that are tenure-track and those that are tenured. One contributing factor to the power issue is the fact that the tenure-track individual invariably has a tenured colleague sitting on the tenure-review committee. Furthermore, Kawalilak and Groen (2010) characterized the tenure-track pathway as "lonely and circuitous, a maze of sorts" (p. 6). As I embark on the tenure-track experience, I can appreciate the concerns expressed by the aforementioned authors. Nonetheless, I cannot help feeling that my current journey is not new, but rather a continuation of the journey that began as a graduate student. Although the compensation for scholarly activities has changed considerably, my daily routine remains remarkably similar to that experienced as a graduate student. Hence, the conceptualization of tenure-track in Hibbert et al. (2010) as the "ten-year road that begins with the decision to pursue a PhD" (p. 80) is an apt description that resonates with my experiences (though I would expand the timeline of tenure preparation to include the completion of a Master's degree). The continuity between graduate studies and employment as a professor has contributed to a greater sense of comfort in tackling the demands of the tenure-track experience; however, it has presented a number of challenges. Drawing on a personal narrative, this paper will outline my journey in the beginning phases of the "ten-year road" to tenure.

The Early Years Prior to the Journey

The decision to enter into the field of education was a circuitous, drawn-out process. After completing high school I was unsure of my career aspirations and, thus, decided to enter into general studies in the Faculty of Arts and Science at the University of Saskatchewan. Having developed a passion for 20th-century history as a child, I decided to pursue the subject as the focus of my studies. In order to investigate historical texts in their original language and further develop the linguistic skills acquired during a high-school exchange program in Germany, I decided to study both German and Russian. The remaining courses in my schedule were selected based on the requirements to transfer into the Faculty of Education. Although pursuing a career as an educator did not seem like an attractive option at the time, the decision to enroll in the courses would prove fortuitous. After completing a BA in history and Russian I taught English in Ukraine for a year, acquiring an interest in the teaching profession and prompting the decision to apply to the Faculty of Education.

After completing the two-year consecutive program at the University of Saskatchewan, I acquired a BEd degree. Subsequently, I worked as a substitute teacher before gaining employment as a regular high-school teacher in a small town in northern Saskatchewan. The three years spent teaching in this environment provided a progressive, supportive environment in which to develop foundational teaching skills. In addition to becoming acquainted with the rigours of teaching, my time in rural Saskatchewan also provided valuable insights into working with Aboriginal children.

Despite enjoying my years teaching a variety of subjects to Grade 9 students, the urge to live and work abroad prompted me to resign from my position. My wife and I became members of an international organization that supports professionals in finding job placements in third-world countries and ventured to Ethiopia for two years. Working at a teacher-education institute in one of the largest cities in the country, I taught English curriculum and instruction courses, supervised teacher candidates during their practica, and developed and administered a professional-development program for elementary-school English teachers. Prior to my second year working at the college, a World Bank-sponsored professional-development program was introduced in the country. All teacher educators were required to complete the intensive course within a three-year period in order to maintain good standing in their position. As I was already familiar with the culture of the institution and the faculty members, I was selected to facilitate the course.

My experiences in Ethiopia were instrumental in directing my career path. In preparation for teaching curriculum and instruction courses and conducting professional development workshops, I engaged in extensive reading about different curriculum theories. The readings helped to elucidate my experiences as an educator and provided greater depth in understanding the different dimensions of curriculum. Moreover, working in Ethiopia provided the first opportunity to engage in pedagogy as an instructor at the post-secondary level. I enjoyed working with in-service and pre-service teachers and teacher educators, and realized I had a passion for teaching about teaching. The desire to further my knowledge about education and gain the credentials necessary to continue working in teacher education prompted me to pursue graduate studies, thus initiating the journey in preparation for tenure.

Research Journey

The phrase "publish or perish" has become synonymous with the process of acquiring tenure. Although the institution in which I am employed prides itself on teaching excellence, the creation of a well-developed research agenda is considered equally important, particularly in the process of attaining tenure. As I work toward developing a research platform worthy of obtaining tenure, my efforts have been strongly influenced by my work as a graduate student.

The most significant influence on my experiences since beginning in the Faculty of Education at the University of Lethbridge has been my incomplete dissertation. At the time I was offered the position as an assistant professor I had not completed my dissertation—I had already written the beginning chapters of the document, collected and analyzed data for the study, and started to write the later chapters; however, a considerable amount of work was required before the document would be completed. Having the pressure associated with an incomplete dissertation hanging over me has influenced all aspects of my personal and professional life; however, it has been most influential in limiting my research agenda.

My employers have been supportive and understanding of my situation and the need to focus on completing my dissertation. They altered my teaching load to facilitate more time for writing and provided clear expectations that the dissertation should take precedence over any other research-related work, in essence releasing me from research activities beyond dissertation-related work. This support has provided comfort and enabled me to focus on the completion of my graduate work, rather than splitting attention between completing my dissertation and establishing a new research agenda. Nonetheless, the fact that I have not yet begun to conduct research since assuming the new position has contributed to a sense of unease. The university has a number of programs in place to support new scholars in acquiring funds and disseminating their research. Moreover, the faculty in which I work employs an individual whose primary mandate is supporting scholars in conducting research. Due to my inability to engage in new research projects, I have not had the opportunity to take advantage of these services. Moreover, as my research-related commitments have been limited to my dissertation, I have not been able to exploit common research interests with colleagues. As a result, the residue of my work as a graduate student has prevented embarking on new research projects, contributing to a sense of falling behind and not exploiting opportunities available.

Although graduate requirements have hindered the advancement of my research program since obtaining a faculty position, efforts during graduate studies have also had a positive influence in shaping the research component of my application for tenure. One of the key benefits of my graduate experience was in providing confidence and guidance in undertaking research. Throughout my time as a graduate student I was employed as a research assistant (RA) or conducted research in concert with my supervisor and other scholars. My first stint as an RA involved assisting my supervisor with a study he was conducting. My responsibilities as part of the job were to transcribe interviews, analyze the transcribed data to identify common themes and trends, and write a literature review. As this was my first exposure to analyzing data and writing a literature review, I regularly consulted with my supervisor for guidance and support. In a subsequent opportunity to work as an RA, I was tasked with assisting my supervisor and two other professors in preparing an article for publication. The article explored how educators in different fields of study (e.g., art education, early-childhood education, and second-language pedagogy) had infused intercultural content into their curriculum and instruction courses. As data was collected from interviews and artifacts produced in the classes taught by the three professors, I was not involved in the data collection or analysis process; however, I was actively involved in various aspects of the writing process. More important than my contributions to the completion of the article was the fact that I was exposed to the process of publishing an article. Throughout the process of submitting, revising, and having the article accepted for publication my supervisor kept me involved. This enabled me to view the entire process of getting published without assuming a prominent role of responsibility.

In addition to providing a smooth induction into the research process, my experiences during graduate studies also provided a platform for experimentation and skill development. Rather than adopting a pragmatic approach in establishing a research agenda (in other words, conducting research to satisfy course or program requirements or acquire remuneration), I engaged in research to further my understanding of my own pedagogical practices and curriculum theory in general. The desire to learn more about the effectiveness of microteaching as an instructional strategy in teacher education incited a research project with students I had instructed in curriculum and instruction courses. Interest in the challenges encountered by international students when studying on a Canadian campus led to a narrative inquiry into the experiences of an international doctoral student. The desire to expand my research into the realm of applied linguistics resulted in conducting a study about the efficacy of task repetition (from an affective and acquisition perspective) in the second-language classroom. Furthermore, curiosity surrounding the impact of infusing critical pedagogy in an English for Academic Purposes (EAP) class led to research tracking improvements in student performance and investigating additional perceived benefits associated with the course. When combined with the two major research projects conducted as part of degree requirements, the aforementioned studies constituted a significant research agenda.

Conducting a multitude of research projects assisted my introduction to academia in numerous ways. As ethics approval was required before conducting any research with human subjects, I became intimately familiar with the extensive process of applying for ethics. Furthermore, as I attempted to stretch my research skills, I embarked on research using different data collection and analysis methods. This resulted in the use of interviews, open-ended and Likert-scale questionnaires, artifacts produced by respondents, language samples, test scores, and texts as sources of data. It also led to the utilization of various research designs or approaches, including hermeneutics, mixed-method case studies, narrative research, and exploratory research. Experimenting with different research designs expanded my awareness about research paradigms, providing valuable information about the underlying foundations and tacit assumptions associated with each paradigm. It also enabled me to better understand my strengths and weaknesses as a researcher and to situate my research within the field of second-language education.

Completing research from different paradigms was also beneficial in terms of the exposure it gave me to scholars from different fields. The breadth of my research agenda meant that I was able to present at conferences with very different foci, ranging from qualitative-based teacher-education conferences to quantitative-based applied linguistics conferences. This resulted in sharing and gaining feedback about my work from diverse audiences, but also in gaining exposure to a range of ideas from alternative perspectives. The result was greater understanding about the relationship between concepts from different fields of study and novel ways they could complement each other.

Teaching Journey

Teaching is at the core of my professional identity; therefore, obtaining opportunities to engage with students in the classroom has always been a high priority. During my time as a graduate student I always sought out opportunities to work as a teacher and teacher educator. These experiences have had a significant influence in shaping my experiences in engaging in the tenure-track process. One of the greatest influences these experiences had was in providing a supportive, mentoring environment in which to develop skills teaching at the post-secondary level.

During the early years of my graduate program I was provided numerous opportunities to teach curriculum and instruction courses. Opportunity was accompanied by mentorship, as my induction to teaching in the program occurred in a gradual, supportive manner. My first exposure to post-secondary instruction in Canada occurred by co-teaching a course with a graduate-student colleague. This meant that responsibilities for planning the structure of the course, implementing lessons, and assessing student work were mutually shared. My co-instructor had taught the course before and possessed a wealth of knowledge about course content and the student population. She was willing to engage in dialogue about the course and provided freedom to introduce content and materials deemed beneficial to student growth. Nonetheless, the fact she already had materials and a basic course structure in place significantly reduced the stress associated with preparing for a new course. Furthermore, the fact that we co-taught the course meant there was an embedded support system in place that was invaluable in planning and delivering lessons, but also in addressing difficulties when they arose.

Although there were inevitable challenges associated with teaching a new course in a new setting, my introduction to teaching at the University of Alberta was a resounding success. The experience was positive and led me to pursue further teaching opportunities within the Faculty of Education. Due to an over-extended teaching load, my supervisor invited me to assist with teaching a fourth-year curriculum and instruction course for second-language majors. Unlike the first experience, where my co-instructor and I were always present in the classroom and adopted a team teaching approach, my supervisor preferred a separation of responsibilities and a clear delineation in the content to be covered—what could be labelled as splitting the credit load. As a result, although we conferred on the material being covered and regularly discussed progress in the course, we were never present together in the classroom and autonomously assigned and graded course work. Despite the different approach to co-instructing the course, the experience shared similarities with my first teaching experience in that I was exposed to new materials and a new approach to teaching, while also having an inherent mentor to engage in discussion about the course and issues that arose.

In addition to the two experiences teaching with the support of a colleague, I also had the opportunity to independently teach curriculum and instruction courses for English-as-a-second-language (ESL) and modern-language (French, Spanish, Ukrainian, etc.) minors on seven occasions in the Faculty of Education. (At the time I was teaching courses at the University of Alberta, students were required to declare a major teaching subject and a minor teaching subject. The minor teaching subject required less subject-specific course credits than the major teaching subject. Moreover, the minor-subject area provided the bulk of the teaching load for teacher candidates during the introductory professional-term practicum, while the major-subject area was the focus of the longer advanced professional-term practicum). The opportunity to teach the same course on multiple occasions was invaluable, as it allowed for continual reflection and revision of the structure and content of the course. Feedback from students was used to adjust the approach adopted in the course; however, the most significant factor affecting the evolution of the course was exposure to new theories and concepts through extensive reading facilitated by my graduate-course work and interest in expanding my knowledge base. Exposure to the work of John Loughran,

Deborah Britzman, Karen Johnson, and Virginia Richardson had a significant impact in shaping my perspective on teacher education. These prominent scholars elucidated the subtle mechanisms that promote the status quo in education and inspired the adoption of strategies to counter such mechanisms. One tactic was the implementation of a constructivist approach to teacher education in which thorough self-analysis is the first step in the journey towards becoming a teacher (Ogilvie & Dunn, 2010). Exposure to the writings of Henri Giroux, Peter McLaren, Alistair Pennycook, and Robert Phillipson helped to contextualize second-language pedagogy and brought a critical dimension to the subject. Moreover, familiarity with task-based language teaching, content-based instruction, and the Common European Framework of Reference (Council of Europe, 2014) was instrumental in shaping the content of the course. Through exposure to new ideas and the constant refinement of practices, the course evolved to the point where it bore minimal similarities to the course I first taught in collaboration with my fellow graduate student.

My teaching experience was not limited to the Faculty of Education. Desiring the opportunity to continue engaging as a second-language educator, early on in my program I volunteered to teach a weekly class to immigrant adult ESL learners. Later on, a fellow graduate student who had been working at the university as an EAP instructor suggested applying to teach in the program. I followed her advice and started in the Faculty of Extension by teaching an academic writing course to graduate students in the Faculty of Engineering. Subsequently, I was offered a position teaching a course for international graduate students who required assistance with their academic language skills before entering into the graduate program. Due to low enrollment, the course had not been offered as an isolated course, but rather had been taught in conjunction with undergraduate courses, with the graduate students also attending additional tutorials. The absence of a course structure meant that I had to develop the course from the ground up. This entailed identifying the overall goals for the course, locating materials, and developing instructional activities.

Developing the graduate-level EAP course from scratch was a challenging experience. Finding resources at an appropriate linguistic level that would be interesting and cognitively challenging for intellectually astute individuals was difficult and time-consuming. Increasingly stringent rules related to copyright made the process much more difficult (University of Alberta, 2015). In the end, open-access programming that addressed contemporary events in a critical manner became the primary resource used. This added an additional layer of commitment, as it required ongoing identification of articles and video clips to be used in class. A further challenge in developing the structure of the class was the use of an external assessment tool. A widely used, standardized academic language-proficiency exam was utilized in combination with performance on course assignments to determine the successful completion of the course. As the course acted as the gatekeeper for acceptance in graduate programs, the exam was considered important and there was significant time spent on preparation. This meant that course activities had to be structured not only to develop general academic language proficiency but also to prepare students to successfully navigate the exam.

Although the absence of a pre-determined structure for the course presented challenges, it also presented opportunities. With the exception of the final exam, there were minimal restrictions on how the course was conducted. This meant I could structure the course according to my pedagogical philosophy. As a result, course materials and activities were designed to be relevant for students. Relevance in this context related both to developing the academic linguistic skills needed to pass the course and to surviving graduate courses in English, as well as to promoting a deeper understanding about academic fields of study and issues that define contemporary society. As such, academic English was the content of instruction; however, it was also the medium through which topics that were relevant to international graduate students were investigated. The fact that I taught the class on a number of occasions meant I was able to experiment with and refine the content and structure of the course. This facilitated praxis and the development of a course grounded in pedagogical theory.

My early induction into teaching at the post-secondary level in a supportive environment has had a significant influence on my journey towards obtaining tenure. First and foremost, the experiences garnered as a graduate student have provided confidence when fulfilling the teaching responsibilities as part of my new role. The fact that I had previously worked with education students on numerous occasions meant that I had experiences I could draw from in confronting new situations. I have dealt with hostile students, resolved conflicts between students in the class, and engaged in the student appeal process. As such, I have confidence that I have addressed difficult situations in the past successfully and can do so in the future. Moreover, having taught numerous courses in the past has provided me with an arsenal of teaching techniques and materials that can be applied to new situations. This has been particularly useful during the current year when tasked to teach four new courses. One of the courses is related to second-language instruction. Similarities to courses taught previously meant that a pre-existing structure and content could be used to create the outline of the course. Even in other courses that were dissimilar to courses taught in the past, previous experiences were beneficial. For example, I taught a course this year related to promoting awareness about social and cultural factors influencing education. I had never engaged with education students about such topics; however, I had introduced critical pedagogy to students in the EAP courses I taught and utilized several activities and readings that were applicable. As a result, my previous teaching experiences provided a foundation from which new teaching experiences evolved.

Despite the benefits afforded by previous experiences, undertaking pedagogy in a new context has presented numerous challenges. One of the difficulties encountered has been navigating a new institutional culture. In previous contexts I had been afforded autonomy to develop the structure of courses. Although syllabi for courses previously taught by other instructors had always been provided and some formerly utilized materials had been shared, in general the perception had been given that I possessed scholarly autonomy to develop courses. Academic autonomy is still preserved in my new setting; however, the structure of the program promotes conformity. When students enter into the education program, they are placed in a cohort with approximately 36 students. The cohorts of students take all classes together and each cohort also takes an identical course load with minor variations based on subject specialization. This means that the same course is taught by numerous other educators. In the spirit of collegiality and program consistency, teacher educators are encouraged to share materials and collaborate. While this creates a supportive environment, it also creates pressure to adhere to institutional norms. Navigating these norms has presented a challenge for me.

Another challenge encountered has been maintaining fidelity with my pedagogical philosophy. Education is a practical endeavour, so activities in a teacher-education program should have some link to practice. Nonetheless, teacher candidates often privilege the act of teaching over the "ivory tower practice" of theorizing and critically investigating practices (Britzman, 2003). In a program that prides itself on the number and length of practical teaching experiences, the emphasis on practical applications in the classroom is even greater. Although I believe teacher-education courses should introduce teacher candidates to instructional strategies and other technical aspects of teaching, I do not believe that the sole purpose of courses is to prepare candidates for successfully completing teaching practica. On the contrary, I believe the university classroom is an important venue to explore issues and develop knowledge about the profession that will enable educators to move beyond being technicians to educational decision-makers and advocates. Therefore, I have been confronted by the dilemma to satisfy the desires of students to solely focus on practical teaching applications or adhere to my philosophy of teacher education and risk receiving poor student evaluations because I have not met their expectations.

Service Journey

Service commonly plays a less significant role in the work of an academic (the breakdown of time allocation at my university is 40% teaching, 40% research, and 20% service) and this has been reflected in my activities to this point in my career. The determination of committee commitments took place at my institution prior to the outset of my employment. As a result, I was assigned to the faculty re-admissions committee at the beginning of the term and only subsequently was named as an alternate to the committee tasked with over-seeing library affairs. The latter committee met once per month, but the times of the meetings often conflicted with my teaching schedule, so I was only able to attend a few meetings. Conversely, I have participated in all activities related to the former committee; however, this has, to date, only consisted of one full day of service. In addition to serving on the two committees I have also participated in faculty councils and other faculty-related meetings. Moreover, I have served as a proposal reviewer for an international conference. Nonetheless, my commitment to service work has been relatively minimal to this point in my career.

The limited service work during my first year in the faculty has mirrored my service-related activities as a graduate student. As it is expected that graduate students will participate in different capacities on committees, I followed through by becoming a member of several organizations. I was a member of the department graduate-student council and served on the university-wide graduate-student association for two years. This experience provided insight into the mechanisms and politics surrounding the functioning of the university. In addition to serving on campus organizations, I also became a member of numerous local, national, and international professional organizations. Membership in these organizations provided opportunities to connect with scholars and professionals within the field through organizational meetings, conferences, and publications. In addition, on one occasion I was invited to provide an extended presentation to teachers in the Alberta Teachers of English as a Second Language organization about task-based language teaching.

Service work also extended to supporting the functioning of conferences and journals. On several occasions I worked as a volunteer at conferences organizing presentation rooms and supporting presenters in any way I could. In addition, I served on the organizing committee for a major international conference hosted by the University of Alberta—the International Conference on Task-Based Language Teaching. Due to my attendance at the three previous conferences, I was able to provide insights about the structure and agenda of those events, assisting in identifying ways the conference in Alberta could maintain continuity while also leaving its own mark. Part of my responsibilities in supporting the functioning of conferences was reviewing abstracts for inclusion in the program. This skill has also been applied in support of a series of journals, as I have been a registered manuscript reviewer.

To date I have engaged in a diverse range of service related activities. Nonetheless, I recognize the inadequacy of the amount of service work conducted and the need to diversify this aspect of my portfolio. I feel the experiences garnered to this point will ensure that going forward I will contribute to the academic and surrounding community in a capacity that stretches beyond teaching and conducting research.

Personal Journey

The decision to pursue an academic position is not just a career choice but also a lifestyle choice, affecting all aspects of one's life. Similar to the teaching profession, work as an academic is never-ending. One can always find more material to read, articles to write, research to conduct, and teaching materials to develop. The key then becomes finding a happy balance between one's professional life and personal life—a delicate balance that is often difficult to strike in a competitive profession that measures performance based on productivity. Finding a balance is further complicated when balancing work life, family life, and the completion of one's dissertation.

Before entering into graduate studies I had been married for four years and had been in a relationship with my wife for over eight years. Our relationship had been weather-tested by travelling across Europe for two months and living in Africa for two years. Both of us had been very busy in our professional endeavours, me as a teacher and her as a registered nurse. We had become accustomed to sharing our lives while navigating busy work schedules. Maintaining a relationship between two busy professionals is one thing, having to do it while also raising children complicates the situation. This was my experience. During the completion of my Master's degree we had our first son, while my second son was born during the first year of my doctoral program.

The work of an academic is demanding; however, it also presents certain benefits. One benefit is the flexibility in schedule. Unlike traditional nine-to-five jobs, the schedule of an academic is not rigidly predetermined beyond teaching commitments and committee meetings. This has been hugely beneficial in raising my children, as it has facilitated being actively involved in their lives. I have coached both my boys in soccer and hockey and attended most of their extra-curricular activities. Moreover, the flexibility in my schedule has enabled me to volunteer at their school and maintain a connection with school-related activities. Furthermore, the flexibility in my schedule has allowed us to never have to rely on daycare or outside help to raise our children, as I have been able to work around my wife's work schedule to ensure one of us is always available to be with the kids.

Although the flexibility associated with an academic schedule has been beneficial, it has not been without cost. The performance requirements in completing a graduate program and obtaining tenure are very high; therefore, alterations in my schedule to accommodate my wife's work schedule and participate in my children's activities must be compensated for in other areas. This has resulted in abandoning hobbies and non-family or professional activities, including sacrificing my desired exercise regimen. It has also presented relational difficulties. In order to facilitate attending my children's hockey, soccer, and other activities, I must spend most of my remaining time developing my curriculum vitae. As a result, date nights with my wife have become few and far between, and our relationship would best be characterized as a tag-team effort based around our children. Although we have a strong relationship, the constant need to work evenings and weekends has become a source of tension and has led to feelings of frustration, as my wife has had to assume greater responsibility for the maintenance of our household. Further complicating the situation is the fatigue associated with maintaining such a busy schedule and the financial burden associated with pursuing an academic career (financial sacrifices have had to be made to facilitate pursuing graduate studies in the manner I have). We both perceive the situation improving once I have completed my dissertation; however, I still understand the time constraints associated with pursuing tenure and understand that time will need to be carefully managed to maintain a balance between my personal and professional life.

Conclusion

The first years of tenure-track in education can be arduous and challenging. Although the process of obtaining tenure officially begins upon acceptance of an academic position, I believe the fluidity between graduate studies and work as an education professor demonstrates the importance of pre-employment preparation for the tenure-track process. In my experience, activities during graduate studies helped to induct me into academia and paved the way for the current journey on which I embarked, a journey characterized by new challenges and obstacles, but also opportunities.

References

Britzman, D. P. (2003). *Practice makes practice: A critical study of learning to teach*. Albany, NY: State University of New York Press.

Council of Europe. (2014). *Common European framework of reference for languages: Learning, teaching, assessment (CEFR)*. Retrieved from: http://coe.int/t/dg4/linguistic/cadre1_en.asp.

Dewald, L., & Walsh, K. (2009). Tenure track athletic training educators: Are they being set up to fail? *Athletic Training Education Journal, 4*, 144–149.

Hibbert, K. M., Stooke, R., Pollock, K., Namukasa, I., Faez, F., & O'Sullivan, J. (2010). The "ten-year road:" Joys and challenges on the road to tenure. *The Journal of Educational Thought, 44*(1), 69–83.

Hirschkorn, M. (2010). How vulnerable am I? An experiential discussion of tenure rhetoric for new faculty. *The Journal of Educational Thought, 44*(1), 41–54.

Kawalilak, C., & Groen, J. (2010). Perspectives – The road to tenure. *The Journal of Educational Thought, 44*(1), 5-9.

Mason, R. T., Casey, C., & Betts, P. (2010). Toward tenure: Developing a relational view. *The Journal of Educational Thought, 44*(1), 85–98.

Ogilvie, G., & Dunn, W. (2010). Taking teacher education to task: Exploring the role of teacher education in promoting the utilization of task-based language teaching. *Language Teaching Research, 14*, 161–181. doi: 10.1177/1362168809353875.

University of Alberta. (2015). *University of Alberta – Copyright information, resources, and guidelines*. Retrieved from: www.copyright.ualberta.ca.

CHAPTER 15

Professor, Student, Mother: Can You Have It All?

Kathy Snow
School of Professional Studies, Education Department
Cape Breton University

Initially, teaching sounds like an easy career, with summers off and a work-day that often ends mid-afternoon. However, as every teacher will tell you, you don't survive in teaching very long if you are in it for the vacations. Ironically, though I knew better, I applied this thinking to my new life as a professor. When I discovered my teaching assignment would consist of approximately nine hours of instructional time a week, as opposed to the typical 3.5–4 hours a day of high-school teaching, I was naively excited about all of my potential spare time. I would be able to dedicate enough time to complete my dissertation and maintain a healthy balance between my family and professional life; after all I was an experienced teacher. I quickly realized that the expectations of a first year as a professor were greater than I had anticipated. The challenges of obtaining tenure and negotiating the triad of teaching, service, and research obligations used to evaluate faculty make for a heavier workload than that of a typical public-school teacher. If demographic comparatives were an indication, the challenges were also increased because I am female. Although education faculties in Canada tend to have a more balanced gender mix, with an average 39% female participation (AUCC, 2007), this is an aberration from the norm in higher education. For the same time period, only one in five tenure-track positions was held by women in Canadian universities as of 2006 (CAUT, 2008). It looked like things were not going to be as easy as

I initially assumed. In light of the increasing output of female doctoral candidates from Canadian universities (second-highest output of graduates in Canada) and the shrinking number of tenure-track positions (education has the smallest number of positions), competition for limited academic opportunities has become a major challenge (King, 2008). With over 60 applicants for the position at the small comprehensive university I was to join, the first hurdle towards tenure was simply getting hired. That accomplished, the next challenge remained: to keep it.

My Story

My path to becoming a tenure-track professor began 20 years ago. Faculties of education often include K-12 classroom experience as a condition of employment. This condition of employment is probably the reason why academics in education faculties in Canada have the oldest average age (AUCC, 2007). Like many of my colleagues, the move to higher education was the beginning of my second career.

Originally from the Maritimes, after substitute teaching in Canadian K-12 schools for a short time, I looked abroad for a more permanent teaching opportunity. After 15 years teaching science and technology in Africa, Europe, and the Middle East, and with the addition of a partner, a dog, and a daughter, our new little family decided to move to Canada to be closer to my aging parents. The poor job market for teachers in the Maritimes had not changed. After a year of substitute teaching and picking up some short-term contracts at a local university, we were starting to rethink our decision to return. Given my level of experience, education, and my stage of life, a professorial position seemed to be the most logical career choice if we wanted to stay in Canada. We moved west, to Manitoba, where I took on a full-time position as an instructional designer and, simultaneously, began my doctoral studies through the University of Calgary. As I had with my previous Master's degree, I began taking distance courses and commuting to the University of Calgary campus for the required residency portions of the degree. We still hadn't achieved our goal of getting back to the Maritimes, but by going west we were getting closer. Six months before my doctoral defense I was offered a tenure-track position in the education faculty of a small comprehensive university back east. Of course, this offer was conditional on the successful defense of the doctoral dissertation I had begun three years earlier. So began my professorial career. With an established career behind me, it looked to friends and colleagues like I was making the next step forward in my professional development. In reality, this decision was fraught with anxiety. I was indeed establishing a new career but at a lower salary, and I was abandoning my recognized professional identity. How would this unfold for my family?

Balancing Parenthood in the Early Years

Balancing personal and professional life with a small child is a challenge for everyone, regardless of profession. However, there is some interesting research that indicates this may be a greater challenge for women in higher education. In a study conducted by Mason and Goulden (2004) female faculty were more likely to be childless or to have fewer than their desired number of children when compared to their male colleagues. The explanations for this included both the delay of child rearing in order to complete educational obligations or, alternatively, the sacrificing of personal relationships for academic success (Clark & Hill, 2010; Solomon, 2011). It was hard to interpret my life as a statistic, but these facts accorded with my own experience. After years of putting family off for education and career and with a very loud biological clock ticking, I had my first and last child at age 37. I had become used to being the "old" mother on the playground, so it was a bit of a relief to discover that my situation was not atypical for women in academia.

That said, as education faculty members tend to be older, those with children are more likely to have had them earlier, during their more secure K-12 teaching career, which means they are entering the tenure process with mature children. Looking around my department I found I was the youngest on staff and the only one with a child under 18. In search of other female faculty in my position—tenure-track with small children—I began to seek out colleagues with similar backgrounds in the broader university. I could not find very many. Wolf-Wendel and Ward (2006) have suggested that many female faculty delay having children until after they have obtained tenure because of the uncertainty around the tenure process. Again, I found this to be true of our campus. There were several recently tenured faculty with new children, though they were generally ten years younger than I was. While I was looking to them for advice, they were also looking to me. This is apparently common. Female faculty with children, regardless of discipline, age, or experience, find they become role models for others as they negotiate their own work life balance because there are so few faculty comparatives (Wolf-Wendel & Ward, 2006). The importance of this group of women for me cannot be understated. Though not an official support group, these women have become important allies. We compare experiences, share strategies, and sometimes just blow off steam. It has also been wonderfully convenient to be able to plan research or have a meeting with someone while our children have a play date.

Making time for the day-to-day tasks of parenthood, particularly since our daughter is small, has been exhausting. According to the literature, being a tenure-track mother appears to be more challenging than being a tenure-track father (O'Laughlin & Bischof, 2005; Solomon, 2011; Wolf-Wendel & Ward, 2006) and fathers are more likely to get tenure than mothers (Mason & Goulden, 2004). Perhaps my fatigue cannot be simply attributed to my age. O'Brien and Hapgood (2012) suggest a cause of fatigue could be the mother's "second shift." The second shift refers to the work done in the home: for example, housework, childcare, and caring for elderly family members. The second shift, according to O'Brien and Hapgood (2012), is predominantly filled by the female spouse. One would think society has changed over time but, according to a survey of McMaster professors (Yates, 2014), which also reflected data reported by Statistics Canada, there remains an unequal sharing between men and women of responsibilities related to domestic childcare. Women spend on average 15 hours a week working in the home compared to 13 hours for men. When one considers issues related to eldercare, the disparity rises; women spend 17 hours and men 11 (Statistics Canada, 2011).

My family is a little different, an aberration from traditional Canadian family expectations, because my partner picks up most of the second shift. We have come to this agreement based on discussions about what makes sense for our family and our choice to put my career goals first. However, literature has indicated our arrangement is uncommon. A quick review of letters to Ms. Mentor, an Ann Landers-style advice column for academics, published in the *Times Chronical of Higher Education*, indicates that women wrestle with complex decisions about life and career balance. Frequently, relationships are sacrificed for tenure or tenure sacrificed for family/spouse career. According to Serrano (2008), both female doctoral candidates and tenure-track professors are often forced to choose between building families or careers. She suggested that the "leaking pipeline" out of academia for women was caused by placing the partner's career ahead of one's own or the decision to have children (Serrano, 2008). These conclusions may explain why so few successful female professors have traditional marriages (Acker & Armenti, 2004). So I may have inadvertently hit upon a successful strategy with a partner willing to take on an unconventional role in the home.

Up to this point I have highlighted the challenges faced by female faculty; however, there have also been some wonderful advantages to having a position with a flexible timetable. Working as a professor has allowed me a lot more control over my time, especially when contrasted with the scheduling commitments of a traditional K-12 school. A few months ago, my daughter's school had a midday event with an open invitation to parents. When I looked around the room, there were very few parents in attendance, which I suspect can be attributed less to a lack of engagement and more to parental employment patterns. Solomon (2011) reports that tenure-track positions are advantageous for women because they allow for more flexibility in childcare. Though I relish these opportunities, I also feel cautious about using them. A recent survey of Canadian university policy conducted by Clark and Hill (2010) indicated a shift in institutional policies across Canada to support women in tenure-track positions, with improved parental leave, delayed tenure clocks, and emergency and regular daycare options for faculty on campus. Nevertheless, I am wary as to how taking advantage of these policies will be perceived. Wolf-Wendel and Ward (2006) claim the normative policy structures found in universities do not serve women well, and their findings are a persistent source of anxiety for me. Will I be taken less seriously in meetings because I stayed home one day last week to take care of a sick child, for example? According to Acker and Armenti (2004), women tend to forgo gender-based policy advantages, such as maternity leave, preferring to negotiate teaching loads and motherhood on their own rather than ask for exceptions. Such decisions can be attributed to fears that people will suspect they are not able to cope with the demands of tenure (Coiner & George, 1998).

Policies may be more progressive, but they fail to alleviate the guilt I sometimes feel about missed bedtimes and weekend work. A professor's timetable may be more flexible, but this does not mean they work fewer hours. On average tenure-track faculty work 60 hours a week (Fogg, 2003), which is a lot of mental distance away from family; the situation is exacerbated when one considers travel requirements, for example, for conference presentations. I should also reiterate the point that I was still working on that pesky dissertation when I started my new job. This first year I have been busy and tired. My strategy was to try to limit my work to the office, so that when I am home I can truly be home. But after a day of teaching and planning and meetings, coming home to role-play the current mini novella my daughter has dreamed up leaves me a little less than enthusiastic. I will never be the super mom, preparing the perfectly arranged fruit snacks for after-school soccer practice, but when I plan carefully I know I can at least make it out to all the games. That realization was hard to accept for an overachiever like me.

Balancing Professional Responsibilities

As with my role in the home, I have had to compromise some of my professional expectations. Celebrating a birthday in conjunction with a conference in Las Vegas might have made me "top mom" for a few days, but it was all part of a balancing act. Bringing your entire family to a conference doesn't make it easy to be a top professor. In a report to the Council of Canadian Academics (Marsden et al., 2012), hereafter referred to as the Marsden Report, it was claimed that having a child might already constitute the first strike against being a good professor. This claim is supported by female faculty reports of being considered less serious about their careers than female colleagues without children, hence, my persistent anxiety. I was very cautious about mentioning the fact that I had a family, let alone a four-year-old, during my initial interview lest it be considered a first strike in the all too competitive job market. Faculty, however, are not officially evaluated by their familial status, but rather by their success in three areas: teaching, service, and research. Regarding these three areas, we again see some statistical anomalies between the genders, and each of these is presented below.

Teaching

The transition to teaching in higher education was the easiest part of my new job. In addition to my years of teaching experience in K-12, I had been working with adult learners in a professional-development capacity prior to my move. According to employment demographics, teaching is a strength for most female academics. Women hold 58% of the lower ranks in university settings, in positions which generally involve heavier teaching load expectations (Serrano, 2008). In contrast to their male colleagues, higher teaching loads are common for female academics at all ranks, and they are more likely to teach lower-level undergraduate courses, where the student needs and enrollments are higher (Mandleco, 2010). These numbers may in part be explained by women's higher participation in part-time and adjunct positions. According to Arnett (2013), the reason why more women take on part-time positions can be attributed to the struggle of finding a work-life balance. Women either cannot commit to the time demands of a full-time professorship, or they cannot obtain full-time employment (Arnett, 2013; Fogg, 2003).

In addition, I was surprised to learn that teaching expectations were different for women. According to Acker (2003), gender biases in Canadian universities presume that women are more nurturing and caring for their students; therefore, they are often expected to "mother" their students. Female faculty are often placed in pastoral roles within departments advising students, which is an important service task, but does not rank as a substantial achievement in terms of promotion and tenure requirements (Mandleco, 2010). The Marsden Report (2012) indicated this same gender expectation can result in female academics feeling devaluated and marginalized. Female faculty choose to respond to these pressures in two ways: by separating personal and professional lives completely (neutralizing gender), or by embracing their role as mothers and professionals (Arnett, 2013). Though I could not find any information that spoke to education faculties directly, I am not sure these conclusions apply to education because this field tends to be a more gender-balanced discipline than others in higher education. Nonetheless, I was told in no uncertain terms by my mother, whose career path I have closely paralleled, that I should "never wear flowers, or flowing feminine clothing" to work if I wanted to be taken seriously. Following her advice, I have the standard rack of black, brown, and, for a hint of colour, blue professional suits in my closet; so perhaps I am a neutralizer. I highly doubt I have been considered the nurturing type but I have been assigned high enrollment, writing intensive courses for my first-year teaching load. Rather than a reflection of my gender, I see my teaching duties as reflecting a rite of passage; as the new person, I expected to be picking up the courses that are perhaps a little less popular with the more established members of my department. I wasn't assigned any early-morning or evening classes, nor was I given less-desirable classroom space. In contrast to some of the anecdotes from colleagues in other departments, I think I fared well in year one. However, because teaching is what I am good at, it is also where I have tended to focus my time. Teaching courses that are entirely new to me, I have spent an unbalanced amount of time on preparation. I find my courses are never ready, never as polished as I would like them to be. In an attempt to regulate my time rather than make use of the flexibility I am afforded, I maintain a strict nine-to-five workday pattern in accordance with my former schedule as a K-12 teacher.

According to literature, professors approach their workday differently. Some, like me, prefer a structured work schedule with fixed office hours, while others adhere to what could be described as a grazing style with a more flexible approach to working (Solomon, 2011). Working more flexibly can mean working more, and it can also make achieving the life-work balance more challenging regardless of gender. Arnett (2013) advises women in particular to ensure they take breaks because they are less likely to do so and therefore more likely to burn out. I have established some pretty firm rules about time, out of self-preservation and an attempt at balancing motherhood and academic life. I don't work on Sunday, I don't check email from 7 p.m.–9 p.m. (generally), and I set daily achievement targets. Because I want to leave the office before 6 p.m., I rarely fail to achieve these targets. Does my teaching suffer because I set these rigid limitations? Women faculty in the Wolf-Wendel and Ward (2006) study reported that having children helped to put work demands into a healthier perspective by encouraging efficiency and moderating expectations of performance. I am not sure if I have reached the efficient state yet; however, I have reached a point where I have realized, in light of my other responsibilities, that it is not in my best interests to always focus on creating perfect lessons. Instead, I would be better off dedicating more time to service, another component of my job which needs more attention.

Service

According to the literature, service is another area where female professors excel. The Marsden Report (2012) states that women appear to perform more of the institutional "housekeeping" tasks. Female professors are also subjected to more pressures for being a "good citizen" than males (Acker, 2003). As with pastoral care of students, service appears to be the lowest priority in the tenure-evaluation criteria, though, at least in my experience, it seems to be one of the most pressing issues in terms of ensuring the smooth functioning of a department. At the beginning of my academic career I was fortunate to be mentored by an older, wiser female professor who told me in no uncertain terms to be strategic about service. She told me to only take service positions that directly relate to expanding my network of connections and furthering my research agenda. Further, she advised me to be cautious about the workload; for example, don't join the program-review committee if your faculty is considering a major overhaul of curriculum. Arnett (2013) reiterated this advice in a discussion on strategizing service as part of the tenure-evaluation process. However, working in a small department in a comprehensive university I want to contribute to the growth and direction of our department. According to Ward (2003), service has a bad reputation, because it is not valued as highly in the tenure process; however, it does provide you with insight into university processes and can give you an opportunity to participate in institutional change. Ward and Wolf-Wendel (2012) claimed that service offers faculty the prospect of agency early in their careers. At the same time, they noted that few female faculty who are heavily involved in service want to move into administrative positions. My colleagues have told me that service expectations in my department are above the norm when compared to other departments on campus because of our small size and our position as leaders in teaching within the university community.

Over the year, I have participated in eight internal university committees, as well as a few more short-term service events. I've stopped using references to specific committees on my curriculum vitae and have instead organized committee service into more general categories; for example, hiring committee appears as one item though I have participated in two. I am not sure of the wisdom of this approach, but it seems less pretentious than listing every committee in my dossier. I have also given two presentations to faculty as part of the teaching and learning department's agenda to raise awareness on teaching techniques. Ward and Wolf-Wendel (2012) discuss how smaller institutions have higher demands for service. Further, they state that the service load increases rather than decreases as one becomes more established. There are guidelines attached to activity reports, which often include suggested percentages for time allocation. The working percentages that seem to best describe my year are 50% teaching and a 30–20% split of my remaining time between service and research respectively. In year one I haven't been able to achieve the more commonly expected 40/20/40 balance of a typical tenured professor. However, in the next year, during the second offering of my courses, I hope to move closer to this goal. Research literature has shown me that the key to success in academia is to not let your research output suffer because of your service and teaching requirements. This goal has been difficult to achieve, because there is no external pressure beyond the looming annual review to encourage me to focus on research.

Research

Of the triad of expectations, research output is the most difficult to maintain but also the most highly valued (O'Laughlin & Bischoff, 2005). When it comes to negotiating time, research falls to the side more frequently for women than men (Ward & Wolf-Wendel, 2012). According to the Marsden Report (2012) women have received fewer Tier I and Tier II Canada Research chairs, honourary doctorates, and other academic recognitions than men. Part of the disparity in research output by females may be related to the fact that they are not applying to the large funding agencies in Canada. Canadian Institutes of Health Research receives twice as many applications from men as it does from women; Natural Sciences and Engineering Research Council five times, while SSHRC is about equal. When success rates are compared, both women and men have comparable results, which indicates women are equally successful when they apply for grants; they are just not applying (Yates, 2014). Why? Using an ecological model to predict publication output, O'Brien and Hapgood (2012) suggest that research output operates in a strong reinforcing feedback loop, in which success is rewarded with further success in an almost exponential fashion akin to population dynamics. In order to establish critical mass in research output, considerable time is needed to develop a research agenda and a track record. Given that the average age for the commencement of a tenure-track position in education is around the early 40s, women confront significant obstacles in establishing a track record. Having completed their first career as a teacher, many face the twin pressures of the biological clock and the need to develop a research agenda. For non-education faculty members, delaying family start until they have achieved research recognition means most women are in their late 30s, a time when fertility drops markedly (Clark & Hill, 2010). This situation has also led to what Bell (2009) refers to as the "female ghetto": women who occupy lower ranking positions with less pay and higher teaching loads. Being promoted out of this ghetto is difficult for women who cannot meet research performance matrices. Female faculty in assistant-professorial positions find it difficult to increase research output because of heavy teaching loads.

I did successfully defend my dissertation mid-year. Previously, when I mentioned that 20% of my time this year was spent on research, I was referring to my dissertation work. Since my defense in the fall, research has fallen somewhat off my agenda as I have raced to catch up on my marking, new course developments, and the committee work I set aside until my defense was done. It has taken a semester to catch up, but now I am starting to think about research again. O'Brien and Hapgood (2012) give me cause for concern, in terms of establishing the positive feedback loop needed to capitalize on my research. Have I been too slow? Am I too late? My colleagues suggested that I spend my first year strategically releasing articles based on my dissertation research while simultaneously developing new projects and partners. They also suggested I present my work at conferences in order to build up my profile. I have done this by participating in three conferences; however, article writing in my research agenda is developing very slowly.

I have dedicated some time this year to building relationships, one of the intangible aspects of a research agenda. Arnett (2013) suggested that it is important for women to leverage their networks to increase research output. Apparently this doesn't come as easily for us as it does for men. Mandleco (2010) reiterates this point and goes on to suggest it is critical for female faculty to seek either a formal or informal mentorship relationship with an experienced scholar who will help them develop a research agenda and a recognized publication record.

The Trade-Off

In reviewing the expectations for both successful motherhood and tenure, the theme that kept presenting itself was that of balance and the determination of what was important when. Although Canadian tenure processes appear more supportive than our neighbours to the south (most Canadian faculty in tenure-track positions get tenure) (Acker, 2003), I am still worried. The McMaster task force identified three key policy areas that impact women's career pathways in higher education: tenure and promotion policy, merit and salary, and leave policies (Yates, 2014). Apparently, I am lucky because in education, polices and conditions are particularly supportive (Aker, 2003). However, according to Acker and Armenti (2004), women cope by working longer, negotiating housework, and by finding support through both formal and informal channels.

Solomon (2011) claims the long hours and somewhat workaholic approach to employment comes naturally to academics regardless of gender, because many of us inherently tie identity to career aspirations. The trade-off is viewed as a temporary state which can result in the following rationalization: "when I get tenure, then I can …" Part of the trade-off can be attributed to the type of institution a person chooses to join. Clark and Hill (2010), who only looked at women, indicate that women may have more success achieving tenure in smaller, predominantly undergraduate universities where the research demands are less burdensome. Interestingly this statement seems to reflect some of the stereotypes for women, disguised as feminism: Choose the less-demanding university in order to ensure success. O'Laughlin and Bischoff (2005) categorize the trade-offs for women in terms of conflicts or competing forces of time, stress, and behavioral expectations. They suggest the key to success is strategizing your way through a series of cost-benefit analyses for institutional fit, teaching, service, and research. There is no question in my mind that these need to be specific strategic decisions. Again, I am lucky that I was hired for a tenure-track position at a small comprehensive university; it may have been the best strategic choice for me. It has given me both the opportunity to grow in a nurturing environment and the pressure to get that dissertation out the door.

Although I have been lucky to receive familial support, it has not come without strain. As my partner can confirm, I am not always fun to be around, especially if a publishing deadline is looming. I have also developed an eye tick, presumably a physiological response to this first year of change. Weinreib et. al. (2012) indicate that, on average, female academics find work more stressful because of personal and professional strain and are slightly less satisfied at work than males. This stress can have serious implications for health. Female faculty are slightly more likely to burn out, fall sick, or suffer from fatigue (Acker & Armenti, 2004). Though I hope this is temporary state for me, I can see that if I do not learn to better manage my time and stress that eye tick may last longer.

Conclusion

Acker and Armenti (2004) point out the three big issues for female faculty are: finding the balance between children and career, negotiating the stress of the tenure-evaluation process, and managing the fatigue of juggling all of these demands in a timely manner. I'm not sure if I can answer the question of whether women can have it all. The variables are complex. According to the literature, chances of success in achieving tenure can be enhanced by choosing the right partner (or choosing not to have one), finding the right time to have a baby (or deciding not to), solidifying a research agenda in the first five years of employment, finding an institution that matches with your commitment level, getting great course evaluations (probably in first year, oversubscribed courses), and strategizing your committee memberships. Negotiating career and life obligations as an academic is not a walk in the park because universities have cultures that are highly competitive. I can certainly say all of these decisions or their ramifications have been presented to me in my first year, and I have negotiated them as best I could, given their context and timing, but this year has indeed been everything but a smooth transition.

References

Acker, S. (2003). The concerns of Canadian women academics: Will faculty shortages make things better or worse? *McGill Journal of Education, 38*(3), 391–406.

Acker, S., & Armenti, C. (2004). Sleepless in academia. *Gender and Education, 16*(1), 3–24.

Arnett, A. (2013). Professor/Mom: Female professors discuss the trials of family life on the tenure track. *Diverse Issues in Higher*

Education (September). Retrieved from http://www.readperiodicals.com/201309/3116650471.html.
Association of Universities and Colleges of Canada (AUCC). (2007). *Trends in Higher Education* (Vol 2: Faculty). Ottawa, ON.
Bell, S. (2009). Women in science: Maximising productivity, diversity and innovation. Federation of Australian and Technological Societies, Canberra, Australia.
Canadian Association of University Teaching (CAUT). (2008). The tenure gap: Women's university appointments, 1985–2005. *CAUT Equity Review* (September) 2–4.
Canadian Association of University Teaching (CAUT). (2010). The changing academy? A portrait of Canada's university teachers, *CAUT Education Review, 12*(1), 1–6.
Clark, C., & Hill, J. (2010). Reconciling the tension between the tenure and biological clocks to increase recruitment and retention of women in academia. *Forum on Public Policy, 2*. Retrieved from http://forumonpublicpolicy.com/spring2010.vol2010/womencareers2010.html.
Coiner, C., & George, D. (1998). *The family track: Keeping your faculties while you mentor, nurture, teach and serve.* Chicago, IL: University of Illinois Press.
Fogg, P. (2003). Family time: Why some women quit their coveted tenure-track jobs. *The Chronicle of Higher Education, 49*(40), A10.
King, D. (2008). Doctoral graduates in Canada: Findings from a survey of earned doctorates 2004/2005. *Culture Tourism and the Centre for Educational Research.* Catalogue no: 81595M. Ottawa, ON: Statistics Canada.
Mandleco, B. (2010). Women in academia: What can be done to help women achieve tenure? *Forum on Public Policy, 5,* 1–13.
Marsden, L., Dodd, J., Ghazzali, N., Konrad, A., Lefebvre, Y., Oldham, G., Wolfson, M., et al. (2012). Strengthening Canada's research capacity: The gender dimension. *Council of Canadian Academies.* Retrieved from http://www.scienceadvice.ca/uploads/eng/assessments%20and%20publications%20and%20news%20releases/women_university_research/wur_fullreporten.pdf.pdf.
Mason, M., & Goulden, M. (2004). Marriage and baby blues: Redefining gender equity in the academy. *The annals of the American Academy of Political and Social Science, 596,* 86–103.
O'Brien, K., & Hapgood, K. (2012). The academic jungle: Ecosystem modelling reveals why women are driven out of research. *Oikos, 121,* 999–1004.
O'Laughlin, E., & Bischof, L. (2005). Balancing parenthood and academia: Work/family stress as influenced by gender and tenure status. *Journal of Family Issues, 26*(1), 79–106.
Serrano, C. (2008). Leaking pipelines: Doctoral student family formation. *Berkeley Undergraduate Journal, 20*(2), 1–20.

Solomon, C. (2011). Sacrificing at the altar of tenure: Assistant professors' work/life management. *The Social Science Journal, 48*(2), 335–344.

Statistics Canada. (July, 2011). Women in Canada: A gender based statistical report (Component of Statistics Canada Catalogue no. 89-503-X). Ottawa, ON: Minister of Industry.

Ward, K. (2003). *Faculty service roles and the scholarship of engagement.* San Francisco, CA: Jossey Bass.

Ward, K., & Wolf-Wendel, L. (2012). *Academic motherhood: How faculty manage work and family.* New Brunswick, NJ: Rutgers University Press.

Weinreib, J., Jones, G., Metcalfe, A., Fisher, D., Gingras, Y., Rubenson, K., & Snee, I. (2012). Canadian university academics' perceptions of job satisfaction – "the future is not what it used to be." In P. J. Bentley, H. Coates, I. R. Dobson, L. Goedegebuure, & V. L. Meek (Eds.), *Job satisfaction around the academic world* (pp. 83–102). Dordrecht, the Netherlands: Springer.

Wolf-Wendel, E., & Ward, K. (2006). Academic life and motherhood: Variations by institutional type. *Higher Education, 52*, 487–521.

Yates, C. (2014). *Women faculty, now and in the future: Building excellence at McMaster university.* Report of the Equity Task Force. Retrieved from http://www.mcmaster.ca/vpacademic/documents/Yates_Report_on_Gender_Equity_January_2014.pdf.

CHAPTER 16

Just Today and Just Tomorrow: Building Capacity on the Tenure-Track in New Brunswick

Lyle Hamm
Faculty of Education, University of New Brunswick

Introduction

It is 9:30 a.m., August 5, 2013 ... I am walking around the faculty looking for my new colleagues who I have been hired to work with, learn from, and support where I am able. At least, that is my objective. I have decided that I will engage them as opposed to waiting for them to interact with me. I know very little about how a Faculty of Education operates, but I am ecstatic to be here and I have many questions. Still, I do not know who my colleagues are or even if I should ask the questions I have because I am not sure if I shouldn't already have some of the answers. After all, I am a veteran educator even though I am a first-year academic. I fear my questions will be received with ridicule from the colleagues whom I do not know yet. I feel caught. At times, I don't know the questions I should ask and worse, I don't know whom to approach to ask the questions that I am unsure of asking.

This field note began my educational journey in the Faculty of Education at the University of New Brunswick (UNB) in Fredericton, where I began the professional transition from being a public-school teacher and administrator with 22 years' experience to my role as a university educator and researcher.

My wife and I left permanent education positions, financial security, and family networks in Alberta, where we had both served in public education for 22 years. By our estimation we had enjoyed meaningful and productive careers in Western Canada. Like many individuals from Saskatchewan in the 1980s and 1990s, we could not obtain full-time and sustainable employment in our home province. We migrated to Alberta at different times, met each other, and remained there—eventually dreaming of retirement near the Rocky Mountains.

When we made the decision to abandon our secure lifestyle, one of our close friends asked us, "Why do you want to leave now and give this up? You are both so close to retirement." By "this" he meant security, property, pension, and friendship. In fact, members of our own family were deeply disturbed with our departure eastward. This fact only added to my anxiety, as I was offered a one-year term position as an assistant professor in educational administration and leadership. This was not a tenure-track academic appointment initially, but I was informed that it would turn into one. I would have to compete for the tenure-track job I desired a few months after my arrival. In that first year, we would constantly remind ourselves to focus on just today and just tomorrow.

Excitement and Uncertainty

A few weeks after we arrived at UNB, I learned that the university faculty and the senior administration were in contract negotiations, but overheard colleagues conjecturing that the stalemate would be resolved before long. I didn't have time to take notice or really invest myself in university politics; I had to begin teaching within a month of my arrival and needed to get course syllabi prepared for September. Little did I or any of my colleagues know that five months later, less than two weeks into 2014, a significant event would occur within our university community. This event would not only affect my life as a first-year assistant professor, but also the lives of hundreds of professors, administrators, and support staff who identified with UNB as their professional home. It was an event that would gather national attention.

Briefly, I was interviewed and offered a one-year term position in June of 2013. I knew, upon acceptance, that it would be advertised nationally as a tenure-track position later that fall. I knew I would compete for it once again. I had applied for several academic positions in the previous two years, but had only received letters in the mail thanking me for my interest and telling me that I had not made the short list of candidates. When the UNB offer was presented to me, I accepted it immediately and unconditionally. I began constructing the adventure in my mind and the process toward acquiring the tenure-track position the following year.

We made our Alberta school district aware of the one-year teaching offer from UNB. They were kind enough to provide a year's leave of absence for both my wife and me. It was great having this small security, but truly, I didn't fancy returning to Western Canada after the effort and the costs associated with moving eastward. Still, the possibility of moving back was always in my mind as I was setting up courses and combing through my dissertation to find the most relevant and interesting ideas to write articles and chapters for publication.

By all accounts, my first year was successful. I taught six courses, submitted several articles, gave presentations at an international conference, and was invited to be a keynote speaker at another New Brunswick conference in early July. The latter conference coincided with the wrath of Hurricane Arthur as the storm turned northward and unleashed its rage and energy on the city and area. With all the conference presenters sitting in a dark room waiting for the lights to return (which took several days), they watched and listened to me as I read my speech in semi-darkness with the aid of my wife's Samsung phone flashlight. It was a cumbersome moment, but in many ways it symbolized and captured my first-year experience crossing the threshold from public to higher education. The entire year I stumbled around in darkness and fog, trying to figure out how to perform effectively within the academy so I could have an opportunity to contribute at this institution for the long haul.

"'You're Hired!' Great. What Now?" (Jiménez, 2012, p. 1)

I set the context above because I am feeling better and have my feet below me again. I finally feel grounded. It is May of 2015, and I am now two months from my 50th birthday and almost a year into my tenure-track position, having secured it shortly after my second set of interviews in March of 2014. Still, I find myself at an interesting and often perplexing crossroads in my career and personal life. Similar to Welsh and Schaffer (2014), who both left secure employment to pursue their elusive tenure-track positions, I constantly wrestle with fear, uncertainty, excitement, confusion, and sometimes even indifference, when I reflect upon the way that I am "being" now. I have been an industrial worker for a mining company, a journalist, a sports coach (mostly hockey), a teacher, and a school leader. I have always enjoyed working directly with colleagues and community members and learning from individuals who do not necessarily share the values or worldviews that I possess.

The last 10 years of my educational service in Alberta was in a community undergoing rapid demographic change. I was motivated to study for my doctorate degree to learn more about how to effectively teach and lead in an increasingly diverse educational and social environment. There are times when I wonder whether I would have continued on in doctoral studies if in fact I wasn't working and living in a "rural-influenced city" (Hamm & Cormier, 2015) that was experiencing rapid growth in linguistic, cultural, and religious diversity (Hamm, 2013). Even while I was deeply embedded within my doctoral research, joining a faculty of education often seemed like an elusive goal. My doctoral studies provided me a glimpse of the type of educational service I believed would challenge and allow me to continue teaching, researching and providing community service beyond my projected retirement date. I did not aspire to be an educator with any regrets after retirement or leave teaching dissatisfied. Most importantly, I wanted an opportunity to work with educators who were in the field striving to become better and who were intent on contributing to positive educational and social change within their schools, communities, and provinces.

Previous Skill Sets and Knowledge Support Academic Growth

Prior to joining the education field, I worked as a reporter, columnist and editor from 1988 until 1990. In my first reporting position, the editor I was working with bluntly pointed out, "Lyle, you may have a BA in English, but you sure can't write." Rather than fire me, she supported and mentored me. Through her guidance and coaching I became increasingly proficient at constructing questions, writing, revising, and conducting interviews with individuals and groups of people. In time, I became a news editor and later transferred many of the journalism skills to my English-literature and writing-pedagogical work in public schools in Alberta. After I moved into educational leadership and administration I tried to provide the same levels of support for the teachers and support staff of the schools I helped lead.

Armed with prior experience and knowledge, on the morning of August 5, 2013, I knew I was going to be much better off in my first academic position if I found support quickly from my education colleagues. I was excited to meet the committee members who interviewed me and the individuals who took time during and after my presentation the previous June to speak with me. During an orientation session with 22 other new academics, many of them hired into tenure-track positions, we were all provided important information at the end of that day. The suggestions included getting support from mentors; selecting and establishing a career path; choosing scholarly projects wisely; selecting service commitments with care; and thinking carefully before taking on extra duties in the faculty. I added two of my own, which included planning enriched and engaging learning activities for my graduate students, and reading and writing every day. I taped these points on the wall above my office desk, where they greeted me each morning when I arrived at work.

Striving for Balance in Teaching, Research, and Service: Does It Exist in Academia?

My first two years have taught me that balance may be an illusion in the academic world. Many new academics find themselves living "an unbalanced life, do not feel a sense of community or collegiality in their workplace and are at the mercy of an unwieldy and vague tenure system" (Greene et al., 2008, p. 43). I experience turbulence at times, but it seems to have been relatively rare; or, I try to make it rare. As a veteran educator and new scholar, I know that the act of educating (in all forms across all contexts, i.e., planning, teaching, research service, and managing time) is a complex activity no matter how you explore and interpret it. I didn't have to obtain a doctorate in education to figure this out. I am determined to accept an unbalanced life as the norm that comes with the tenure-track position. I believe my previous educational, coaching, and journalism experiences prepared me for a role in higher education. However, the fact is, this job is challenging, confusing, complex, and creates excessive anxiety for me. Some of this anxiety motivates me; some of it debilitates me. But at this point, I believe it is because I am still grasping to understand the culture; I am still trying to learn about the institution and the bureaucracy that I am now a part of.

Okay, I Am Here ... Kindly Mentor and Support Me

Receiving positive collective mentoring from colleagues has been crucial for me, and it is the idea of mentoring or being mentored that has promoted my reflection mostly these first 22 months at UNB. Having been a mentor for young reporters, athletes, and new teachers earlier in my life, I know the value of helping someone connect quickly to an organizational culture (Schein, 2004). Institutional connection helps new members of an organization feel immediate success in their multiple roles and a sense of belonging on the team they are working with. I agree with Welsh and Schaffer (2014) that "[t]here is ... no single story of the road to tenure" (p. 26). The narrative that I am constructing has been filled with success and not necessarily in published articles, established research programs, and extended community service at this point. Yes, these areas of my professional life are developing, but they are developing slowly. I am building capacity in many areas in my new academic life. I am constantly aware that I have to be patient and move forward cautiously as I set my courses, craft my pedagogy, and construct my research program.

Teaching

I have experienced equal amounts of tension, confusion, stress, and uncertainty, given the new expectations I have accepted as part of my tenure-track appointment. Yet, I still cling to the thought that guided me as an educator for 22 years. That is, I can only do what I can, and perform what I must, given the sources of energy that I have to draw from. I have known for a long time that I must take care of myself. Balance hasn't arrived yet. I am not confident that it ever will for me. I am a late starter in higher education. I have committed myself to learning the rest of the way and staying as healthy as I can.

Transition From Active Classroom Teaching to Online Pedagogy

I served 22 years in public-school classrooms, gymnasiums, and administration offices, often waiting for an audible signal so I could eat my lunch, go to the washroom, and then eventually go home after the students had left for the day. I am delighted and fascinated with the freedom and autonomy that I now have to construct my working environment and how I function within it to serve my students and the faculty. There are no bells that automatically direct me to where I need to be teaching, supervising, and meeting with others. Instead, I have found there are more flexible teaching arrangements here at UNB than in K-12 public education, especially when most of my teaching to date has been in the online environment. I have enjoyed this new reality, but cautiously. I have to keep my focus on how I am using my time and energy each day, each week, and each month. I document everything. I conceptualize and construct priority lists every two to three weeks in my field notes.

As I mentioned, my teaching experience so far at UNB has predominantly been in online distance education through the Desire2Learn (D2L) online platform. My students are graduate students—mostly educators themselves, working in classrooms and schools across Canada, and even around the world. My courses are designed for them to engage when they have the space and time to be productive with their learning colleagues. Initially, this reality created considerable anxiety for me as I had been teaching and providing educational leadership face-to-face in K-12 public schools my entire career. I had taken two courses online through my graduate studies and did not find the format satisfying for my learning, but the technology has improved since that time.

Looking back to that first month of teaching online, I wonder how I survived. I had been preparing in my mind, on the long drive east, how I would engage and challenge my adult students in my university courses. I had outstanding university teachers while I was a graduate student at the University of Lethbridge and at the University of Calgary. I was drawing from their methods of forming authentic relationships, delivering course content through inviting pedagogy for safe engagement, and always working to encourage my students to go beyond the syllabus in their research. I even had some success working for the University of Lethbridge in the summer of 2010 while teaching a face-to-face course in their leadership program.

"You Will Be Teaching Online Courses, Lyle"

I quickly found out that graduate students would be the least of my worries; in fact, they would be my allies. I found teaching online very challenging and time consuming that first few months. September 2013 was a pedagogical nightmare for me as I had to quickly adopt new technologies and construct an online social-pedagogical presence (Kezar & Lester, 2009; Smith & Sivo, 2012). Even though I had extensive D2L online support located just down the hallway from my office, I still isolated myself in my office, crafting long lectures in text wondering constantly how best to deliver them. With the help of my wife, I published course files to the D2L framework along with learning activities and discussion questions, and waited. I waited and watched my computer. Sometimes, I would forget to click one icon when uploading content, and then I would have students emailing me wondering where the file was or wondering how they could enter into a discussion that I forgot to open up. My frustration and anxiety was at its highest level in mid-September when I couldn't help the students who were new to the program and new to online learning. For the first time in my teaching career, I could not help my students adjust comfortably in my course within their graduate program.

I apologized a lot that first month, but I was upfront with students. I told them I was new to the university system and had never taught an online course. Fortunately, there were students nearing the completion of their degrees who were coaching me, as I was trying my best to teach them and facilitate our discussions. It was in these moments of students supporting me that Paulo Freire's words rang sharply when he suggests, "The teacher is no longer merely the-one-who-teaches, but one who is himself taught in dialogue with the students, who in turn while being taught also teach. They become jointly responsible for a process in which all grow" (1970, p. 80). I was fortunate to have empathetic graduate students in my courses, who were patient with me, while I established my footing and formed the early stages of a new pedagogical process in my educational ways of being.

Setting the Intellectual Bait

Teaching online, in many ways, is like fishing. I imagine what my students look and sound like, where their schools and communities are, and the educational complexity they face each day. In my lessons, I try to construct what I would coin "intellectual bait" in every attempt to enhance their critical engagement of my courses. I infuse humorous anecdotes about teaching and leadership; I employ what Freire (1970) and Kincheloe (2005) might call critical-constructivist questions and case studies that I believe will challenge their thinking and keep them in the deep dialogical discussions longer than what I present as minimum standards. Early on, I constantly inquired about online pedagogy with colleagues who were also teaching online or in a position of supporting teachers. I asked them about the strategies they used to engage their students. Again, I didn't want to let my guard down and paint them a portrait of an incompetent teacher. I was careful in asking them the types of questions that would give me the responses I thought I should be looking for. I did not let anyone know that my wife had to help me publish my course files each week for the first month of my UNB experience.

When I was finally able to complete the uploading tasks myself without error, I felt a sense of accomplishment. This may sound like there was no support in my faculty; that is absolutely false. I simply would not ask for additional support because I didn't want people to know about my digital shortcomings. So, when I did conjure up enough courage, I carefully selected individuals to ask questions regarding how they prepared and taught online courses. I always received their unconditional support. But as a first year, term-appointed, neophyte academic with 22 years of teaching and leadership experience behind me, I was afraid to let anyone know about my lack of confidence and sense of despair early on. Can this be attributed to my own arrogance? Pedagogical insecurity? I don't know. But then and now, I simply feel fortunate to be working with the people I am serving with. I now know I shouldn't have been as silent as I was.

Selecting Mentors

A suggestion that was provided me, along with all the first-year professors in our orientation session, was to acquire support from mentors and peers in our respective faculties immediately. The mentoring relationships that I have described have been crucial for my service and academic development at UNB. The way I was initially mentored, coached, and supervised when I began teaching shaped the way I provided leadership and support to the teachers I worked with as a school-based administrator. Further, my K-12 mentoring relationships also impacted how I coached and developed athletes in the sports I contributed to. Thus, the mentoring relationship cannot be understated or go unexplored in the new experiences I am having at UNB. When I think about how I have been mentored these past 22 months, it does not in any way parallel the explicit nature of mentoring in public K-12 schools I served in, or even how I learned that mentoring should be conducted for new teachers. Yet, without the mentoring I have received here, I would still be lost in the dark.

For instance, I was assigned a mentor in the school system when I began teaching in 1991, and even when I became a vice-principal in 1999. In later years of service, my administrative partners and I always matched up a new teacher with a more experienced teacher who worked in a similar subject area or shared many of the same interests. The more support we placed around a teacher, the better they were able to function within their multiple roles. I have not been assigned a mentor at UNB; I have found individuals myself to work with and align my research, thinking, and writing.

Some researchers have found that mentoring is often absent in university institutions or not provided in an effective manner (Greene et al., 2008). These researchers describe how this reality creates gaps in support that leave many new faculty members lost and wondering about how the institution and faculty operates and what their educational priorities might be. The fact is, "when faculty are engaged in open and communicative dialogue, they often experience a more friendly and helpful climate with their colleagues" (Fritschler & Smith, 2009, as cited in Trower, 2012, p. 124). A helpful climate in any institution may propel individuals to step outside their comfort zones and engage in activities or take on responsibilities that help them build capacity in their roles. That has been my experience at UNB.

Direct and Indirect Mentoring

My experience to date has been a mix of direct mentoring and gentle nudging (Welsh & Schaffer, 2014). Though I have not been assigned a formal mentor, I find myself among many supportive and collegial colleagues. Interestingly, if I were to call some of them mentors, I am not sure they would recognize themselves as serving that role for me. I have received unconditional indirect mentoring from many of them. I have been invited by several colleagues to join with them in their research activities, to supervise their graduate students with them, and to be part of the graduate-thesis process, which includes thesis defenses. These have all been opportunities for me to learn from my experienced colleagues.

At first, I thought forging collegial relationships was my responsibility and part of my role as a new scholar. Later on, I wondered why they had invited me to support them in their work. After all, I was a novice researcher and university teacher; I believed I had little to offer them, especially some of the senior professors and researchers I worked with. I believe now they were sympathetic to my transition. But again, why was I offered immediate support? Yes, I have described how I went seeking for this support in my first month at UNB. But I could have been turned away as easily as I was accepted. Why was I able to secure the mentoring relationships that I am now enjoying and benefitting from, while at the same time building what I am hoping will be life-long friendships?

Relationship Building Has Been My Priority

Upon reflection, I think the early success I experienced at UNB was due to my anxiety when I began and the uncertain questions that I posed to colleagues when I arrived. My questions increased my engagement and professional contact with my colleagues and opened up safe spaces to interact with them. I believe they observed an educator who was interested in learning and grasping the organizational and institutional structures quickly. At 50 years of age, one never knows how much time they have left to work with colleagues, serve their students, nourish their intellectual spirit, and contribute a piece for educational change in our country. Indeed, I was in a hurry and I still am. But I was fortunate to be invited to belong. The invitations were many and various. "Lyle, you would be good on that committee"; "Lyle, your academic interest supports my graduate student"; "Lyle, we have a similar interest; we should write together"; "Lyle, this local school could use your support." My colleagues opened doors just a crack and invited me in. It was up to me if I wanted to walk through those doors. I recognized the seeds they were offering for the mentoring relationship, and grasped them, and I have firmly planted them within the complexity and confusion of my first two years. I did not know if the relationship would last or what service I could provide my colleagues in the work they were performing. The uncertainty created anxiety within me. It may also have signaled some questions within colleagues, as my sense from emails to them and hallway conversations, that were so focused on working together and getting together, may have been a slight boundary challenge. I was actively seeking to help them and to learn from them. Tenure was not in my mind in my first year; getting the tenure-track position was. But you don't get the next position unless you have a sense of what is going on in the institution. I had to establish support. I was receiving supportive responses to my questions. I began to feel confident responding to my students' questions, and my courses were going well. I was producing writing from my dissertation that was being considered for publication. I was contributing to committees. I had momentum at the end of 2013. Then it crashed, when, collectively, the faculty at UNB went on strike in January of 2014.

Darkness Leads to Light

Walking with colleagues in darkness at extreme temperatures in the middle of January affects a person's mind, body, and spirit in ways that are difficult to describe. If I could choose one word to describe the experience, it would be "erosion." As each day of the three-week strike passed, a little piece of what I had been building was weathered, eroded, and slowly disappearing. To say the first month of 2014 was the worst month of my educational life would be true. Here I was, trying to learn how to build my capacities as a university professor and, at the same time, getting ready to compete for the tenure-track position in a second set of interviews. My courses stopped, my writing stopped and my service stopped. It was over. It was dead. I firmly believed this. I felt despair. I felt shame. I would go back to my former life, I thought. Collectively, we waited for news each day from our negotiators, but progress was slow. We trudged together in cold weather and snow as the public hurled insults through the media, and while driving passed us on the picket line.

On the other hand, the experience was enlightening, character building, and relational. As we trudged together I met colleagues from many faculties who were wonderful people. Without the picket line we might never have met. We talked about our teaching and research, initially. As the temperatures descended even further and we ran out of shared professional experiences to discuss during our three-hour walking shifts, the conversations became more personal. I met friends now, not just institutional colleagues. I asked many when their next shift was and looked forward to continuing our conversations from the previous ones we had. Our dialogue held the frigid temperatures at bay. I learned about family members, their doctoral programs, and the friends we had in common in other institutions in Canada. Out of the darkness of that month, life-long friendships were forged and solidified. A strike does that to humans. It makes them stronger and more resilient. It became a wonderful experience.

Service

I still feel fragmented here. Some days, everything comes together in crystal-clear fashion. Some days, I am working through fog, wondering what I am doing, and if what I am doing is enough to even be considered for a promotion to associate professor when I am up for it, as my colleagues remind me.

I had a discussion recently with one of my colleagues and I asked several questions. "How much is enough? I mean, what is expected of an assistant professor? I don't mean simply to reach promotion and eventually tenure. What exactly should I be doing outside of the teaching that is assigned to me? How much should I write? Where should I send my writing to? What counts as solid academic writing and what does not count?" I am always wondering along these lines. After I have completed my planning, teaching, and assessments for the week, what should I spend most of my energy and time doing? I want to stay here, and the elusive breakdown of 40/40/20 related to teaching, research, and service is not easy to define at this point in time for me. Simply speaking, I am striving to build a meaningful program of research; I am striving to build highly engaging and relevant courses for our students in graduate studies; I am looking for schools who might be interested in working with me. I am trying to survive.

I miss schools. I miss the children and the teaching and the sports programs, and I miss the intensity. I need to be in schools, working with teachers and administrators for my own professional satisfaction. It is still where I feel most comfortable. Early in my first year at UNB, I was invited to be part of a provincial action research project in several schools. I was fortunate to meet many schoolteachers and created some strong connections in the community. Later, I was invited to become part of a school-professional learning community with teachers who were interested in understanding similar realities in their school that I had experienced in my former ones in Alberta. The projects ended, the learning community moved on to other topics, and I was once again outside on the perimeter of schools.

I believe the permanent avenue into schools will be through the participatory action research project that I have planned and that I have gathered funding to conduct this spring. It has taken almost two years to get to this point. When I started this job, I reminded myself of barriers that exist when entering a research setting and the gradual process of setting up a research study in an unfamiliar setting. I had experienced this during my graduate studies, and the knowledge I brought forth from those experiences has at least allowed me to retain my patience in working to establish my program.

Research on Demographic Change

I described earlier in this writing that, had it not been for the rapidly changing community environment I lived and worked in, I might not have continued on in doctoral studies. I am glad I stuck with it. I have been a seeker of information and knowledge my entire life, and I have long been curious to learn more about how people adapt to continuous change in their environments. When I sought interview advice from my supervisor early in 2013, it was noted that my background was well suited to New Brunswick because it was undergoing rapid demographic change in many of its communities.

Getting the job meant that I had interest and experience in research that would be relevant for the community and province I was working in. It is within these emerging realities that I have worked to build a research program where I will draw from the research I conducted in Western Canada and apply it within the context of New Brunswick, and eventually Atlantic Canada. I hope.

Fortunately, I have met individuals who share similar interests with me related to how students and teachers understand diversity and what those understandings may reveal about the nature of their educational experiences in this province, region, and across Canada (Hamm, Peck, & Sears, 2015). My anxiety has been lessened significantly through my research partnerships where I have received support and guidance from some colleagues. I do worry that I burden them because they are embedded in their long-established research programs and operate at high capacity, whereas I still function as a beginner. The biggest mistake I feel I am making is trying to keep up with them, when I know realistically I cannot at this time. I have to proceed slowly. It is the same advice I offered new teachers in the schools I served in as an administrator. Gently move forward, build capacity, be resilient, and look for opportunities to collaborate with and support colleagues (Hamm & Cormier, 2014). Above all, breathe and be happy. A career, I have learned, is fluid, and the time goes by rapidly.

Closing Remarks

I have enjoyed working on this reflective journey, and it could not have come at a better time. I am finishing my teaching for this year and, finally, I will get a break from preparing lessons and facilitating discussions. I will be able to fully engage my research program that has taken almost two years to construct. I have received support and approval to enter into schools and investigate the educational realities of research participants in this Atlantic province. Have I done everything that I could have and should have been doing since that field note on August 5, 2013 (that started this chapter)? I believe I have. Am I motivated to continue working with an eye for tenure? I know I am. As Jiménez (2012) suggests, "(G)etting an academic job feels like winning the lottery" (p. 1). I believe this now. I can and will live with the uncertainly and venture deeper into the unknown tenure-track territory. I have enjoyed every second of the last 25 years. But I would like 25 more.

References

Freire, P. (1970). *Pedagogy of the oppressed*. New York, NY: Continuum.
Greene, C., O'Connor, K., Good, A., Ledford, C., Peel, B., & Zhang, G. (2008). Building a support system toward tenure: Challenges and needs of tenure-track faculty in colleges of education. *Mentoring & Tutoring: Partnership in Learning*, 16(4), 429–447. doi:10.1080/13611260802433791.
Hamm, L. (2013). Intercultural research and education on the Alberta prairies: Findings from a doctoral study. *Journal of Educational Thought*, 46(3), 219–231.
Hamm, L. D., & Cormier, K. (2014). Building instructional capacity: The new face of professional development. *Canadian Association of Principals*, (Spring) 21–23.
Hamm, L., Peck, C., & Sears, A. (2015). *"Don't even think about bringing that to school": New Brunswick students' understandings of ethnic diversity.* Paper presented for the Annual Conference of the Canadian Society for the Study of Education, Ottawa, ON.

Hamm, L., & Cormier, K. (2015). School leaders face complex racial issues in diverse schools and communities. *Antistasis, 5*(1), 41–45.

Jiménez, J. (2012). "You're Hired!" Great. What Now? *Chronicle of Higher Education, 59*(4), 1–5.

Kezar, A., & Lester, J. (2009). Supporting faculty grassroots leadership. *Research in Higher Education, 50,* 715–740. doi:10.1007/s11162-009-9139-6.

Kincheloe, J. L. (2005). *Critical Constructivism.* New York, NY: Peter Lang.

Schein, E. (2004). *Organizational culture and leadership.* San Francisco, CA: Jossey-Bass.

Smith, J., & Sivo, S. (2012). Predicting continued use of online teacher professional development and the influence of social presence and sociability. *British Journal of Educational Technology, 43*(6), 871–882.

Trower, C. (2012). *Success on the tenure track: Five keys to faculty job satisfaction.* Baltimore, MD: John Hopkins University Press.

Welsh, K., & Schaffer, C. (2014). Embarking on the tenure journey at age 50. *The Delta Gamma Bulletin, 81*(1), 26–31.

CONCLUSION

Tenure-Track Advice

From the initial conception of this book we were careful about advice. We wanted readers to form their own opinions because we were cognizant that the immersive experience of the authors is prone to personal bias and myopia. Authors were highly constrained, by the editors, around the inclusion of advice. However, the authors clearly are in a position to offer advice, which led to this chapter.

This chapter was developed from advice provided by the authors. The editors sorted the advice into themes. Some was contextually dependent and had very few authors making the suggestion. Other advice arose many times and transcended contextual details—such as how institutions can improve. Interpretation of the themes created two challenges for the editors. First, the advice needed to be generally applicable, beyond the scope of those who contributed to a theme, but reasonably reflect the limited number of voices. Second, the editors are immersed in the tenure-track process and, while this perspective was usually beneficial, care was needed to avoid sympathetic editorial bias. These issues were not overly pronounced, however, because of the clarity of themes that emerged.

The advice begins with a focus on the beginning of the journey—starting out. This is followed by advice for addressing personal, methodical (or technical), and cooperative approaches. A final segment, where there were many contributions, provides advice regarding institutional strategies that address the initial stage of their most important resource—their faculty members.

Starting Out

If you only absorb one piece of advice, it surely must be the succinct aphorism: "Stay positive! Breathe! Focus!" It borders on humorous that its author offered three pieces of advice and called it one! Nevertheless, while the chapter author who proposed this was apologetic about its overly simple tone, it speaks to personal attitude once you have committed to the tenure-track process. That "keep going" attitude is the one thing that is common to all experiences in the tenure-track.

Many of the authors have noted the significant impact of moving to the tenure-track position. It is not unusual to feel less effective, if not incompetent, while navigating a new environment. It takes more than a year to overcome this and may take the entire three years of a renewable term. In effect, one has likely been a high performer in a previous position and now has to struggle through every detail to achieve anything at all. It is quite likely that, in striving to survive the first year or two (or three), your partner and/or family will not appreciate the personal strain that is being coped with.

In terms of advice, it is one thing to recognize what is happening and another to actively implement strategies to address the situation. Recognize that physical, emotional, and mental health need to be included in the list of priorities and that life-work balance requires effort—and, perhaps, should be considered a task within the working role. Some form of exercise regime, perhaps as simple as a daily walk, can help with the physical aspect. Emotional elements benefit from having people to talk to, but not just colleagues; it is important to have a confidant who understands that quick-fix responses underestimate your situation. They need to listen, allow venting, and, at most, suggest baby steps. The mental aspect is fundamentally challenging because academics, generally, work with a mental capacity that can't simply be turned off. Lying in bed and having final daily "should have" thoughts is very difficult to address in a direct manner. However, you may find that developing personal mental time helps. A diary or journal can facilitate recognition of detrimental patterns before they cause too much trouble, or in a manner that allows one to seek help in a timely manner. Overall, health is not an isolated component; it is part of the larger journey, and all of the advice given in this chapter will address health in one way or another.

Progress in tenure-track terms requires looking for small but achievable opportunities, within the university. These may emphasize service roles where a degree of caution is needed to avoid too much service. However, presentations, sharing, and seeking opportunities that build your repertoire will create an academically fertile situation. While the steps may initially be small, this facilitates time to develop the courses you are likely to teach several times in the tenure-track years. In terms of teaching, learn from your students who have a broad perspective of what other professors are doing with their courses.

Student-opinion surveys should be handled carefully. Recognize that many people have animosity towards them, and you should anticipate having responses that irritate you and undervalue you relative to your own personal expectations. That said, a process of reflection and objective evaluation helps address shortcomings and revisions of the course. Thinking ahead to a tenure application, it has got to be better to demonstrate that you took action in response to student feedback than not.

Write regularly, even though much will not be directly publishable. A pattern of regular writing practices a skill that is fundamental to good scholarship. One way to ensure this practice is to stay abreast of current academic writing in your field and to create article summaries or idea collections for your use in one form or another. Book reviews are frequently sought—while these won't help you achieve tenure per se, the practice of writing will ultimately serve you well. As mentioned earlier, consider setting aside time each day for a diary or personal journal. This has two benefits because it provides a degree of therapeutic attention and catharsis, and a way to look back and see how much progress you have made (something one can easily lose sight of). It may also be a focus of conversation if you periodically share your writing with a confidant. A diary moves the locus of attention away from you, and while it remains personal, can allow a degree of objectivity.

While writing is important, so is ongoing professional reading. Several authors identified this issue, but one said it succinctly, stating: "It is said that it takes seven years, reading one hour a day, to become an international expert in an area. Most of us did at least an hour a day when we wrote our doctoral thesis. But the bar has now gone up! So, keep reading. The reading informs both the teaching and the writing."

Personal Life

Academia allows the boundaries between work and life to blur. The flexible hours around teaching, use of mobile devices, and travel for conferences all have benefits, but also have potential to infringe on what was previously defined as personal space. Care is needed to focus on accomplishing goals and tasks, while avoiding obsession that invades one's personal life. It sounds straightforward to those unfamiliar with academia, but it is a challenge to those who arrive in academia, even if they have a plan to address it.

Another piece of advice that authors provided is to recognize the need for a long-term perspective. The tenure-track is not six months, and there is no need to try to accomplish everything quickly. In particular, academia has cycles through the year, and caution needs to be exercised that decisions are not unduly influenced by the momentary state of affairs. If one of the most significant long-term plans, starting a family, is in your foreseeable future then consider how "family friendly" different universities are before choosing to join one. Avoid too much delay, when starting a family, because there are potential consequences if you allow work to infringe too much. When you do have family, give additional attention to the work-family balance. This has been studied extensively and the amount of advice available far exceeds this chapter.

Lastly, "be good to yourself." Arrival in academia is a reflection of considerable effort. There is an implication that the effort has to continue. However, you are not a young student anymore, this is not a temporary situation, and this is the way things will be for many years. It is natural to rise to the occasion, but do it with a realistic vision of who you want to be as a long-term academic.

Methodical (or Technical)

Advice in this segment was the most diverse, which likely reflects different perceptions of pathways to tenure. Experiences, learning, and personal development reflect different contexts and perspectives. In all cases, however, the advice was provided with specific action combined with a specific reason. For the reader who is contemplating the tenure-track, recognizing the diversity of commentary is a form of advice. For those readers who are in the tenure-track, the reason that is provided will help judge if the action is suited to your situation.

An overall piece of advice was to "beware of the tenure-hype" and be objective about it. This fits well with advice to read the collective agreement, and any other institutional documentation, that defines tenure. This may not resolve all your questions (What are "creative products"?) but gives an objective voice that is not swayed by personal stories you may hear from colleagues. If there are presentations provided for people preparing to apply for tenure, it may be beneficial to attend them in the first year or two with due care to consider the details with an objective perspective that fits your timeframe.

Read a style guide to get an overall sense of the style goal of writing. Read and write daily and make article summaries. The summaries serve for future use of the article but also as a record that reminds you that you have been reading.

Set achievable goals, and refine your definition of *achievable* as you gain experience. Consider setting these goals with short-, moderate-, and long-term schedules. As one specific example that arose in the advice provided: Use evaluations to guide alterations of courses.

Cooperation and Collaboration

Advice that emphasized cooperation fell into two categories. First, there was advice that addressed the potential for isolation in academia. Second was advice directed toward collaboration and work with particular colleagues. In this segment, we address these in this order.

Offices provide a workspace, but the walls are barriers to meeting other faculty members. While one necessarily has to focus to get work done, you also need to be visible and develop relationships. This goes beyond participation in meetings, which are focused on particular tasks. It was advised that many faculty members face challenges, and conversing allows you to realize you are not alone. Developing relationships may require you to take the initiative; for example, suggest having lunch together, but aim for social elements to be as authentic as possible.

Finding a mentor can provide a person who can help with developing scholarship more rapidly. In the simplest form, this may be a writing partner who can critique your writing and provide critical feedback, but in a constructive and enabling fashion. Another approach is that they may be a person who can help appraise opportunities by providing you with a sense of the big picture of your role. At a more elaborate level, one can develop co-authoring, co-teaching, and co-researching opportunities as the relationship develops.

Institutional Challenges

Advice for institutions received far more thoughtful consideration than any other aspect. The overwhelming message from the collective voice is that institutions are in a position to improve the tenure-track experience. This segment contains a wide range of advice that is not interpreted as context dependent because of the degree of institutional similarity. The wide range of advice was seen as reflecting the number of opportunities to implement changes that would make differences in varying degrees.

Orientation programs are beneficial, but they need to be followed by some form of regular conversation, not necessarily frequently but more than once a year. Guided conversations would allow for discussions of expectations and interpretations, such as how much service is appropriate for tenure, and provide a means to recognize when issues of isolation, mental health, and general wellness need to be addressed. It was suggested that many elements of orientation go beyond the institution, such as how to find a doctor or dentist. There may be ways to mitigate some of these issues, such as temporary access to student health facilities that may exist on campus.

It was suggested that circumstances can arise that call for modifications of the terms of the tenure-track contract. The advice was directed toward having institutions facilitate special needs, if they arise. This could be implemented using employee-assistance programs, by allowing them to modify the terms of a tenure-track contract, if the need arises. It could be implemented in other ways, but the point is to have a protocol, and making new faculty aware of it, whereby if they find themselves in a circumstance that does not fit with perceived institutional norms, they are aware of a course of action to address the need. One specific area, but not the only one that raised this advice, is to make institutions more family friendly.

This might require special dispensation but would address the challenges of balancing academia with motherhood, fatherhood, and parenting more generally. (Does parental leave change the end date of the tenure-track contract?)

Institutions can have a role to play in, or at least be conducive to, providing potential mentors and support for mentorship practice. They could use "cluster hiring" as a means to address isolation, particularly where the specific type of scholarship may isolate a scholar. This could also be melded with support for the cluster—especially where the scholarship itself is necessary for institutional change.

Consider updating the tripartite component of research. This advice may reflect the focus on education faculty members, but there seems to be a need for engaging professional practitioners, providing leadership, and supporting the community. This is service when viewed through a traditional lens of an expert extolling their wisdom on those in need. However, it is not service when it becomes a bilateral sharing of expertise from different perspectives. In this view, research becomes a perspective that focuses on using systematic investigative approaches oriented toward developing theoretical understandings. The view, while not definitive, points to the need for consideration of what constitutes research in the 21st century.

Overwhelmingly, the collective advice is indicative of a need for institutions to clarify the concept of tenure! What is the current value of: Community engagement? Leadership in an area of teaching? Program development for the institution? Program development beyond the institution but in your field of scholarship? What role does prior experience have in tenure? The answers may be obvious to those who have been through the tenure process itself. However, from a tenure-track perspective, a large number of voices have spoken to the challenge of comprehending what is required for tenure. Talking to colleagues does not clarify the issue and only points to an historic record that lacks clarity. Often colleagues will explain that you never know with tenure applications because they are peer reviewed across the whole institution, and it depends on who is on the committee, and which faculties may be influential in the view of scholarship, and who else is in the pool of tenure applicants. This, more than anything else, seems to fuel the rumor mill of tenure speculation and defies the systematic nature of inquiry that universities are based on. That defiance is surely something institutions could address.

Other Advice

Two pieces of advice were given that do not fit into any of the other categories. One relates to pensions, and the other is based on the experience an author had developing a chapter for this book.

Pension advice requires care, and this segment will not give specific advice. What we will do, however, is acknowledge that anyone considering a move into higher education should seek professional advice around pensions. There is a fundamental distinction between two kinds of pensions: defined value, and defined benefit. The former is essentially a system where what you contribute, along with its growth, is what is available when you retire. The latter is not constrained in the same manner; it defines what you get from the pension and is valued based on the collective contributions of the group. It is also important to know that some universities allow one to continue with teacher pension plans and others do not. If this choice is available, you need professional advice because the impact of details such as "highest five years of salary" can have a financial impact through all your years in retirement. At the same time, if you will reach the ceiling for years of service, then starting a new pension may circumvent the ceiling.

Final Word

The word "author" is derived from "authority," and the editors have benefited enormously from their interactions with so many authorities. The publisher also assisted from the earliest stages and gave constructive advice. We also benefited from the constructive feedback of reviewers who invested considerable time in assessing the book. We were also delighted that the production team, particularly the copy editor, invested their time in our professional learning. It has been a wonderful experience, and a significant time commitment, that has provided considerable insight into the world of tenure-track.

This brings the advice full circle because, as the first piece of advice in this segment implies, attitude is the singular common element you will live with throughout the tenure-track. As editors, our "learn from the authors and publisher" approach was an attitude that paid an enormous dividend. Thank you!

Contributors

This section lists the authors of chapters in alphabetical order, with the one exception of the writing group that submitted a chapter. In that particular case, they have a biography for the group as a whole.

All contributors have the academic requirements to be in tenure-track. They also have or are on track to have the academic requirements for tenure. In some cases, they have not completed their doctorate; however, in those cases, they are sufficiently far along that there is an expectation that they will have a doctorate by the time they apply for tenure.

Cecile Badenhorst is an Assistant Professor in the Faculty of Education in the Adult/Post-Secondary programs at Memorial University. She teaches courses on academic literacies and adult teaching and learning to undergraduate students; and advanced research methods and research writing to graduate students. Her broad research interests are academic literacies, and graduate and faculty research writing and productivity. She has published three books in this area: *Research Writing* (2007), *Dissertation Writing* (2008), and *Productive Writing* (2010); and has published peer-reviewed articles on graduate and faculty writing.

Lee Anne Block is a teacher educator at the University of Winnipeg. Her research and teaching are focused on how we name and engage with difference in educational locations and on cultural sustainability. She recently completed *Gandhi, Globalization and Earth Democracy*, a course on sustainability with Vandana Shiva, in residence at Navdanya, India. The experience at Navdanya was praxis, cultural theory, and agricultural action combined. She has a Master of Arts from the Ontario Institute for Studies in Education, University of Toronto, and a doctorate from the University of North Dakota. For twenty years, she was a classroom teacher in Winnipeg.

Joan M. Chambers is a professor in the Faculty of Education at Lakehead University. She teaches elementary science and environmental education to teacher candidates in the BEd program. In the graduate program, Joan teaches introductory and qualitative research-methods courses; science, technology, society, and environment (STSE); and science curriculum. Her research interests include primary science education, environmental education, and literacy for young children, climate-change education, and student mental health and well-being. Though she completed her BEd in 1985, she chose to stay home with her children, entering graduate school 15 years later. She began her academic career in 2009.

Cam Cobb teaches in the Faculty of Education and Academic Development at the University of Windsor. His research focuses on such topics as social-justice issues in special education, co-teaching in adult-learning contexts, and narrative pedagogy in the arts. Over the past two years his work has appeared in a variety of journals, including the *International Journal of Bilingual Education and Bilingualism*, the *International Journal of Inclusive Education*, the *British Journal of Special Education*, *Exceptionality Education International*, *Cinema: Journal of Philosophy and the Moving Image*, and the *F. Scott Fitzgerald Review*.

Frank Deer is an Assistant Professor and current Director of Indigenous Initiatives in the Faculty of Education at the University of Manitoba. Frank holds an earned PhD in Educational Administration from the University of Saskatchewan and is published in the area of Indigenous education. Frank has been awarded funding from the Social Sciences and Humanities Research Council of Canada for his work in ancestral languages. As current President of the Canadian

Association for the Study of Indigenous Education, Frank has worked with scholars from across Canada and abroad. Frank has previously served as a classroom teacher in Northern Manitoba and in the inner city of Winnipeg.

Lyle Hamm is an Assistant Professor in Educational Administration and Leadership at the University of New Brunswick. He teaches face-to-face, online, and blended pedagogy courses in teacher supervision, educational theory, school culture, leadership theory and leadership in culturally diverse schools. His research, broadly speaking, focuses on the impact of demographic change on teachers, students, administrators, schools, and community members. In 2015, he was presented with the Allan P. Stuart Award for Excellence in Teaching at UNB.

Victoria Handford is an Assistant Professor in Education (Leadership) at Thompson Rivers University. She teaches face-to-face, blended, and online, and has developed courses in all three delivery modes. Tory held multiple roles in education prior to moving to her university position. She was a teacher, vice-principal, principal, education officer for the Ontario Ministry of Education, and program officer for the Ontario College of Teachers. Her research interests are leadership and trust within schools and school districts. Tory is the Director of the Executive Program for Leadership in Education at Thompson Rivers University. She has a husband and three sons who keep her entertained—and busy.

Lloyd Kornelsen has worked in the field of education for the past 28 years, primarily as a high-school social-studies teacher. In addition to teaching, he has developed curricula, facilitated international practica, and, as an adult educator, acted as a conflict mediator and trainer for both local and national organizations. His recently published book, *Stories of transformation: Memories of a global citizenship practicum*, is based on research for which he was awarded the Manitoba Education Research Network award for outstanding achievement in education research. Currently, Lloyd is as a member of the Faculty of Education and Director of the Global Education Project at the University of Winnipeg.

Onowa McIvor is maskiko-nihiyaw from Norway House Cree First Nations and also Scottish-Canadian. Onowa is an Assistant Professor and the Director of Indigenous Education in the Faculty of Education at the University of Victoria. Onowa's research focuses on Indigenous language and cultural revitalization, sociocultural aspects of language learning and language education; second-language acquisition; and cultural-identity development and maintenance. However, her most important job is raising two young daughters, with the help of her extended family.

Peter Milley is Assistant Professor of Educational Leadership at the Faculty of Education, University of Ottawa. He completed his PhD in educational administration in 2005 at the University of Victoria. He has published on the moral, political, emotional, and aesthetic dimensions of educational leadership, drawing theoretical inspiration from the critical-theory tradition. Peter has significant professional experience in executive leadership development, policy research, and both adult and workplace learning from a successful career in the Canadian federal public service and post-secondary institutions. He has researched, presented, and taught in numerous countries, including Brazil, China, the Netherlands, Singapore, and the United Kingdom.

Greg Ogilvie is an Assistant Professor in the Faculty of Education at the University of Lethbridge located in Lethbridge, Alberta, Canada. Since contributing his chapter, he completed his PhD at the University of Alberta. Greg has worked as a high-school teacher, an instructor of English for academic purposes (EAP), and as a teacher educator in Canada, Ukraine, and Ethiopia. He has published articles about task-based language teaching, constructivist teacher education, and intercultural education. Greg's research interests include educators' conceptualizations of "interculturality" and "criticality" and their pedagogical impact, and the ways that social justice can be infused into education at all levels.

Greg Rickwood is an Assistant Professor in the Physical and Health Education and Education Departments at Nipissing University. He is an Ontario certified teacher and physical education specialist, with an extensive teaching background in elementary and secondary schools. Greg's research agenda examines the relationship between elementary- and secondary-school cultural systems and school-based physical-activity opportunities. He recently acted as a Consultant for

Physical and Health Education Canada to collect needs-assessment data that assists Ontario's secondary physical-education teachers with curriculum delivery. Additionally, Greg developed the junior-kindergarten curriculum for Ontario's daily physical activity document, "AtMyBest."

María del Carmen Rodríguez de France has been a visitor to the land of the Coast Salish and Straits Salish people and their communities for 20 years. Born and raised in Monterrey, México, Carmen's career in education and related fields spans thirty years, with participation in a broad range of educational, community service, and research activities. As a former international student, and as an immigrant, she is mostly interested in approaches to teaching and learning that promote education for diversity along with respect for ways of knowing and being in the world.

Carmen holds a Master's degree and a PhD from the University of Victoria. Currently, she is an Assistant Professor in the Faculty of Education at said university, where she facilitates courses within the Indigenous Education Unit and the Department of Curriculum and Instruction. Her research interests center on Indigenous curriculum development throughout the lifespan, and Indigeneity and social justice, to name a few.

Margarida Romero is an Assistant Professor in Educational Technologies at Université Laval. She was awarded her European PhD in Educational Psychology by UMR-CNRS France and Universitat Autonoma de Barcelona in Spain (Extraordinary PhD Award in Psychology). Her research interests are educational technologies in primary, secondary, and tertiary education, with a special focus on digital game-based learning (DGBL). In particular, her current focus of research is the study of the contribution of intergenerational digital game-design activities to collaborative learning in formal and informal educational settings.

Trish Rosborough is from the Kwakiutl Nation on Vancouver Island. Prior to her appointment to the role of Assistant Professor of Indigenous Education at the University of Victoria, Trish was Director of Aboriginal Education for the British Columbia Ministry of Education. She completed her doctoral studies in 2012 at the University of British Columbia. Trish's research area and life passion is Indigenous language revitalization. She is an adult learner and speaker of her mother's first language, Kwak'wala. Trish is a mother of five and grandmother of nine.

Manu Sharma is a Teacher Education Instructor and Practicum Supervisor at Brock University, and has previously taught at the University of Toronto and the University of Windsor. The chapter in this book was written while she was working at the University of Windsor. She teaches in the BEd program and the Master's program. In addition, she has taught with the Toronto District School Board, and internationally in Antigua and Barbuda, Germany, Japan, and Tanzania. Her research focus and interests are in teacher education, equity initiatives, teacher development, social-justice pedagogy, deficit thinking, and international teaching experiences. Currently, she is on the executive of the Canadian Association for Teacher Education, and she is the President of the Canadian Association for Action Research in Education.

Timothy Sibbald is an Assistant Professor in the Schulich School of Education at Nipissing University. His focus is primarily in mathematics education, which was founded in experiences as a high-school math teacher and prior experience in remote sensing research. While his current research focuses on mathematics education, he also studies his educator experiences that arise as his career progresses. He is, currently, the president of the Ontario Association of Mathematics Educators.

Kathy Snow is an Assistant Professor in the Education Department of Cape Breton University's School of Professional Studies. She teaches in both the pre-service teacher BEd and the graduate programs within the department. Kathy's research interests center around facilitating access to education through technology for non-traditional learners at all levels. In addition to Kathy's work at CBU, she serves as the co-editor of the *Journal of Professional, Online, and Continuing Education* (JPOCE—formerly CJUCE), serves on the executive board for the Canadian Network for Innovation in Education, and is heavily involved in community outreach for science-education literacy.

Memorial's Education Writing Group (Memorial University of Newfoundland)

Gabrielle Young, Sharon Penney, Jennifer Anderson, Cecile Badenhorst, Nancy Dawe, Jacqueline Hesson, Rhonda Joy, Xuemei Li, Heather McLeod, Sylvia Moore, Sharon Pelech, Sarah Pickett, Mary Stordy, and Dorothy Vaandering.

Over five years ago, a group of members from Memorial University's Faculty of Education began meeting to share their writing and discuss the writing process. The group meets regularly, and each member takes a turn hosting the meeting. There are no strict deadlines and action items for the meetings; instead, each member takes a turn checking in with the group and asking for feedback or advice on their writing. It is a relaxed and open setting where networking and socializing are as welcome as producing results. The group deliberately set forth to create an environment of non-criticism—we can give feedback but not criticism, and we agree to promote support rather than competition. Through this process, the writing group has served to foster a sense of belonging.

At present, the group is entirely female; however, male faculty members have participated in the past, and all members come from diverse areas of teaching and research, such as post-secondary education, science, special education, human kinetics, counseling psychology, and social studies. The group has successfully published several papers, and as we have worked together we have mentored each other, learned how others write, and incorporated that learning into our own writing. Through this process we have developed a growing confidence in ourselves as researchers.

The writing group offers support to fellow faculty members, not only when it comes to writing, but also when it comes to common concerns such as negotiating contracts, navigating the tenure process, or asking questions about benefits. Members have also found it useful to discuss half-formed research ideas and ask other members for practical advice on the logistics of grants and research designs. What makes this writing group unique is the supportive and collaborative environment. In an academic setting, and especially for those on the tenure-track, research and writing tends to be competitive and performed individually. This group specifically wanted to overcome that individual experience and turn academic writing into a positive practice.

It is rare for writing groups to lasts as long as ours. While the membership of our group and the structure of our meetings have changed over time, our faculty of education writing group continues to gain momentum. We feel this is because we value productivity, yet understand the importance of nurturing a safe space where individuals can make a connection and support each other. In the process of developing and maintaining our writing group, our colleagues have become supportive peers and friends who we can continually count on to help navigate the ebbs and flow of our academic careers.

Index

ability, 13, 33, 45–46, 65, 69, 82, 142, 157, 204, 208, 215
academia, v, 1–2, 6, 9, 13, 29–30, 32–35, 37, 56, 68–70, 75, 79–82, 85–86, 88–90, 92–94, 107, 114, 131, 133, 139, 143–146, 148–153, 156, 193, 200, 222, 231, 235, 237, 242, 245–246, 268–269, 271
adaptation, 131–132, 182, 187, 190, 193, 214, 217
  adaptive cycle, 182, 187–190
administration, 32, 67, 89, 148, 186, 190, 250, 252, 254, 278
age, 33, 38, 46, 49, 64, 95, 146, 151, 193, 205, 214, 234–236, 243, 259, 264
auto-ethnographic, 6

balance, 4, 7, 23, 34, 38, 42, 77, 79, 82, 93–94, 97, 131, 136, 143–144, 149–151, 153, 155–156, 171, 193, 199–202, 230–231, 233, 236, 239–240, 242, 244–245, 253, 266, 268
  out of balance, 136

capacity, 17–18, 45, 53, 81, 136, 171, 183, 193, 229, 239, 246, 254, 258, 262–263, 266
  community capacity, 18

collaboration, ix, 2, 8, 48, 61, 64, 69, 75–77, 79, 89, 91, 98, 103, 105–106, 114, 124, 139, 211, 225, 269
complexity, 195, 205, 214, 256, 259
conceiving. *See* family
contract, 53, 80, 137, 155, 179, 185, 204–205, 250, 270–271
co-publishing, 122, 123
co-teaching, 76–77, 97, 114–115, 117–125, 223, 270, 276
criterion, 18, 24, 43, 46, 59, 160, 188, 241
critical pedagogy, 125, 167, 169, 171–172, 222, 227
culture, 26, 44, 47, 59–60, 79, 85, 89, 96, 103–106, 163–164, 170, 174–175, 184, 186, 191, 217, 219, 227, 253–254, 264
  dominant culture, 44, 47, 161
  Indigenous culture, 96
  institutional culture, 217, 227

dialogue, 8, 57–58, 106, 113, 116–118, 120–122, 168, 223, 256, 258, 260
difficulties, 42, 48, 83, 89, 105, 145, 223, 227, 231
disempowered, 35
dissertation, 19, 25, 39, 41, 43, 49, 60, 124–125, 159, 177, 189, 211, 220–221, 230–231, 233–234, 238, 243–244, 251, 260

diversity, 1, 50, 56, 58–60, 121, 164, 176, 183, 189, 246, 252, 262–263, 269, 279

ecology, 180–182
email, 33, 141, 152, 212–214, 240
embodied knowledge, 162, 172–175
experiential, 195, 232

family, 7, 32–36, 42–43, 48, 56, 63–64, 89, 94–95, 99, 105, 131, 143, 150–151, 156, 163–164, 193, 195, 203–204, 206, 209, 214, 230–231, 233–236, 238, 243, 245–247, 249–250, 260, 266, 268, 270, 278
  caregiver, 34
  childrearing, 94
  children, 7, 30–32, 34, 36, 63, 94–95, 97, 100, 111–113, 129, 133, 148–149, 151, 163, 203, 207–208, 219, 230–231, 235–238, 240, 245, 261, 276
  father, 52, 63, 150, 163, 207, 236
  maternity, 150, 155, 205, 237
  miscarriage, 151, 157
  mother, 30, 42, 52, 83, 95, 98, 100–101, 146, 150–151, 201, 235–236, 239, 280
  parenting, 271
  pregnancy, 150–151
  second shift, 236
  spouse, 137, 140, 142–143, 203, 236
First Nations. *See* Indigenous
funding, ix, 20–21, 35–36, 53, 67–68, 70, 87, 130, 139, 142, 147, 175, 180, 189, 242, 262, 276

gatekeeper, 226
gender, 2, 5–6, 56, 58, 156, 233, 237, 239–240, 244, 246–247
  gender equity, 6, 246
global citizenship, 163–165, 169, 171–173, 176–177, 277
goals, 14, 75, 86–87, 119, 122, 184–185, 191–192, 225, 236, 268–269
graduate studies, 30, 43, 81, 201, 218, 220–221, 230–231, 255, 261–262

health, 7, 14, 22, 34, 36–39, 52, 67, 83, 112, 149, 183, 208, 245, 266–267, 270, 276

depression, 34–37, 39, 82, 168
energy, 33, 43, 70, 100, 102, 107, 118, 136, 147, 172, 251, 254–255, 261
fatigue, 231, 236, 245
mental health, 14, 36, 38, 266, 270, 276
holistic, 114–115, 123–124
home, 7, 21, 30, 32, 34, 36, 43, 51, 63, 88, 95, 98, 102, 107, 137, 143, 154–155, 170, 202, 209, 213–214, 236–238, 250, 254, 276

identity, 9, 24, 27, 42, 47, 49, 51, 56, 59–60, 90, 92, 165, 181–182, 185, 194, 223, 235, 244, 278
immigrant, 51, 54, 56, 59, 225, 279
implementation dip, 210
Indigenous, vii, 17–24, 26, 28, 61, 76–77, 93–109, 276–280
  two worlds, 94, 107–108
induction, 180, 221, 223, 226
international, v, 32, 51–52, 54, 58–61, 67, 84, 98–99, 111, 146–147, 149, 152, 159, 164, 186, 210–211, 219, 222, 225–226, 228–229, 251, 267, 277, 279–280
  France, vii, viii, 77, 93, 145, 147–148, 153, 156, 279
  Mexico, 39, 149
  South Africa, 14, 51–52, 55–56
  Spain, viii, 131, 145, 147, 149–151, 153–154, 156, 279
interview, 69, 112, 137, 153, 181, 238, 262
  hiring, 4, 6, 36, 102, 186, 204, 241, 271
isolation, v, 59, 77, 79, 90, 185, 269–271
isolated, 42, 59, 67, 100, 225, 256, 267

judgments, 24

lifelong learning, 146
life stage, 46
  mid-life, 174, 180, 185
lifestyle, 137, 230, 250
lived experience, 6, 121, 131, 165, 175, 203
loneliness, 79, 90
loss, 51, 57, 150–151, 185, 189

maladaptive traps, 182, 188–190
meetings, 25, 55, 66, 133–134, 140, 150, 174, 180, 211–212, 228–230, 237–238, 269, 281
mental health. *See* health
mentor. *See* mentoring
mentoring, 60, 67, 70, 75–76, 90–92, 123–124, 201, 223, 243, 254, 257–259

narrative, 23, 51, 57–59, 80, 115, 121, 123, 162, 172–173, 180–181, 193–194, 218, 222, 254, 276
    narrative inquiry, 123, 172–173, 222
navigate, 98, 100, 124, 160, 169, 171, 175, 226, 282

office, 33, 37, 64, 67, 83, 88, 97, 111, 120, 138, 150, 179, 209–211, 238, 240, 253, 256
online, 20, 54, 58, 84, 117, 138, 150, 255–257, 264, 277
organization, 2, 8–9, 52, 54, 60, 75, 96, 131, 134, 136–137, 141–143, 187, 211, 219, 229, 254
    building, 32, 36–37, 42, 52, 87, 94, 97, 101–103, 106, 124, 129–130, 139, 169, 188, 237, 243, 254, 259–260
    lists, 136, 206, 255, 275
    structure, 13, 45, 65, 75, 85, 131, 140, 169, 213, 223–227, 229, 281
othering, 55, 57–59
outdated, 14, 34, 38

parenting. *See* family
partnership, 19, 21, 90, 97, 102
pathways, 80, 193, 244, 268
pedagogy, 18, 23, 42–43, 47–50, 108, 115, 120, 122, 125, 164–165, 167, 169, 171–173, 177, 219, 221–222, 225, 227, 254–255, 257, 276–277, 280
    critical pedagogy, 125, 167, 169, 171–172, 222, 227
    digital, 257, 279
    storytelling, 132, 164–165, 172–173, 177
peers, 4, 46, 83, 100, 104, 159, 163, 185, 257, 282

peer review, 14
perception, 44, 66, 227
personal. *See* family
personal mission, 113, 145–146
planning, 22, 24, 36–37, 91, 114, 120, 123, 134, 150, 180–181, 183, 192, 201, 223, 238, 253, 261
politics, 49, 53, 56, 60, 85, 130, 165, 188, 229, 250
portfolio, 67, 113, 229
practitioner, 61, 79, 139, 143, 146, 157, 174–175
pregnancy. *See* family
preparation, 7, 14, 33, 68, 86, 102, 113, 124, 133, 137–138, 141, 155, 188, 195, 200, 206, 210, 212, 218–220, 226, 231, 240
    course preparation, 155
    tenure preparation, 218
presentation, 48, 111, 117, 150, 229, 253
profession, ix, 6, 9, 18, 21, 24, 26, 33, 35–36, 42, 146, 148, 214, 219, 228, 230, 235
progress reports, 22
proposals, 37, 53, 68, 141–142, 181, 196
protective system, 191–192
psychology, 80, 108, 144, 180–182, 184, 191, 281
    developmental psychology, 180–181, 184
    guilt, 64, 191, 237
    motivation, 68, 204, 209
    optimism, 184, 194
    pressure, 20, 22, 33–34, 38, 53, 149–152, 217, 220, 227, 242, 244
    stamina, 33
    stress, 83–84, 86, 89, 140, 149, 184, 193, 217, 223, 244–246, 254
publishing, iv, ix, 77, 88, 102, 119, 123, 135, 151, 161, 221, 244
    publish, 35, 67, 81, 87, 149, 220, 257
    publish or perish, 67, 149, 220
    revise, 8, 115, 123
    revising, 221, 252

recovery, 36, 107, 193, 195

reflection, 55–56, 114–115, 121–122, 131–132, 140, 146, 164, 187, 193, 224, 239, 254, 259, 267–268
reflective of, 29, 200
relationships, 9, 44, 48, 64, 67, 86–87, 90, 97–99, 106–107, 129, 132, 139, 142, 157, 166, 171–172, 176, 184–185, 190–191, 202, 235–236, 243, 255, 257, 259, 269
research, 1, 4–6, 9, 14, 17–21, 23, 25–28, 30–32, 35–37, 39, 41–43, 45–46, 48, 51–54, 57–58, 60, 66–70, 75–77, 79–85, 89, 93–94, 96–97, 99–100, 102–103, 108–109, 115–116, 118–119, 122–124, 130, 133, 135–136, 139–143, 145–147, 149–156, 159–161, 166, 168, 170, 172–175, 177, 179–183, 185–192, 194–195, 201, 210–213, 220–223, 228–230, 233, 235–236, 238, 241–246, 252–255, 258, 260–263, 271, 275–281
revisiting, 161, 172

self-
 self-actualized, 7, 140
 self-discipline, 192
 self-doubt, 82, 161, 191
 self-efficacy, 184, 194, 200–201
 self-regulation, 184, 192
 service, 1, 4–6, 14, 17–18, 21, 23–27, 32, 35–36, 41–42, 44, 49, 52, 54, 56–57, 66–67, 70, 77, 84, 88, 93–94, 96–97, 99–100, 107, 115, 124, 132–133, 147–150, 152, 156, 160–161, 165, 172–173, 175, 177, 179, 183, 187, 190, 201, 206, 210–211, 219, 228–229, 233, 238–242, 244, 247, 252–254, 257–261, 267, 270–272, 278–280
social justice, 41, 45, 49, 119–122, 125, 278–279
 social-justice, 26, 104, 117–122, 276, 280
Social Sciences and Humanities Research Council of Canada, 18, 31, 276
 SSHRC, 18–19, 21, 31–32, 53, 139, 161, 211–213, 242
standardized testing, 167

stigma, 35
storytelling, 132, 164–165, 172–173, 177
stress. *See* psychology
structure, 13, 45, 65, 75, 85, 131, 140, 169, 213, 223–227, 229, 281
 course structure, 65, 223, 225
student, 5, 14–15, 18, 25, 31–32, 35, 37, 52, 64–66, 70, 77, 82, 98–99, 112–114, 117, 125, 140, 142, 149–150, 157, 166, 170–173, 176–177, 180, 186, 201, 205–206, 209–210, 218, 220–223, 225–226, 228–229, 239, 246, 255, 259, 267–268, 270, 276, 279
 graduate student, 15, 35, 52, 64, 77, 113, 180, 218, 220–221, 223, 225–226, 229, 255, 259
 student evaluations, 64, 66, 149, 228

technical skills, 204, 214
tension, 47, 97, 106, 163, 171, 214, 231, 246, 254
tensions, 42, 54, 105
theory, 36, 39, 45–46, 115–117, 123, 144, 171, 176–177, 182, 211, 222, 226, 276–278
time commitment, 66, 211, 272
traditional, 6, 34, 98, 119–120, 230, 236–237, 271, 280
travel, 20, 24, 112, 148, 215, 238, 268
two worlds, 94, 107–108

uncertainty, v, 2, 51, 77, 82, 89, 106, 135, 181, 207, 217–218, 235, 251, 254, 259
vague, 55, 185, 192, 253
vulnerable, 29, 35, 149, 187, 195, 232

weekend, 43, 148, 237
work culture, 85
work-life balance, 79, 82, 143, 149–151, 153, 155–156, 201, 239

Education

Series editors: Nicholas Ng-A-Fook and Carol Fleuret

Our educational series seeks to advance thought-provoking research within the broader field of education. Scholarly works in this series examine educational research from a multidisciplinary perspective and addresses a variety of issues in the field including curriculum studies, arts-based education, educational philosophy, life writing, foundations in education, teacher education, evaluation and counselling.

Previous titles in this collection

Janna Fox, Mari Wesche, Doreen Bayliss, Liying Cheng, Carolyn E. Turner, and Christine Doe (eds.), *Language Testing Reconsidered*, 2007

Ruby Heap, Wyn Millar, and Elizabeth Smyth (eds.), *Learning to Practise: Professional Education in Historical and Contemporary Perspective*, 2005

Henry Davis Mchenry, *From Cognition to Being: Prolegomena for Teachers*, 1999

For a complete list of our titles in this series, see:
press.uottawa.ca/series/contemporary-society/education.html

www.ingramcontent.com/pod-product-compliance
Lightning Source LLC
Chambersburg PA
CBHW061345300426
44116CB00011B/1999